REPUTATIONS

OLIVER CROMWELL

J.C. Davis

Professor of English History
University of East Anglia

A member of the Hodder Headline Group
LONDON

Distributed in the United States of America by
Oxford University Press Inc., New York

First published in Great Britain in 2001
This impression reprinted in 2003 by
Arnold, a member of the Hodder Headline Group,
338 Euston Road, London NW1 3BH

http://www.arnoldpublishers.com

Distributed in the United States of America by
Oxford University Press Inc.,
198 Madison Avenue, New York, NY10016

The advice and information in this book are believed to be true and
accurate at the date of going to press, but neither the author nor the publisher
can accept any legal responsibility or liability for any errors or omissions.

British Library Cataloguing in Publication Data
A catalogue record for this book is available from the British Library

Library of Congress Cataloging in Publication Data
A catalog record for this book is available from the Library of Congress

ISBN 0 340 73117 6 (hb)
ISBN 0 340 73118 4 (pb)

2 3 4 5 6 7 8 9 10

Production Editor: Anke Ueberberg
Production Controller: Bryan Eccleshall
Cover Design: Terry Griffiths

Typeset in 10 on 12 pt Sabon by Phoenix Photosetting, Chatham, Kent
Printed and bound in India by Replika Press Pvt. Ltd.

What do you think about this book? Or any other Arnold title?
Please send your comments to feedback.arnold@hodder.co.uk

Contents

General editorial preface

Hero or villain? Charlatan or true prophet? Sinner or saint? The volumes in the Reputations series examine the reputations of some of history's most conspicuous, powerful and influential individuals, considering a range of representations, some of striking incompatibility. The aim is to demonstrate not merely that history is indeed, in Pieter Geyl's phrase, 'argument without end', but that the study even of contradictory conceptions can be fruitful: that the jettisoning of one thesis or presentation leaves behind something of value.

In Iago's self-serving denunciation of it, reputation is 'an idle and most false imposition; oft got without merit, and lost without deserving', but a more generous definition would allow its use as one of the principal currencies of historical understanding. In seeking to analyze the cultivation, creation and deconstruction of reputation, we can understand better the wellsprings of actions, the workings out of competing claims to power, the different purposes of rival ideologies – in short, see more clearly ways in which the past becomes History.

There is a commitment in each volume to showing how understanding of an individual develops (sometimes in uneven and divergent ways), whether in response to fresh evidence, the emergence or waning of dominant ideologies, changing attitudes and preoccupations in the age in which an author writes, or the creation of new historical paradigms. Will Hitler ever seem *quite* the same after the evidence of a recent study revealing the extent of his Jewish connections during the Vienna years? Reassessment of Lenin and Stalin has been given fresh impetus by the collapse of the Soviet Union and the opening of many of its archives; and the end of the Cold War and of its attendant assumptions must alter our views of Eisenhower and Kennedy. How will our perceptions of Elizabeth I change in the presence of a new awareness of 'gendered history'?

There is more to the series than illumination of ways in which recent discoveries or trends have refashioned identities or given actions new meaning – though that is an important part. The corresponding aim is to provide readers with a strong sense of the channels and course of debate from the outset: not a Cook's Tour of the historiography, but identification of the key interpretative issues and guidance as to how commentators of different eras and persuasions have tackled them.

Preface

This book would not have been possible without the support of many people. I am grateful to the Arts and Humanities Research Board and to the University of East Anglia for combining to provide me with a year of research leave in 1999–2000. I am indebted to the School of History at UEA and its members for financial, moral and intellectual support. The British Library, Cambridge University and London University libraries, as well as my own university library, have all responded to my requests with efficiency and generosity.

My Special Subject students, over many years, have questioned and challenged my own received 'wisdom' on the great issues of the English Revolution and Oliver Cromwell. I hope that some of the enthusiasm for those issues, which they perpetually rekindle, comes through in this work. I want to thank Anthony Fletcher, Willie Lamont and John Morrill for their friendship and support, and specifically in relation to this project. Drafts of some chapters were read by Glenn Burgess, Kate Davis, Damaso de Lario and Jonathan Scott, to all of whom I am indebted for far more than their criticism and support on this occasion. Providence brought me Jane Ramsbottom, for whose word-processing skills and good-humoured energy I am humbly grateful.

Understanding other human beings is always a process, never an end point. With all its faults, for which I alone am responsible, I hope that this book might encourage others to engage in that process in pursuit of Oliver Cromwell.

The Civil Wars 1642–1651. From Richard Ollard, *This War without an Enemy: A History of the English Civil Wars*. London, 1976

|1|

Enigma or hero?

In the later eighteenth century, when the redoubtable Dr Johnson decided not to persist with a biography of Oliver Cromwell because so much had already been written about him, he left a question waiting in ambush for all others who would take up that pursuit. What more can be added to the knowledge and understanding to be derived from even the most careful scrutiny of the records of Cromwell's deeds and words? What new perspective may be usefully added to the apparently infinite variety of judgement and interpretation built, more or less firmly, on those records? What is the case for a fresh examination of his reputation?

It is, of course, in important ways essential to the health of our intellectual life and our political culture that we should never close the book on enquiries of this kind. In the words of the police bulletin, it should always be a case of 'investigations pending'. This is all the more important when the subject of our enquiries has been depicted, as we shall see Cromwell frequently has, as a defining exemplar (for better or for worse) of the national character; or as a central figure in the shaping of English – and British – historical destinies; or as a figure to be invoked as either inspiration or warning in the face of time's challenges. The vigour of Cromwell's reputation has given it a life and force of its own at both popular and academic levels and, since it can arouse extremes both of anger and of devotion, we do well to keep it under observation. In large part, though not entirely, those extremes have followed the currents of intellectual passion and conviction as they have coursed through our history. So we have had a Restoration Cromwell; Whig, Tory, Romantic, Chartist, Nonconformist, Liberal, Catholic, Labour Movement, Marxist and Revisionist Cromwells. In the second quarter of the twentieth century both antifascists and fascist sympathizers saw the prototype of the modern dictator in the Lord Protector. The American, French and Russian revolutions all excited further speculation on his historical meaning. Was he the liberating force of rebellion or the strong man of order, curbing the excesses of revolution and repressing its *élan vital*. One might be tempted to read the history of Cromwell's reputation as an endorsement of the view that every generation makes, and ought to make, its own past; that full use should be made of history's plasticity by each generation for its own benefit. 'Damned to everlasting fame', we could, in line with this view, expect a continuing progression of Cromwells to emerge as time passes. (Not long to wait now for the Cromwell of the Third Way!) But the history of Cromwell's reputation does not quite bear this out. Alongside the more extreme depictions, and even stubbornly inherent in many of them, have been acknowledgements that the record is not infinitely malleable; that some sort of balance has to be struck. What that balance has been and what it might be will be principal themes of this book.

The 400th anniversary of Cromwell's birth in 1999 came when some of the more dramatic aspects of his career seemed peculiarly relevant to questions currently being raised about the United Kingdom, its future and character. The unity which he imposed by conquest on England, Wales, Ireland and Scotland might be contrasted with the present movement towards devolution within that union. His record in Ireland might be set against what – in our optimistic moments – we might regard as first steps towards some resolution of Ireland's troubles. The nation's political institutions – Parliament, the House of Lords, the monarchy, the relationship between church and state – all seem to be open to reconsideration and the pertinence of Cromwell's record in this regard is obvious. Finally, as an embodiment of military strength, he raises important questions about such capability and about this archipelago's place in Europe and the world.

Yet the most important argument for a re-examination of Cromwell's reputation relates to the assumptions underlying the framework within which interpretation of his life has now operated for some considerable time. Both of the two key assumptions involved influence our understanding of and approach to the past and, for that reason, they are worth exploring more fully here. There is general agreement, first, that Cromwell is one of the great figures of British history and yet also, second, that the nature of that greatness is shrouded in paradox. The discussion of his reputation continues to be dominated by these two themes – the capacity for paradox and the invocation of greatness. But are these safe and helpful bases on which to build our interpretations of the life of a figure so central to our history?

The notion of Cromwell as a paradox – combining opposed qualities, pursuing contradictory goals and trying to reconcile conflicting outcomes – is by no means new. His contemporaries frequently saw him as a paradox of virtue and vice, encapsulated in one version by Edward Hyde, Earl of Clarendon's image of him as a 'brave bad man'. Nevertheless, the paradoxical has become a major and insistent feature of more recent interpretations of his life and achievements. In a popular but serious biography first published in 1934 but still in print in the 1970s, John Buchan placed Cromwell's greatness in the first rank but the character of that greatness remained puzzling because 'Paradox is in the fibre of his character and career'.[1] In Christopher Hill's important and influential Historical Association pamphlet of 1958 Cromwell was a man of paradox and his paradoxes reflected those of the English Revolution.[2] For John New it was the paradoxes of Puritanism which Oliver epitomized and the title of a collection of texts for undergraduates which New edited in 1972 was *Oliver Cromwell: Pretender, Puritan, Statesman, Paradox?*[3] The concluding chapter of Antonia Fraser's long, impressive and popular biography of 1973 is an essay on the paradoxes comprising a character with 'so much of paradox in it'.[4]

In many respects, it is not surprising that the paradoxical continues to inform our assessments of Cromwell down to the present day. It not only appeals to our sense of irony but it also reflects many genuinely puzzling features of Cromwell's actions and career. No man rises as dramatically as he did without being, in some sense, ambitious and yet he baulked at what might be thought the final prize, kingship. He fought for civil liberty and the rule of law, but, in power, appeared to intimidate judges. A believer in the majesty and authority of Parliaments, he used the sword to turn one out – in contravention of a law which he had himself supported – and was complicit in the purging of others. He was extraordinarily willing to support liberty of conscience, yet came to be regarded by many of the sects as their enemy, an apostate who had betrayed the godly cause. He looked like the prime agent in the destruction of the ancient constitution – King,

Lords, Commons, Church of England – but went on to build something not dissimilar to it. He was a man of war, capable of exultation and ruthlessness in violence, but also a peacemaker, seeking to heal and settle. In the end, if accounts of his deathbed utterances are to be believed, he may even have proved a paradox to himself; God's Englishman in doubt about his state of grace. In all of these – and many other – ways we can find material for sustaining the image of Cromwell as paradox. There is truth in these depictions but beyond their identification of the puzzles and complexities inherent in any assessment do they advance our understanding of the historical Cromwell?

In fact, paradoxicality is deeply unsatisfying as a final historical assessment for a number of reasons. The contradictoriness of the paradox, while it may illuminate the problem, never explains or resolves it. It is essentially a restatement of the problem. On the one hand, it can be banal. We may all be presented as paradoxes to our children, parents, wives, husbands, teachers or students. It explains too little. On the other hand, it explains everything as well as nothing. Confronting a problem – why did Cromwell do this when he appeared to intend that? – we turn the problem into a paradox and assume that it has some explanatory force. Pressed a little harder to deal with more specific issues, the problems come back, elbowing their way out of the envelope of paradox. For example, the paradoxical Cromwell's forte was military and political leadership. He was a man who would lead and command others into life-threatening and bewildering situations, could persuade others to suspend their judgements and follow him on trust. But people do not follow; will not readily come to a settlement with; are not greatly motivated by; do not trust and will not fight and die for a paradox. So while some of his contemporaries were clearly baffled by Cromwell, to rest on the paradoxical as the key to his achievements merely deepens the problem as to the leadership and clarity of purpose on which so much of his significance must be built. In the end, to invoke paradox may be no more than to concede complexity, either in particular moments or over time, or both. Cromwell's maturity spans the 18-year trajectory of major political and institutional collapse (1640–2), devastating civil wars (1642–51) and the desperate attempt to claw back some stability and order in the aftermath of intracommunal violence on an unprecedented scale. Involved in this too are the events which come nearest in our history to those of a great revolution, the destruction of the old landmarks and the attempt to reconstitute the governmental landscape on a new basis. Complexity is obviously heightened and darkened by moments of extreme pressure, rapid development and urgent moral dilemmas such as these. Does the label paradox enable us to penetrate these complexities – and specifically Cromwell's role in relation to them – or does it shield us from them?

The second assumption common to most assessments of Cromwell down to our own day is that of his greatness. There is something surprising about the persistence of this assumption, given that we live in a climate of ironic scepticism in which professional historians are cautious to the point of niggardliness in awarding the epithet 'great', and in which one of our primary expectations of biography is that it will expose weakness and debunk the mythology of overblown esteem. It is striking then that Oliver Cromwell's reputation seems to escape these norms. Norman Davies, in a work intended to be an end of millennium retrospect on a thousand years of British history, *The Isles: A History*, described him as 'one of the greatest figures of English history'.[5] Also in 1999, the President of the British Academy, introducing the Ralegh Lectures, described Cromwell as a colossus dominating British history. Such assessments have been in vogue for over a century. Sir Charles Firth, in what many professional historians would still regard as one of the most balanced verdicts on Cromwell, told his Edwardian readers that Oliver was the greatest figure of his generation, albeit too much of a partisan to be a national hero.[6] A generation later, John Buchan cast that reservation aside and, ignoring the issue of dynastic legitimacy, cast the Lord Protector as 'The greatest of English monarchs ...'.[7] Writing at about the same time, Sir Ernest Barker thought that Cromwell shared the laurels of his period only with Shakespeare.[8] We might expect the annual Cromwell Day Addresses, organized by the Cromwell Association, to reflect this positive tone and indeed they do. In 1963 Michael Foot observed that Cromwell's greatness was multifaceted, appealing to widely different groups: the great revolutionary; the man of order; the religious hero; the founder of English national greatness.[9] For C.V. Wedgewood, as late as 1971, Cromwell was, even from this elevated plateau, 'steadily gaining prestige as a national figure'. In line with her recently published biography, Antonia Frasier in 1973 wanted to extend Cromwell's greatness from the public to the private sphere. Drawing attention to his 'private greatness' she emphasized his charm, knowledge of men, respect for women, his goodness as a family man and his virtue. Finally, we might observe that, while some informed military assessments in the 1970s rated Cromwell coolly, in comparison with, for example Fairfax, more recent ones have elevated him to 'military genius', 'the Greatest Englishman'.[10]

There are two features worth noting about this aspect of Cromwell's reputation, his greatness. One is, as we have seen, its long life and ubiquity. Whether positive or negative his reputation has, since his death, been pushed to the extremes of 'greatness'. If he was bad, he was extremely bad, greatly evil; just as he was, in the role of the champion of virtues, heroic. It is hard to find a single case of a sustained argument for Cromwell's mediocrity.[11] The second noteworthy feature of his 'greatness' is its persistence. Serious minds may be coy about conferring 'greatness' on any individual past or present, yet Cromwell seems to escape this embargo. Even those who would distance themselves from what they see as the nature of his achievements continue to assert his greatness. This should tell us something about our own generation and the uses that it might have for this particular reputation. Why do we want to construct a *great* Cromwell?

The answer to that question may be of interest to the social commentator, the sociologist or the anthropologist but, as historians, we need to know – especially in re-examining such a reputation – what we mean by 'greatness' and what it can mean in ways which are helpful and satisfying for our understanding of the past. In this case two pairs of related qualities have been most commonly used to establish, for good or ill, Cromwell's 'greatness'. The first pair are moral qualities and godliness. In moral terms key issues have been Cromwell's honesty or hypocrisy; bravery and boldness or indecision; personal ambition or self-effacement and public spirit; cruel ruthlessness or compassionate sensitivity. Carlyle saw him as stumblingly, inarticulately, honest and sincere; a monument of rough-hewn integrity. For others, he was the epitome of machiavellian deceit, manipulation and hypocrisy; the great dissimulator. The massacres of Drogheda and Wexford suggest to some the kind of viciousness we might now associate with what we would call 'war criminals'. For others, Cromwell represents a military discipline careful to minimize casualties and the impact of military activity on civilians; a commander of great compassion. 'God's Englishman' has been associated with qualities of godliness and tolerance since his own times. Again, these qualities can be seen in either a positive or a negative light. Cromwell is either one of England's great religious enthusiasts, or a wonderful adept in the exploitation of religious language, gestures and practice. These two categories – morality and godliness – are linked, as the themes of hypocrisy and sincerity illustrate. And they both pose problems for us as assessors of this reputation at the opening of the twenty-first century. Do moral judgements – rather than morally neutral historical judgements, if such things are possible – tell us more about ourselves than about the historical figure who is ostensibly the subject of our enquiry? The question may be put another way. Cromwell is a morally charged figure. Goodness – obedience to the will of God as he saw it – was central to his self-identification. Is it appropriate that we should assess his greatness in terms of his moral qualities and achievements? How are we equipped to do it? Our secularism, our distance from the living God Cromwell endeavoured to serve, is so pronounced as to bear comparison with the legitimacy of one culture, gender or sexual orientation passing moral judgement on the experience of another. Cromwell submitted himself to the judgement of God. What is the authority by which we might make moral judgement of him?. It may be done but it begins to look like an impertinence; the assumption of an authority for which we have no warrant. But appraisal in terms of historical role, meaning and significance may be a different matter.

Here we come to the second pair of categories – again connected ones – by which Cromwell's greatness has most commonly been assessed: his skills as a leader and his success. Cromwell came to leadership at a late, but not untypical age, his mid-forties. He impressed at every level of military command from captain of a troop to commander-in-chief. Military authority and political leadership went hand-in-hand for him from the outbreak of civil war in 1642. As soldier, politician and statesman, Cromwell showed the ability to develop skills appropriate to addressing – if not always of resolving – some of the most serious, and possibly intractable, problems ever to have faced his country. To acknowledge these skills is relatively straightforward. When we turn to assess them, however, we are immediately pushed towards the fourth category, that of success. Furthermore, to ask whether Cromwell, as soldier, politician or statesman, was a success, is immediately to raise two further questions. How lasting was his achievement and how does it bear up against that of comparable figures? To illustrate the difficulty with regard to the first of these questions: a chain of argument could be built up that without Cromwell, and his abilities as leader, Parliament would not have won the civil war, the old constitution would not have been overthrown, Ireland and Scotland would not have been conquered, and a union of the old kingdoms under the Protectorate and our first written constitution would not have been forged. And yet within two years of Oliver's death the whole structure had collapsed and vanished. The kingdoms were restored. In England, the ancient constitution of King, Lords, Commons and the Church of England came back virtually unchanged. In the end, it might be argued, the victors in the civil wars had destroyed themselves and their cause. In the spring of 1657, with a reasonably enthusiastic parliament offering Cromwell the crown, we might count him a success in reconciling the nation to his rule. Move the perspective on three years and it looks much more like abject failure. Where do we place his 'greatness' on this spectrum?

Roger Howell, who had thought more than most about Cromwell's reputation, began his biography of Cromwell (1977) by pondering on the question of greatness.[12] He suggested two sets of considerations. First, most people are shaped by the historical environment of their time but some individuals reverse that process and shape that environment. To have such leverage, he suggested, there must be a fit between their temperament as individuals and the times in which they live. Greatness, in this sense, is therefore related – not to universal standards – but to the relationship between an individual and a specific historical context. Howell's second set of considerations, however, related to those individuals who not only shape their own world but change the course of history, men and women whose achievements resonate beyond their own time. This kind of greatness would appear to depend upon the individual's ability to rise above the limitations of their time, to shape and possibly reshape the world in which they live, or to intervene decisively in historical development.

We need to bear in mind this second set of Howell's considerations but our primary focus will be on the first and, with it, on the historian's responsibility for placing their subjects, and their reputations, in their appropriate historical context. Informing this enquiry is the belief that it is not, in the end, 'greatness' around which the historian's assessment of a figure like Cromwell should be built. Rather we should assess him in terms of his capacity both to reveal the tensions of his day and to tell us about the meaning of continuity and change in his time and beyond it. Ultimately, the fascination of Oliver Cromwell is not dependent on whether he can be made into an heroic figure. We soon get bored with our heroes. The only ones to continue to hold our gaze are those whose feet of clay are revealed and who thereby cease to be heroes. The fascination of Cromwell rests on his ability to take us, intelligently and constructively, to the central dilemmas of one of the critical periods of English and British history. It may be his achievements and status in politics, religion or war which raise him to the point where he can take us on that journey, but it is what he does once there which makes him distinctive amongst his contemporaries and which continues to fascinate us. To take this journey it is essential to maintain the interplay between event and context, individual and environment. Cromwell is no Icarus figure who breaks free from the atmosphere of his times and operates at some transcendent level before the inevitable fall back to earth. We will need to think of him as rather more like ourselves, caught, most of the time, in the mesh of the limitations of his society and therefore condemned to repeat what he had found to be the deficiencies of others. Examples of such effective constraints are not hard to find, as we shall see, in the relationship between government and parliament; consent and effective administration; military and civil authority; in the balance between religious liberty, decency and order, or in the pursuit of an ambitious foreign policy and its sustainability for a poor society. Nevertheless, while it is right to acknowledge the continuing influence of such limitations and constraints, we also need to be alert to observe Cromwell pushing against their boundaries.

Cromwell's reputation has moved through extremes: from darkness to light and, latterly, towards paradox which seeks to embrace something of both. In every case it has moved towards the extreme of 'greatness': great darkness, great light and great paradox. Since, however, we find neither greatness nor paradox entirely satisfactory categories, it is time to look at Cromwell's reputation and our appraisals of it again.

|2|

Why Cromwell's reputation matters

The record

A fresh look at Cromwell's reputation must begin with the record on which that reputation should ultimately rest. The aim of this chapter is to give an overview of Cromwell's life, to present you with a narrative or biographical outline. Inevitably, even the most cautious and barely factual narrative will be held together, as a story, by judgements and interpretations. It is intended to give substance to these in the chapters which follow this. But we need also to confront the problem of documentation. Almost always, the historian, like the politician, national leader, commercial manager and scientist, has to face the problem of not having all the information we would ideally desire. We must make as much intelligible sense as we can on the basis of the evidence, partial as it may be, which is available to us. The documentation which remains available for any individual life is deficient in its own particular way. It would be wise then for us to begin with a sense of the particular documentary deficiencies on which both the factual and the interpretative accounts of Cromwell's life must be based.[1]

Two problems need to be taken into account. One is the patchy coverage of the records relating to Cromwell's life. The other is the prism – or prisms – of interpretation through which they have been refracted to us from a very early date; the points at which the reputation was, and still is, taking over from the record. Cromwell's life, like the lives of even the most obscure of us, left traces in official records and, because of his eventual prominence, it was bound to leave more than most. Still there are inevitable gaps, losses and omissions. In other cases, reputation has

intruded on the record and the documentation has been inter-
fered with. In the parish register of St John the Baptist,
Huntingdon, where his baptism was recorded on 29 April 1599,
some later hand has written, 'England's plague for five years'.[2]
Similarly, the admissions register of Sidney Sussex College,
Cambridge records that 'Oliver Cromwell of Huntingdon was
admitted Fellow Commoner on 23 April [1616], tutor Mr
Richard Howlet'. Much later someone else added to the same
record, 'This was that great impostor, that most accursed
butcher, who when the most pious King Charles I had been dis-
posed of by foul murder, usurped the throne itself, and for the
space of almost five years, under the name of Protector, tor-
mented the three Kingdoms with unrestrained tyranny.'[3] The crudity of this kind of interference with the record alerts us at once
but it was clearly intended to influence the way in which an otherwise neutral record was read. We will need to be equally alert
to more subtle attempts to achieve similar ends. At the other end
of the spectrum, some records have not survived. Other information which we would like to have was probably never recorded.
It is very difficult, for instance, to chart Cromwell's income and
wealth throughout his life because most of the appropriate
records are lacking. Cromwell left no political memoirs: a particular problem since many accounts of him have been influenced
by the memoirs of his contemporaries, several of them hostile to
him. He is unlikely ever to have set down his views on constitutional issues in any systematic way and yet these issues are critical to his record as Lord Protector. Like other politicians, much
of Cromwell's work was done through informal meetings and
conversations. Some record of a handful of these is available to
us and it is invaluable, but the many other meetings and conversations which there must have been remain blank on the record.
Of documents in his own words, modern editions assemble
almost 1000 items. We can be reasonably sure of the letters but
his speeches were almost always delivered without notes and,
given their length and tendency to ramble, must have been a
nightmare for those attempting to record them. His speeches as
Lord Protector were more likely to be recorded in shorthand
notes. Where we have more than one record of one of his
speeches, they can differ considerably. An example is his speech
of 27 February 1657 to a large group of officers who had come
to express their opposition to his accepting the crown. Here, we
have at least the advantage of being able to compare two versions

and to note where they confirm each other. Where we have only
a single version we need, of course, to exercise due caution.
One needs to be equally, if not more careful in the use of contemporary memoirs by other hands. These sometimes come from
hostile pens or were compiled after the Restoration when some
distancing from Cromwell and the interregnum regimes was frequently thought politically wise. The account of the life of
Colonel John Hutchinson by his wife Lucy can be taken to illustrate the memoir as politics by other means since Mrs
Hutchinson was determined to vindicate her husband in his
opposition to many of Cromwell's actions and politics. The
memoirs of Edmund Ludlow illustrate the same point with an
additional twist. Ludlow was a military and political colleague of
Cromwell's and a fellow regicide. As a committed republican,
however, he was appalled by Cromwell's expulsion of the Rump
and his memoirs, compiled in exile after the Restoration, were
written to show the personal ambition behind Cromwell's apostacy and its consequences. They were not published until 1698
and then in a much bowdlerized form in an edition probably by
John Toland. Yet it was Toland's edition which was to be the
basis for all subsequent editions until very recently and it gave
currency to a hostile account of Cromwell which not only pitted
republican integrity against machiavellian self-aggrandizement
but a rationalist Whig against a religious enthusiast.[4] Two sets of
distorting lenses confront us then in documents of this type: one,
the animus of Ludlow against Cromwell; the second, the spin
given to Ludlow's account by a later editor. Even in the case of
the editing of Cromwell's own words, we need to be aware of
deficiencies. Carlyle, the first editor of Cromwell's letters and
speeches, was a careless, self-indulgent and intrusive editor.
Abbott, the most comprehensive editor of Cromwell's words,
was neither as thorough nor as helpful as one would wish.[5]

There are in consequence several key issues on which the
nature of the documentation, or its sheer absence, leave us struggling to make as much meaning as we reliably can of the clues
available to us. For example, Cromwell's marriage in 1620 to
Elizabeth Bourchier, the daughter of a substantial London fur
dealer who was establishing himself amongst the landed society
of Essex, remains underdocumented. We do not know how it was
arranged and are left clutching at the possible network of connections which might have made such an advantageous and suitable move possible for a young man with little solid achievement

behind him or secure prospect ahead. Religion is obviously a key issue for Cromwell and much of the record of his own words is infused with, and even directed by, religious sentiment, but of his own religious practice we know little. When did he cease to use the Book of Common Prayer? Did he ever use the Directory of Worship approved by the Parliament of which he was a member in 1645?

Equally, there are key events or passages in his life for which documentation barely, if at all, exists. Much of Cromwell's youth is, in this way, impenetrable. As John Milton described it, Cromwell grew up 'in secret at home ... in the silence of his own consciousness, for whatever time of crisis was coming, a trustful faith in God, and a native vastness of intellect'. Even the last part of this reads as speculation gone too far and we have to be aware of the tendency to paper over the gaps with speculation or hoary old stories, of doubtful provenance, passed uncritically from one account to another. Despite the fact that the reasonably full contemporary records of Lincoln's Inn show no evidence of Cromwell ever having been a student there, it has been repeatedly asserted that he was.[6] When, on 4 June 1647, Cornet Joyce secured the person of the King before escorting him from Holdenby House to Newmarket, what, if anything, had passed between Cromwell and Joyce beforehand? The truth is that we do not know and, however we balance the probabilities, a speculative element remains. When, on the evening of 11 November 1647, Charles I escaped from captivity at Hampton Court only to end up in further confinement in Carisbrooke Castle on the Isle of Wight, it was to move from the custody of one kinsman of Oliver Cromwell, his cousin Edward Whalley, to that of a slightly more distant kinsman, Robert Hammond. Was Cromwell complicit in the escape of Charles and his eventual destination? We do not, finally, know. A list of events or decisions where the absence of clinching documentation frustrates our attempts at definitive explanation would have to include Cromwell's involvement (or non-involvement) in Pride's Purge; the expulsion of the Rump in April 1653; the adoption of the Instrument of Government in the same year; the considerations behind the setting up and final abandonment of the Major-Generals scheme in 1655–6; and the part played by military pressure in the rejection of kingship in the spring of 1657. All of these are crucial issues in Cromwell's political career and they bear heavily on the construction of his reputation. Nevertheless, despite all of these gaps, omissions and problems, there remains a substantial body of material on the basis of which we can reconstruct much of Cromwell's life; the movements of the mature Cromwell on an almost daily basis; his thoughts on many things at different stages of his life and, even in several critical circumstances, his motivation. But we need to exercise some caution, to recall that at many points documentation is sparse, needs to be weighed carefully and that there is a natural tendency for interpretation to outstrip evidence and that this tendency must be resisted.

Born on 25 April 1599 and baptized four days later, Cromwell was the second son, but the only one to survive, of Robert Cromwell and Elizabeth Steward. Robert was MP for Huntingdon in 1597 and served as a county JP. So he was the head of a family of local governing rank, itself a junior branch of a Cromwell dynasty briefly dominant in the region but now in decline. The Cromwells' rise to dominance in Huntingdonshire had been associated with the secularization of church property, particularly in the first phase – the 1530s and 1540s – of the extended process we know as the English Reformation. Indeed, one branch of the family had changed their name from Williams to Cromwell in order to underline their kinship with Thomas Cromwell, Henry VIII's chief minister and architect of the break with Rome. Enriched by the despoliation of the Church, their fortunes had eventually been undermined by an extravagant pursuit of court patronage and the sheer fecundity of several generations of the family. Robert, Oliver's father, was a younger son in a family of ten children. Oliver in turn was the surviving brother amongst seven sisters. The strain of providing something for so many siblings in successive generations had the natural effect of stretching the family's patrimony. Without injections of fresh resources, downward social mobility was almost inevitable.

The family's home in Huntingdon was itself a house which had been ecclesiastical property. Oliver attended the local grammar school which was supervised by Dr Thomas Beard, an ardent believer in God's providential interventions in the world and in the virtues of an unflinching hostility to the Pope and all his works but, in this and all other respects, conforming to the mainstream beliefs and practices of the Church of England. Two days before his seventeenth birthday, Oliver went up to Cambridge and was registered at Sidney Sussex College as a fellow commoner. Oliver's father and uncle had both been students at Queen's College in the same university but by 1616 Sidney

Sussex may have had a more godly appeal. The statutes of the college required the Master and Fellows to abhor 'Popery and all heresies, superstitions and errors' and the master, Samuel Ward, personified such rectitude. As a fellow commoner, Cromwell enjoyed a more privileged diet and accommodation than the normal fee-paying undergraduate or pensioner. He left Cambridge in June 1617, soon after the death of his father, without completing his studies or taking a degree (but neither of these outcomes was uncommon in the period).

What he was doing in the next three years remains a mystery. Was he studying the law? More particularly, might he have been studying civil law as a subject relevant to one whose patrimony was tangled up with ecclesiastical property?[7] It has been repeatedly suggested that Cromwell attended Lincoln's Inn, or, because of its family connections, Gray's Inn. There is no documentary evidence to support either speculation. The idea that Oliver spent these years in dissipation of various kinds, like the stories of childhood precocity and physical combats with Charles Stuart in boyhood, must be set aside as totally unsubstantiated and coming, at best, from sources with axes to grind.

On 22 August 1620 Cromwell married Elizabeth Bourchier, the daughter of a wealthy London furrier, at St Giles Cripplegate. Bourchier had established a presence in Essex, where he rented a substantial manor house from the Earl of Warwick, within easy reach of Cromwell's Barrington cousins. Cromwell was to maintain close links with this area. His sons were sent to the school at Felsted in which Warwick maintained a direct interest. His choice of bride may therefore be an early manifestation of the influence of the overlapping kinship, social, political and religious networks which were to be of critical importance to him throughout his life. Whatever the source of its inspiration, the marriage of Oliver and Elizabeth was to prove a solid and fruitful one, a relationship on which Cromwell leant throughout his career.

The couple settled in Huntingdon where they began to raise a family and, no doubt, to play a part in managing the family's interests. In 1628 Cromwell was elected to Parliament as one of the MPs for Huntingdon. His contribution in the House of Commons was undistinguished: a rehashing of an old controversy in the context of much more serious concerns about 'arminianism' and what was perceived to be its counter-reformation threat. Meanwhile, his social and material fortunes were slipping beneath his feet. In 1628 the senior branch of the family were forced to sell Hinchingbrook House, the principal family seat, symbol and site of their former glories. In Huntingdon, the remodelling of the borough's charter in 1630 left him excluded from the central institutions of the town's government and his intemperate protests landed him in trouble with the Privy Council. The melancholia, which had led him to consult a London physician in 1628, must have deepened as honour and power in the urban community of which he had always been a member slipped away from him. His response, which looks like an acceptance of defeat, was to sell up and move the five miles to St Ives where he became a tenant farmer. It has been suggested that one reason for the choice of St Ives was the recent appointment of an old Cambridge friend, Henry Downhall (who had been a godfather to Cromwell's eldest son, Richard) as vicar there. If this was the case, it would confirm Cromwell's religious conformity at this stage since Downhall was essentially a conformist and served as a Royalist army chaplain during the civil war. At some time in these years Cromwell experienced a spiritual conversion and it has recently been suggested that this was possibly during his time at St Ives under the influence of lecturers like Job Tookey or Walter Wells.[8] But the evidence is fragmentary and circumstantial.

Cromwell's social standing in his mid-thirties was then ambiguous but with every sign of deterioration. Potentially, he was well connected: a cousinage which included John Hampden and Oliver St John (Hampden's barrister in the case brought against him for non-payment of shipmoney), the Barringtons and was linked on to the circles of Warwick, the Earl of Holland and Viscount Saye and Sele. On the other hand, he was at best a member of the urban gentry in a small provincial town. In Huntingdon he had become embroiled in disputes over endowments and the remodelling of the town's charter. In both cases he had been humiliatingly defeated. In St Ives he held no office, was a tenant rather than a landlord, had few dependents and worked for a living. He looked downwardly mobile and the political and social networks on whose margins he existed appeared to be in long-term eclipse, excluded as they were from royal favour, as the King's personal rule assumed settled form. If Cromwell did contemplate migration to the New World, the reasons are not hard to find. In religious terms, we need to be cautious about ascribing some hidebound Puritanism or intransigent nonconformity to him. In these years he became one of the godly – identifying himself with an advanced Protestant piety which was sceptical about religious forms and scruples over them but which was also committed to service to a living God who raised His saints from the barren wilderness and directed their footsteps through life. It was the godly in this sense, whose piety recommended them one to another, with whom he was most critically networked.

If Cromwell's spiritual condition in the 1630s was to have been rescued from a blackness, a darkness, there was also a double transformation in the fortunes of himself and of the political and social networks to which he was connected. In 1636 the death of his maternal uncle, Sir Thomas Steward, left him heir to long-term leases and the administration of tithes associated with the cathedral at Ely. There the family moved and Cromwell proceeded to involve himself in improving their position and in the operation of various trusts associated with the cathedral. He became one of the more substantial members of Ely's urban community but it is worth reminding ourselves that this was still a small, provincial town dominated by its cathedral, and when Cromwell was later referred to as 'Lord of the Fens' it was a sneer suggesting a modest fish in a barely existent pond. He became involved in the disputes over fen drainage but his position appears to have been one of concern that adequate compensation be provided for commoners likely to lose rights rather than one of outright opposition.[9] He paid his shipmoney, coexisted with the ecclesiastical authorities, showed some concern over the maintenance of lectureships and preaching but, in the main, got on with what must have been much more comfortable material circumstances for his growing family in the later 1630s.

The second transformation, in the fortunes of the political networks to which Cromwell was linked, came with the collapse of the King's government in the aftermath of a disastrous policy in Scotland and failure in both the 'Bishops' Wars'. Cromwell was elected twice, for both the Short and Long Parliaments, in 1640 as an MP for Cambridge. He had only been made a freeman of that borough at the beginning of the year. The evidence as to why Cambridge chose him is lacking. The most plausible suggestion is that he was recognized as being linked with Warwick and through him to Warwick's brother, the Earl of Holland who was Chancellor of the University.[10] Be that as it may, at the age of 41 the tempo of Cromwell's life and the record of that life in official documentation suddenly increased. By 1641 the administration which had governed England in the 1630s was in collapse, its ministers in flight or facing trial, the institutional and fiscal machinery which had sustained their policies was being dismantled and legislation to redefine the relationship between the elements in the parliamentary trinity was in progress. There was a great deal of work for MPs to do and Cromwell, like many others, was quickly drawn into it. He rapidly found himself on a substantial number of committees working alongside John Pym, Denzil Holles, Oliver St John and John Hampden. He was prominently associated with justice for those who had suffered at the hands of the episcopate in the 1630s, in particular for John Lilburne. He became involved in moves to reform the Exchequer and moved the second reading of a Bill for annual parliaments. But his main interest remained religion and he, with the younger Henry Vane, promoted the introduction of a Bill to abolish episcopacy, the Root and Branch Bill, which passed through their hands into those of Sir Arthur Hesilrige and was introduced to the floor of the House by Sir Edward Dering. In September, Cromwell spoke critically of the Prayer Book. In this sense, then, he was taking an advanced position on the sensitive and divisive issue of what to do about the Church of England. He has been represented, at this stage of his parliamentary career, as something of a lone operator and a loose canon. Certainly he made blunders but it is more likely that he was being used as part of a larger political network and may sometimes have been cast in the role of a forlorn hope, someone whose job was to test political reactions before more senior figures in the network committed themselves. He greeted the Protestation of May 1641, which was designed to alert Protestant England to the dangers of a combination of popery and arbitrary rule and to unite the nation against that threat, with unqualified enthusiasm. He watched the uncertain progress of the Grand Remonstrance in November 1641 with some anxiety. The Irish insurrection of October 1641 alarmed him and he was forward in contributing to the scheme to send an army to Ireland funded by loans made on the security of lands which would be confiscated once the rebels were suppressed.[11] From February 1641 he was seeking information about the character and implications of Scots demands for religious uniformity between their kingdom and England. These were the first signs that the British dimension of the crisis engulfing his countrymen was impinging on him.

The Irish rebellion may have made Cromwell's zeal look more mainstream than it would otherwise have appeared but the

Grand Remonstrance polarized Westminster and gave the King the beginnings of a resurgence of support in the political nation. Cromwell was riskily forward in seeing this combination as akin to a call to arms. He was early in urging that Parliament should put itself and the nation in a state of defence. In mid-July 1642 he sought authority to raise two companies of volunteers in Cambridge. In August he seized the colleges' plate to prevent it being sent to the King. This was all before war had been formally declared and, had peace broken out, Cromwell could have found himself in a position of considerable embarrassment.

But war did come and Cromwell threw himself energetically and unreservedly into it. By the end of August 1642 he had mustered a troop of cavalry at Huntingdon and he kept on steadily recruiting. In October he was inconclusively and inconspicuously at the battle of Edgehill. By February of 1643 he was a colonel in the Eastern Association, commanding his own regiment and, despite panics about supply, support and the strength of the enemy, he began to make a sustained impact on the campaign in the eastern counties. He secured a number of strategic points: in April 1643 Peterborough, Crowland Abbey and Burghley House; in May, Belton; in July, Gainsborough and in October, with Sir Thomas Fairfax, he won a decisive victory at Winceby in Lincolnshire. From Essex to the Humber, the east of England had been made relatively safe for Parliament. With William Waller's campaigns in the west country, Cromwell's efforts stood out against a much more mixed, even threatening, backcloth. He was rewarded by being made Lieutenant-General and second in command, under the Earl of Manchester, of the armies of the Eastern Association.

Parliament's overall lack of confidence in their capability versus the King had led them to draw in the Scots as allies and the price for this had been the Solemn League and Covenant and joint management of the military effort against the Royalists. On 5 February 1644 Cromwell took the oath of the Covenant and two days later he was appointed to the Committee of Both Kingdoms, the agency for Anglo-Scots war management. The year 1644 was the one in which Cromwell moved from a regional to a national stage in terms of the intertwined political and military aspects of the war. In July he played a decisive role in Parliament's victory at Marston Moor, by far the most important set piece battle of the war to that point. For the first time an outright parliamentary victory began to appear possible and minds began to turn to the political consequences of such a victory. On 13 September Cromwell prefigured some of his concerns with a speech in the Commons on provision for tender consciences in any future religious settlement. Late in October the indecisive follow-up to the second battle of Newbury, and the failure to secure from the Royalists the strategic stronghold of Donnington Castle, confirmed to Cromwell and like-minded colleagues that senior commanders on the parliamentary side had reservations about pursuing the campaign and the war to a comprehensive victory. Army members of the Committee of Both Kingdoms were asked to report on the conduct of the campaign to Parliament. In doing so, Cromwell described the Earl of Manchester's attitude as one of 'backwardness to all action'. Manchester, according to Cromwell, saw the war as coming to an end not in victory but in an 'accommodation'. He was unwilling to pursue the King's forces after Newbury or to risk all on an attempt to recover Donnington Castle.[12] While numerous witnesses came forward to support Cromwell before the Commons committee investigating the issue, Manchester responded with countercharges against Cromwell in the House of Lords. A full-scale public row between senior commanders in Parliament's armies and between the two Houses seemed to be in prospect. On 9 December, when the committee investigating the charges was due to report, Cromwell rose in the House to make a major speech which had a long-lasting impact on his reputation both positively and negatively. The speech did three things. First, it sought to move away from personal recriminations: everybody had made mistakes. Second, it pointed to the necessity of bringing the war to a speedy conclusion if Parliament was not to exhaust the nation and lose their political support. Third, it suggested that the relationship between Parliament and its armies should be reorganized and that, as part of that process, members of both Houses should give up any direct military role. The motion then put by Henry Vane and Zouch Tate (the chairman of the committee) was to prove the first step towards the Self-Denying Ordinance by which all members of Parliament were required to give up their military posts. Simultaneously, a reorganization of the army leading to the establishment of the New Model Army under the command of Sir Thomas Fairfax was carried forward.

In theory this should have brought an end to Cromwell's military career as it did to that of Sir William Waller under whose command he was campaigning in the early months of 1645. On

17 April 1645 he returned to Windsor to surrender his commission, ahead of the due date of 12 May, but the Committee of Both Kingdoms ordered him to continue campaigning. His commission was extended for 40 days and thereafter had to be renewed periodically so that Cromwell's command was the most subject to public scrutiny of any in Parliament's armies. The position of Lieutenant-General of the horse in the New Model remained unfilled and it was to this post that Fairfax eventually and enthusiastically appointed him. Cromwell was not given a longer-term commission until 1647 and although his formal commission lapsed in July 1646 he remained on the army payroll.[13]

At the battle of Naseby in June 1645 Cromwell's cavalry and his capacity to control them in the field were amongst the decisive factors in Parliament's victory. At Langport, a month later, he was again decisive in destroying the Royalists' ability to sustain a field army in the west. The rest of the civil war was a matter of reducing the strongholds still held by the King's supporters. From the fall of Bristol in September 1645 until the surrender of Oxford in June 1646, Cromwell was preoccupied with this work and his commission was repeatedly renewed to enable him to complete it. By midsummer 1646 the war had been won and Cromwell dropped out of active service, returning to Westminister for his first sustained period there for four years. Three issues were of central concern to him in the next period. How to make peace with security, the first of these, involved negotiating a reasonable settlement with the King and making sensible provision for military security. The second involved ensuring the proper role for Parliament in such a settlement and in the future government of the country. Cromwell had already, in April 1646, denounced his army colleague, Henry Ireton (soon to be Cromwell's son-in-law), for not reporting to Parliament a Royalist attempt to draw the army into direct negotiation with the King. The third issue was religion. In October 1646 the legislation abolishing episcopacy was finally approved by the two Houses and it was expected that the Presbyterian system recommended by the Westminster Assembly would be enacted and implemented. The critical question was how narrowly conceived this system would be. Already Cromwell's attempts to gain recognition for the problem of 'tender consciences' had run into difficulties in Parliament and some of the versions of his despatches after Naseby and the fall of Bristol which were published by Parliament had omitted his remarks in favour of liberty of conscience. These three issues – settlement, Parliament (and the army) and religion – were, of course, linked and it is their interplay that forms the context for Cromwell's actions over the next few years.

By early 1647 a dominant group in the Commons, led by Denzil Holles, began to implement a plan for the resolution of all three issues. A Presbyterian system of church government, but one barely acceptable to the Scots, was to be imposed on the nation and religious order and uniformity were to be restored. The New Model Army was to be disbanded and from it a new army was to be recruited for service in Ireland. All officers in any future armies would have to accept the Presbyterian church. A settlement would be reached with the King which would restore much of the *status quo ante bellum* and take the heavy costs of the military establishment off the backs of the taxpaying classes. There were two problems with this scheme. The first was that of reaching any kind of settlement with a king who was determined to use every advantage to secure the position and future strength of the crown. The second was the army. Anxious about substantial arrears of pay, which Parliament showed no signs of paying, indemnity from criminal prosecution for acts of war and for provision for widows, orphans and wounded soldiers, the soldiers were in no mood for their concerns to be brushed aside. Early modern armies were incipiently mutinous and the parliamentary armies of the first civil war were no exception. Between May and September 1646 there had been disorders amounting to challenges to the military chain of command in 22 counties in England and Wales. With the army owed something in the region of three million pounds in arrears of pay, 1647 was always going to be a difficult year.

Despite the fact that Cromwell was ill with 'an impostume of the head', as both an MP and a military commander he was inevitably drawn into mediating between Parliament and the army. On 20 March 1647 he assured the House of Commons that the army would obey its orders and comply with their plans for disbandment, redeployment and reorganization. Such assurance may, however, have been premissed on the assumption that Parliament would respond to the army's reasonable grievances. The soldiers wanted their pay and, if they were to be redeployed, to serve under the old commanders. They petitioned for their grievances to be met before Parliament's plans were implemented. Fairfax was ordered to suppress the troopers' petition and on 29 March 1647 the Commons passed a 'Declaration of Dislike' describing the promoters of the petition as 'enemies of the state'. Such provocation was not likely to strengthen the hands of the moderates in the army. On 16 May Cromwell, at Saffron Walden with the army, urged compliance with Parliament's authority but found the rank and file organizing to ensure a proper hearing for their grievances and increasing numbers of officers doubtful about their ability to push the rank and file into compliance with what many felt to be unfair or dishonourable terms. On 21 May he reported to the Commons with a request to encourage army moderation by making moves to redress the soldiers' grievances. Contemptuous of the warning implicit in Cromwell's statement the Commons voted, on 25 May, that the army should be disbanded in the first two weeks of June. Cromwell's position was still that parliamentary authority must be upheld and that, in the end, the army must obey its masters but on 29 May around 100 officers reported to the army's Council of War that the army could not be disbanded without serious disorder. The commanders of the New Model were now faced with an unenviable choice: to risk losing control of the army or to defy Parliament's inflexibility. A general rendezvous of the army was called for 3 June at Newmarket but meanwhile Cornet Joyce acting apparently without orders from a superior secured the store of artillery at Oxford and then moved on to make safe the person of the King who had been held at Holdenby House by a detachment of troops under Presbyterian officers. Out of his depth, Joyce appealed to his superiors for guidance and in the meantime complied with the King's request to be taken to Newmarket. This was a momentous shift in the balance of political forces but what Cromwell's role in it was is far from clear. Joyce had met Cromwell in London on 31 May but there is no evidence that he was acting under Cromwell's instructions. Nevertheless, this was a decisive moment for Oliver. He knew that, for the time being, it was impossible to reconcile Parliament and the army and threw in his lot with the latter. Nevertheless, two major objectives remained uppermost with him over the next six months. The first was that of restoring discipline in the army and preventing its politicization in the direction favoured by the radical civilian movement, the Levellers, who were suggesting what looked to Cromwell like the dangerous design of a wholly new political order. The second objective was to get a parliamentary settlement back on track by hammering out a moderate settlement acceptable to the army and to the King and capable of being put into law through Parliament, the strategy of The Heads of Proposals. The price for order in the army was that its leaders should be seen to be listening to the soldiers' reasonable grievances and representing them to the civilian authorities. At the same time, Cromwell was insistent that there could be no constitutional *carte blanche* and that therefore settlement must involve a deal with the King and the maintenance of parliamentary authority. However, the army had edged into identifying itself as an independent and distinct political factor. The Rubicon of collective disobedience of parliamentary orders had been crossed.

On 4 and 5 June six regiments of cavalry and seven of infantry assembled on Kentford Heath at Newmarket. Fairfax addressed each regiment in turn. The Solemn Engagement of the army was endorsed: they would not disband until their grievances as soldiers and their rights as subjects had been cleared. A General Council of the army, consisting of two officers and two representatives (agents or agitators) for each regiment as well as the staff officers would be responsible for the army's future dealings with Parliament.[14] To bring pressure to bear on Parliament and its enemies in that assembly, the army began a slow and rambling advance towards London. In response the House of Commons began to look to the safety of the capital and discussed the formation of a new army based on the City's trained bands with which it might confront the New Model. The victors in the first civil war were coming close to the brink of civil war amongst themselves. It was a situation in which the Levellers, seeking liberty of conscience and the radical constitutional reform which might guarantee it, could imagine that the old forms of government were dissolving and that the army might form the vehicle for delivering a new order derived from the will and consent of the people, the Agreement of the People. The Army's *Declaration* of 14 June reflected some of this thinking. It announced, in a famous phrase, that the New Model was no mere mercenary army and called for the establishment of the just rights and liberties of the people. The present Parliament should be purged of malignants, an end to its term should be set and 'a more equal representative' be elected following a redistribution of constituencies. In mid-July, meeting at Reading, the Council of War debated terms drafted by Henry Ireton working with John Lambert, Lord Saye and Sele and Lord Wharton for submission to the King, The Heads of Proposals. On 20 July, 11 MPs who had been identified by the army as plotting to restore the King and to form a new army in alliance with the Scots to achieve their ends asked leave of Parliament to go into exile. Less than a week later, on 26 July, a large number of their supporters invaded the House of Commons and Lenthall and the Earl of Manchester, the speakers of both Houses, with 57 MPs and eight peers fled to the army for protection. The remainder of the Commons, known as 'Pelham's Parliament' because they elected Henry Pelham speaker, tried putting a bold face on things. They forebade the army to come within 30 miles of the capital, reactivated the Committee of Safety, recalled the 11 MPs and began measures to recruit an army to defend themselves and the capital. It was all too late. The New Model Army was advancing on London. At this point, desperate to bring stability to a dangerously volatile situation, the army commanders, including Cromwell, sought to press ahead with The Heads of Proposals. It was a strategy designed to reconcile satisfaction of the army, agreement with the King and a parliamentary settlement. But if it was to prevent further civil war it needed to be settled quickly. The Proposals were presented to the King who, sensing political opportunities in the confusion of those who had defeated him in the field, failed to realize that time was not on his side in that there had to be a resolution of the current crisis as a matter of urgency. What is striking about the Proposals is their moderation. There would be limited constitutional change (mainly designed to make parliaments more geographically representative and regular), safeguards against royal tyranny although in the longer term much of the royal prerogative would remain intact, and the old church, complete with bishops, and the Prayer Book, would be restored in combination with liberty of conscience for those Protestants who wished to remain outside of the state church. On 2 August, with the army now close to Windsor, The Heads of Proposals were published. On 4 August the New Model occupied the Tower and Southwark and two days later the MPs who had fled to the army were escorted back to Westminster. The General Council of the Army meeting on 18 August endorsed a remonstrance calling upon Parliament to consider The Heads of Proposals and to dissociate itself from the actions of the 'Pelham Parliament'. It was understood that, if these conditions were complied with, the army would withdraw from the capital and on 27 August its headquarters were moved to Putney where they were to remain until mid-November.

These months of mid-summer to autumn 1647 were a crucible of crisis and political education. Cromwell was far from being a dominant figure but his realization that there were those on the parliamentary side who could bring the situation to the brink of renewed civil war, into the precincts of violence, must have left its mark on him. He played his part in keeping the army under control and in furthering a plan for parliamentary settlement through The Heads of Proposals but he was by no means the sole, or even the prime mover in these schemes and the notion that he was the central figure, manipulating these events to his own advantage, must therefore be seen to fall short of the mark.

On 7 September 1647 Parliament submitted its own proposals (the Newcastle Propositions) to the King only to be told by him that he preferred The Heads of Proposals. The promoters of the Proposals took this response as encouragement to put their terms forward as a series of Bills for legislation as part of a parliamentary settlement. In October such legislation was brought forward, primarily at the instigation of Lord Wharton and Viscount Saye and Sele with whom Cromwell and Ireton were in close collaboration. Their Bills were intended to cover each of the 16 'heads' of the Proposals. Sensing that a political settlement was in prospect, the Levellers began to push for a full discussion of a more comprehensive and radical constitutional settlement and for the full settlement of military grievances. A statement of the latter was presented by the agitators of five regiments of cavalry to Fairfax as The Case of the Armie on 18 October. This was to form the basis of discussions to be held by the General Council of the army at its regular meeting later in October. In the event these issues became conflated with the wider constitutional ones of the first Agreement of the People drafted by the Leveller leaders and forming one of the bases of the famous Putney debates held in the last days of October and the first of November. These debates have often been depicted as the more or less unsuccessful attempt of the conservatives, Cromwell and his son-in-law, Henry Ireton, to defeat the radical, proto-democratic Levellers. But an equally important dimension was Cromwell's attempt to keep the army behind the strategy of his allies, The Heads of Proposals, to achieve a moderate settlement which might be endorsed by the army but would be legitimated and implemented by Parliament. The Levellers proposals, by contrast, would have to be legitimated by the people and imposed by the army. It was clear that there were members of the General Council who were reluctant to make settlement dependent on the agreement of Charles I and who, therefore, were willing to contemplate some degree of radical constitutional change. The debates ended inconclusively but from the army commanders' point of view with a need to reassert military unity and discipline.

On 8 November the General Council agreed that all agitators should return to their regiments and, the following day, that there would be a general rendezvous of the army at three separate sites. Two days later the King escaped from captivity at Hampton Court, eventually making his way to the Isle of Wight and renewed confinement in Carisbrooke Castle. His scheming with the Scots for a renewal of the war was now well known and his actions threatened to undermine the entire strategy of the alliance of which Cromwell was part. With a new risk of war it was even more imperative to re-establish army unity and discipline. The three rendezvous – at Ware on 15, St Albans on 17 and at Kingston on 18 November – were reassertions of exactly this type, with Cromwell playing a particularly vigorous role at Ware. Reporting these events to the Commons on 19 November he vented his frustration with the King by referring to the Norman Yoke, a view which suggested that the Stuart monarchy was directly descended from the Norman Conquest. On 24 December the Council of Officers voted in favour of prosecution of the King and on 3 January 1648 Cromwell vigorously supported the Commons motion that all negotiations with the King should cease. Distrust was now subverting the strategy which had been pursued since mid-1647. In late December the King had rejected the four constitutional Bills presented to him as he was finalizing an Engagement between himself and the Scots.

By the spring of 1648 it was clear that there would be further war but, in a resolution of 28 April asserting that there would be no alteration in the fundamental constitution of the kingdom, the Commons sought to prevent that war from becoming a revolutionary one. From May until mid-November 1648 Cromwell was fully occupied as commander of the cavalry of the New Model Army; first in suppressing insurrection in South Wales, then in the campaigns leading up to the battle of Preston (17 August). This was the first major engagement in which Cromwell had overall command. It reveals his tactical daring, his devastating vigour and his economy with his own forces. The Scots force was virtually annihilated with minimal casualties amongst Cromwell's troops. There followed a brief mission to Scotland to

ensure the disbandment of the remaining Scots forces and then a
protracted siege of Pontefract Castle, one of the few strongholds
stubbornly held on to by recalcitrant Royalists.

Providence had clearly spoken in the dramatic finality of
Preston and there was considerable anger that the King and those
who had supported him in the second civil war had not only been
responsible for the unnecessary spilling of blood but had defied
God's will in effectively denying the judgement of Providence in
conferring victory upon Parliament in the first civil war.
Nevertheless, the attempt to find some settlement which could be
endorsed by the King, the army and Parliament was not yet aban-
doned. At St Albans in early November 1648, the Council of
Officers had discussed what to do about Charles. Ireton had
drafted a remonstrance declaring the King's blood guilt and calling for justice but Fairfax was strongly resistant to it and its
implications. It was decided that a final approach should be made
to the King. On 15 November he was presented with what were
essentially The Heads of Proposals revived. The following day,
fatally, Charles rejected them, apparently still deluding himself
that he had room for manoeuvre. Two days later the Council of
Officers adopted Ireton's remonstrance with only two votes
against it. Cromwell remained absent in the north while these
events took place but a sense of their inevitability is unlikely to
have been lost on him. To salvage something close to the original
design of mid-1647 would require management of not only
Parliament but also of an angry army in which his son-in-law
seemed to have shifted to the radicals and was negotiating with
the Levellers over a settlement envisaging a new constitution via
an Agreement of the People. The King had effectively put himself
outside of any realistic political equation.

On 20 November the army's remonstrance was presented to
the House of Commons which shelved it for a week only to
adjourn debate on it until 7 December. Three options now faced
the army: a dissolution of the Long Parliament by military force;
a purge; or continuing in the hope of persuading Parliament that
Charles Stuart must be dealt with. On 5 December, while a group
of officers and MPs were debating this issue, the last alternative
was in practice ruled out. The Commons voted for continued
negotiation with the King, effectively, in these circumstances, for
his restoration. The following morning Colonel Thomas Pride,
acting on behalf of the army, carried out his famous purge.

Cromwell arrived back in London on the evening following

Pride's Purge. He accepted what had happened but to what extent he had been consulted beforehand it is now impossible to say. His own wrestling with the dilemmas of the future had gone on through November 1648 as his letters bear witness. Providence had dealt dramatically with those who had defied its clear judgement in the outcome of the first civil war. It seems likely that Cromwell had come to the conviction that the King and his misguided supporters must be dealt with firmly but that in early December 1648 he was not yet clear what that meant in detail and in practical terms. Part of our problem is that we do not know the extent to which menacing moves in December 1648 were designed to push the King into a more compliant negotiating position. However that might be, Charles had demonstrated his inflexibility, or his courage, sufficiently by the end of December to make it clear that there could be no compromise. On 1 January 1649 the trial of the King was approved by the Rump and Cromwell did not shirk his part in the responsibility. He was active and unwavering in his eventual commitment to seeing the trial and execution through and, thereafter, consistent in his defence of it as Providential and necessary, though those categories substantially overlapped in his mind. Despite its reduction to attendance by a handful of members he was less persuaded of the necessity of abolishing the House of Lords and sought to stabilize the new republic on as traditional a basis as possible. Of the eventual membership of the Rump, two-thirds were uncommitted to the Purge or to the execution of the King. Cromwell was foremost amongst those who persuaded moderates who had avoided complicity with the regicide to resume attendance at the Commons in the early months of 1649.[15] The Council of State set up to run the new republic was to elect a new chairman every month and Cromwell acted as the first of these. It is significant that Henry Ireton and Thomas Harrison, hardliners for a resolute dispensing of justice to the King and his principal supporters were excluded from the Council. By contrast, more conservative figures, including five peers, three judges and two senior lawyers were included. The Agreement of the People hammered out as a compromise between army officers, MPs, some lawyers and the Levellers (who walked out of the negotiations in disgust) was presented to the Rump on 20 January 1649 and then ignored. There was to be no written constitution.

To its enemies the republic looked like the outcome of a military coup, a tyrannical usurpation of established forms, unrepresentative and without the capacity to establish a new legitimacy. The Levellers denounced it as a betrayal, a military tyranny ruling by will, rather than law, and a vehicle for the ambitions of Cromwell – the arch-traitor – and the 'Grandees'. To its supporters it was a commonwealth, a republic, liberating its citizens and their energies for achievements which might parallel those of the classical republics of ancient Rome and Greece. The full fruits of this republican vigour were to be seen in the military and naval achievements of the years 1649–52 and in the former of these Cromwell played a leading part.

From mid-1649 to late 1651 he was once more a campaigning soldier and his military exploits in these years established his reputation both as a commander of genius and, more controversially, for a kind of ruthlessness. The first objective was to secure Ireland but, before this could be done, discipline within the army had to be reasserted and the threat of insurrection against the republic, possibly led by the Levellers who were most vociferous in condemnation of it, had to be prevented. In March the Leveller leaders were arrested and it may well have been Cromwell who was most determined to break them as a political force. On 15 March he had been named as commander-in-chief of an expedition to be sent to Ireland and on 30 March he accepted this commission. His preparations were deliberate and prolonged, and amongst them was a determination to secure military order in England. In May he and Fairfax led a force drawn from the New Model which was to crush mutinous troops at Burford in Oxfordshire.

Cromwell's preparations for the expedition to Ireland were protracted partly because Ireland had so often been the graveyard of English military ambitions but also because he knew the importance for military discipline of securing adequate provision of money and materials. He also knew that it would be a campaign of sieges and that, if, as was necessary, the campaign was to be concluded swiftly, it was essential to be well equipped with good artillery. In the meantime, he attempted to further divide the already divided ranks of opposition to the English republic in Ireland. His key success here was to win over Roger Boyle, Lord Broghill, one of the most substantial landowners in Ireland and previously a Royalist. As Cromwell's preparations neared completion, on 2 August 1649 an English army under Colonel Michael Jones destroyed a field army of their Irish opponents at Rathmines, just outside Dublin. That his own campaign would be one of siege warfare was confirmed in Cromwell's mind as was the necessity, if disease and problems of provision were not to take their toll in a long drawn out series of sieges, of acting decisively. His forces landed at Dublin on 15 August and, within a month, he was summoning the first major stronghold, Drogheda, to surrender. The subsequent storming of the city on 11 September, along with the taking of Wexford in October, has become amongst the most controversial aspects of Cromwell's military career. Close to 3000 were slaughtered in both cases. Was this justified by the conventions and exigencies of contemporary warfare or were these more or less indiscriminate massacres and were innocent civilians put to the sword? Nothing of similar severity occurred in the rest of Cromwell's Irish campaign and the terror of Drogheda and Wexford may have, intentionally or not, played a part in that. On the other hand, at Clonmel in April 1650 Cromwell was out-thought by the defenders of the town and the New Model received some of its most severe casualties of any campaign under his command. Nevertheless, by the time he left Ireland in late May 1650, the combination of military vigour and diplomacy had achieved what was seen as a great success and on his return to England he was greeted in triumph as a conquering hero, a great servant of the English republic.

He did not have long to rest on his laurels. Soon after the regicide, the Scots had provocatively proclaimed Charles II not simply King of Scotland, but of Great Britain, France and Ireland. Charles landed in Scotland on 24 June 1650 and it was clear that the Kirk party, who for the moment dominated Scots politics, were determined to mould him into a Presbyterian monarch of Britain. For the English the question was whether to wait for them to act or to engage in a pre-emptive strike, carrying the anticipated war on to Scottish territory. Fairfax could not reconcile himself to a war of aggression against England's Protestant and apparently loyalist neighbours. Despite the attempts of a committee, including Cromwell, to persuade him otherwise, on 25 June Fairfax resigned as Lord General of the New Model Army. On 28 June, the day that he was appointed to succeed Fairfax, Cromwell left London and began the march north. The commander opposing him was a seasoned and wily soldier, David Leslie, who retreated to the well-defended line of Leith–Edinburgh, stripping the territory north of Berwick of supplies and forcing Cromwell to rely on provisioning by sea for which the most suitable access was the east coast port of Dunbar. Leslie's strategy was to sit tight and let hunger and sickness in Cromwell's army do the work. Cromwell's problem was how to draw Leslie out of his strongholds before that happened. A series of feints to the west and even to the north of Leslie's positions were undertaken to achieve this but without success. But Leslie's political masters, repeatedly interfering with and purging his army to produce a more godly force, also urged Leslie to be more trusting in the Lord and to adopt more aggressive tactics. Cromwell, in a series of declarations, messages and taunts, attempted to play on these divisions. So a discursive context for the military campaigning was the question of which disposition of church, state and crown – the Scots or the English – was most likely to meet with God's providential favour and which side was more trusting in Providence. By the end of August 1650 Cromwell's forces had been indeed reduced by 25 per cent through sickness. Leslie at last moved in an attempt to cut him off from his supply lines through Dunbar. In the event he succeeded in trapping Cromwell and his men in Dunbar itself. The Scots were reputed to outnumber the English by a factor of two to one and the ground they occupied appeared to give them every military advantage. But, by a combination of tactical vision, energy and decisiveness, Cromwell spotted a temporary weakness in his enemy's dispositions and exploited it to the full. The result on 3 September 1650 was an astonishing triumph, which Cromwell ascribed to divine providence; victory plucked from the jaws of defeat. Three thousand Scots were killed on the field, 10,000 taken prisoner. The English casualties were minimal, perhaps as few as 20 dead. It was Cromwell's most astonishing military achievement.

One outcome of Dunbar was to precipitate a political crisis in Scotland which strengthened the hand of Charles Stuart as the only unifying prospect for the disparate alliance which made up the Scots forces. Lambert had defeated the armies of the Western Association of Scots and Edinburgh was taken in late December, but from February to May 1651 Cromwell was ill. The newly crowned King and his supporters began vigorous recruiting and in May seized power so that the Committee of Estates was dominated by Royalists. Cromwell's strategy was now to open the path to the south for the Royalist/Scots forces while shutting off their potential supply of reinforcements from the north. By taking Perth and Dundee he forced his opponents to begin the move south. As July turned to August, the Scots advanced into England and a carefully coordinated response was put into action. Cromwell split his force into two, setting off in pursuit with one half while George Monck used the other half to take aggressive advantage of the departure of Scots forces into England to secure central Scotland and prevent further recruits being sent south. From Leith, Thomas Harrison, without waiting for further word from Cromwell, set off south, shadowing the Scots army as it advanced down the west of England. In the meantime, county militias were being assembled in southern England to block the Scots' road to London. Once the Earl of Derby and the prospect of substantial English recruitment for the Royalists were defeated in Lancashire, it was clear that Charles and the Scots were entering a trap from which there was little prospect of escape. Taking refuge in Worcester, they were surrounded by a much more substantial English force. Again, Cromwell looked for two things: to inflict crippling defeat on the enemy and to do so, as much as possible by guile, at minimal cost to his own forces. In the event, he feinted across the bridges spanning the Severn to draw the Royalists out and then redisposed his forces to strike them in the flank. The result was overwhelming. While Charles escaped dramatically into exile, barely a few dozen of his Scots supporters reached their homeland. The rest were killed or captured and transported. It has been estimated that, of an adult male population of 200,000, Scotland lost a devastating 10 per cent in the campaigns of these years. As in Ireland, resistance in Scotland was broken. The rest was a mopping-up operation.[16]

The impact of Worcester and Dunbar on Cromwell's military reputation, heightened for his contemporaries by their coincidence of timing on 3 September 1650 and its anniversary in 1651, was enormous. The Scots who had intervened, almost with impunity, in England in 1640 and 1644–6 now found themselves faced with conquest and enforced union on English terms. It was Cromwell's last campaign and a triumphant one. The armies of the republic and their Lord General gathered laurels but, apart from legislation against swearing, neglect of the sabbath and adultery, the Rump had achieved little by way of reform. Within a few days of his return to life as a London-based politician, Cromwell was serving on a committee of the House to consider elections. Informally, he held a series of meetings to look for longer-term solutions to the problem of a lasting settlement with some claim to legitimacy. A recurrent theme in the discussions was whether English legal systems and modes of governance required an element of the monarchical to work more naturally. Despite these conversations, Cromwell continued to believe that Parliament, or what was left of it, must itself find the solution if such a thing were to have legitimate authority. He also sought reconciliation with ex-Royalists, whose hopes of a restoration were now at a low ebb, by means of a generous act of indemnity or pardon. Further objectives for him at this time were settlement of the church, and John Owen, who had been his chaplain in Ireland, was commissioned to head an attempt to draft a set of proposals, and reform of the law. The Rump was to disappoint his expectations, and those of many of his colleagues, with respect to all of these objectives. Meanwhile it had dramatically expanded the navy of which Sir Henry Vane was the principal commissioner. From April 1652 the navy faced its greatest challenge in war with the Dutch. The eventual outcome was another victory for the English republic and Vane, who was committed to the sovereignty of the Long Parliament and the republic, probably saw the navy as some sort of counterweight to the power and influence of the New Model Army. Cromwell had no appetite for the Anglo-Dutch war as a conflict between Protestant states and his irritation and that of his comrades with the Rump's distraction from reform continued to grow. On 13 August 1652 he and his fellow officers petitioned Parliament to adopt a 14-point programme of reform including: spreading the gospel; reforming the law; adopting more stringent financial controls; ending begging and vagabondage; paying military arrears; making provision for widows and orphans; and setting in train the arrangements for a new Parliament. Ten months later very little had happened to realize these proposals and on 1 April 1653 the Rump's decision not to renew the Commission for the Propagation of the Gospel in Wales seemed to fly in the face of the first of them. Replacing the Rump now assumed first priority.

The problem was how to move to a new representative assembly without giving conservative opinion the opportunity to undo all that Providence, the army and a purposeful minority had achieved. At one extreme, a return to unfettered, free elections could be the prelude to a rapid restoration of the ancient constitution. At the other was the prospect of either continuing with the Rump, co-opting or recruiting new members as required, or holding 'elections' which were controlled in such a way as to cast doubt on their legitimacy. It was a circle around which discussion revolved in an increasingly frustrated manner. Dissatisfaction with the Rump bore down on the seemingly intractable problem of finding a successor which would have the support of the political nation but yet advance a revolution for which that nation had no appetite. On 19 April a meeting of officers, including Cromwell, and about 20 MPs agreed that the Rump would suspend further action on a Bill for a new representative pending further discussions. On the following day Cromwell and his colleagues were startled to receive the news that the House was proceeding with a Bill for new elections. Whether the 20 MPs had been unable to restrain the rest or not, this looked like a promise betrayed. What was in the Bill before the House we do not know since it has not survived but this has not prevented a great deal of speculation by historians. On that day, 20 April 1653, Cromwell took the fateful action of turning out the Rump in anger and by military force. The underlying context was broad dissatisfaction and army frustration with what had come to be seen as an unrepresentative body which had denied itself the saving attribute of having pursued godly reformation as one of its main priorities. The specific nature of the trigger for its expulsion, a broken promise or something in the Bill under discussion, remains unclear. Whatever its cause, the expulsion of the Rump had severed the last connection with the ancient constitution, the remnant of the Long Parliament. Constitutional experiments would have to be tried. Whatever they were, they would have to deal with the hostility not only of the old Royalists, the moderates alienated at Pride's Purge, the Levellers broken in 1649, but now also of the republicans, or commonwealthsmen, who had viewed the Rump as a legitimate instrument of republican development.

Even before these precipitate and unplanned developments, a number of officers had wanted the Rump to give way to an interim unelected body. The dilemma was what form that body should take and what its brief should be. For the immediate running of day-to-day domestic government a small Council of State, at first of 10 members, later of 13, was set up. John Lambert was its president with Cromwell an active member. The constitutional resettlement of the country was left in the hands of the Council of Officers, an assembly of senior officers with Cromwell usually in the chair. The records of their discussions are no longer extant but it seems clear that Cromwell's primary aim was to get governing authority back into safe, and preferably reforming, civilian hands. As a medium-term solution it was decided to call an assembly with both executive and legislative functions, roughly representative of the country as a whole but consisting of nominated rather than elected members. It was to be a British assembly, with members drawn from Scotland and Ireland, as well as England and Wales and would eventually make way for a more traditionally representative institution at some future date. The Council of Officers chose the members, only 15 of whom had been nominated by the congregations of which they were members. It was a civilian body from which lawyers were excluded and much closer in its social composition to the natural and traditional rulers of the shires than some enthusiasts might have hoped.

Nevertheless, Cromwell's opening speech to the Assembly, on 4 July 1653, stressed the providences which had brought them to this point, hinted at the role of the Assembly as a divine instrument in what might well be an apocalyptic moment and called for toleration of the saints. Within the 140 strong membership of the Assembly there was a core of enthusiasts for whom these were signals for them to get on and do God's work. Outside of it, many saints and godly congregations saw Cromwell's expulsion of the Rump as godly work and this as the moment when God's people might leave the wilderness behind and achieve the promised land; and they wrote in some numbers to tell Cromwell so. He refused to sit in either the Assembly or on its Council of State. The civilians were to be left to their own devices and they soon found themselves pulling in different directions. About 40 of them vigorously pursued a radical agenda: wholesale law reform, including the abolition of Chancery; the eradication of the last vestiges of popery and prelacy; and the end of tithes as a means of maintaining a national ministry. The major part of the Assembly, willing on the whole to embrace moderate reform, became increasingly alarmed, as did Cromwell. As early as 22 August, in a letter to Charles Fleetwood, he was beginning to identify the Nominated Assembly as a mistake, his folly. The radicals appeared to threaten ministry and property. The Assembly's attitude to taxation caused anxieties about the funding of the army. On 1 November the Assembly elected a new Council of State; 113 members voted. The lowest number of votes cast for a moderate councillor was 62; the highest for a radical was 58.[17] It was a reminder to the moderates in the assembly of their numerical potential. In late autumn senior officers had begun to draft a written constitution and, on 13 November, John Lambert presented the Instrument of Government to the Council of Officers. A month later, on 12 December, the moderates in the Assembly engineered a submission of their authority back to Cromwell and the experiment was wound up. Four days later, in a rather austere ceremony, Cromwell was installed as Lord Protector under the terms of the Instrument of Government.

The Instrument had been drafted principally by Lambert but was also the product of reiteration and negotiation. Initially, the title of 'King' was part of it but Cromwell had rejected that. Still, for many of the saints, especially radical millenarians like the Fifth Monarchists, and for the republicans, the adoption of the Instrument was the moment of Cromwell's greatest apostasy. However austerity might mask the reality, the return to a single person, as a key element within the constitution, smacked of a return to monarchical forms; the adoption of a formal constitution spoke for others of a rejection of the fluidity of saintly and Providential rule. It was the moment when Cromwell's reputation for scheming ambition and personal aggrandizement took hold. But the Instrument was yet another attempt to find a 'safe' basis for civilian rule and in some significant ways it harked back to The Heads of Proposals and even to the settlement which many had hoped for in 1641. Responsible or 'coordinate' government required the single person to rule with powers with respect to finance, the appointment of senior officials and command of the army, constrained by a Council elected by Parliament and a powerful, single chamber Parliament. If it was a move towards regal forms, and in a formal and ceremonial sense it inevitably was, it was in the direction of a firmly limited monarchy. Further proof of this was given when Cromwell met his first Parliament in September 1654. Elected on a franchise with a more restrictive property qualification than the old Commons and with a very substantial redistribution of seats away from the small boroughs in favour of the counties, it was bound to reflect the traditional ruling classes in all their shades of conservatism and moderation. Substantial reforming legislation had been enacted by Protectoral ordinance in the nine months before Parliament met and this, plus the origins of the constitution, became immediate bones of contention. After eight days of acrimonious debate, Cromwell spoke to the House again. He asked members to formally recognize and to work with the regime while offering in turn to consider constitutional revision provided that four fundamentals – rule by a single person and

Parliament; liberty of conscience; regular elections of parliaments and joint control of the military – were respected. About 80 MPs refused to accept the 'Recognition' and so excluded themselves. The constitutional debates which ensued ran into two major obstacles. The first was that of religious toleration and its extent. Most MPs wished, as they saw it, to restore religious order and the case of James Biddle, a unitarian imprisoned for blasphemy in December 1654, seemed to be an opportunity for firm action. The second issue was the Instrument's provision (clauses 27 and 28) for a standing army of 30,000 men as a prior charge upon state revenues. Some reduction in the size of the army was part of Cromwell's long-term strategy for the civilianization of government, but precipitate attempts to slash its size and jeopardize its funding only alienated what was still the key element in his political support. On 22 January 1655 he dissolved the House, accusing them, in a disappointed speech, of 'disettlement and division, discontent   and   dissatisfaction'   and   comparing   them unfavourably with the Rump.

What followed was a year of mixed fortunes. The navy, developed by the Rump and inherited by the Protectorate, delivered victories in the Mediterranean and off the African coast. But the Hispaniola expedition of 1655, an attempt to establish an English base in the Caribbean from which to harass the Spanish, was a worrying disaster, when God's face might have turned away from his Englishmen. At the time it overshadowed the occupation of Jamaica which was far more important in the long-run for the British presence in the Caribbean. News of the massacres of Protestants in the mountains of Piedmont roused Cromwell (and John Milton) to think again that God might have an international mission for his Protestant champions. Success in crushing an abortive Royalist rising in March was followed by worrying intelligence of conspiratorial alliances of Royalists, Levellers, commonwealthsmen and Fifth Monarchists which rippled through the summer. To meet the needs of security but also perhaps as a means of finding a cheaper alternative to a standing army, even perhaps to find a means whereby the goal of godly reformation might be more effectively pursued (and a jealous God be appeased), in August 1655 Cromwell began to commission the Major-Generals. The country was divided into 10, then 11, regions each with a Major-General supported by a core of seasoned soldiers and with the task of recruiting and training a regional militia. The first priority was security and in the medium-term it was anticipated that such a function could be shifted from an expensive national standing army to regionally responsive militias. Indeed over the summer of 1655 some 10,000–12,000 men of the New Model Army were disbanded. But the initial and recurrent costs of the regional militias were to be met by a tax on those who had been active Royalists, the decimation tax, to be collected under the authority of the Major-Generals. This necessarily involved them in civil administration, identifying 'Royalists', assessing their wealth and income and levying the tax. Rather than a move from centralized to regional security, this looked too much like the heavy hand of centralizing government imposed on the localities. It was a perception reinforced by the Major-Generals' involvement in the policing of communal activities and the reformation of manners. Given conventions of thought which saw the appeasing of a watchful and potentially angry God as a necessary part of the nation's security, such involvement was almost inevitable but the desire to use the new system to push for the reformation so long postponed also played its part. However good its intentions, the system's performance and effectiveness were patchy and it became a public relations disaster of some magnitude. Reconciliation with the natural rulers of the countryside, delinquents or not, was rendered virtually impossible by the threat of overbearing military rule which the system, and its possible extension, came to represent. At the same time, the judges were beginning to question the legal validity of Protectoral ordinances in respect to taxation and treason. The government needed the endorsement of statute law if its policies were to have a legitimacy which could be recognized by the courts.

As the war with Spain was spreading from the Caribbean to Europe, the decision was taken in the summer of 1656 to call a Parliament for September of that year, earlier than was required under the terms of the Instrument of Government. The influence of the Major-Generals on the elections appears to have been negligible, if not counterproductive, and about 120 of the candidates returned had to be excluded from sitting. Clauses 14–16 of the Instrument could be seen as providing some warrant for such exclusions and they seem to have been decided by the Council rather than the Lord Protector. But such exclusions meant that the politics of Pride's Purge still hung over the Protectorate and it was clearly an issue which would have to be addressed. Cromwell's lengthy opening speech on 17 September 1656 stressed the importance of the conflict with Spain, billed as the nation's inveterate enemy and the need for security and reformation at home.

Despite the exclusions, the session began well. There was support for the war and for reasonable security measures. It was soon clear that there was also a will to stabilize the regime on a civilianized basis. At last an opportunity appeared to be on offer whereby a deal could be struck between Cromwell and the local governing classes, a deal driven by their ideas and therefore possessed of a legitimacy it could not claim as long as it was imposed by the military. Sindercombe's plot to assassinate the Protector, reported to the House by John Thurloe in January 1657, may have underlined the vulnerability of the regime and the desire to get it on to a more stable, inevitably traditional, basis. Early in the Parliament there had been a motion to make the Protectorate hereditary, a suggestion sharply dismissed by Cromwell's brother-in-law and member of the Council, John Desborough. Two other issues impinged on this. One was the Major-Generals to whom there was broad opposition amongst MPs. Cromwell quickly signalled, through his son-in-law, the MP John Claypole, his willingness to abandon the system. The other was the case of James Nayler, a potential leader of the Quakers, who had been arrested for blasphemy after riding into Bristol in what looked like an imitation of Christ's entry into Jerusalem. In October 1656 the House had taken upon itself to try Nayler in a deliberate attempt to assert its authority over religious issues and to stem what was seen as a worrying tide of religious nonconformity and religious excess. Nayler's case simultaneously posed the problems of liberty of conscience and of the constitution: how could a single-chamber assembly be checked if it set out to control the consciences of the godly?

In January 1657, on to a vote congratulating the Protector on escaping Sindercombe's plot on his life, John Ashe, an obscure backbench MP, had tagged an amendment in favour of a return to something like the 'ancient constitution'. A month later, on 23 February, the House voted, by 150 to 52, in favour of offering Cromwell the crown and setting up a second chamber. On 27 February about 100 officers made their opposition to proposals to amend the Instrument clear to Cromwell. In an angry response, he berated them for their inconsistent and frequently ill-thought out harassment of him and made the powerful point that, if liberty of conscience, which was dear to them all, was to be maintained, they needed a second chamber as a check on the otherwise unfettered power of the Commons. Cromwell's searing fury had its effect. On 5 March a much more conciliatory army deputation met with him. The road was open to a degree of constitutional revision. It was clear that a majority in Parliament were looking to a reversion in the direction of King, Lords and Commons. On 25 March they voted by 123 to 62 votes to offer Cromwell the crown. A week later the Humble Petition and Advice was offered to him as an all-or-nothing package. On 3 April he replied in terms of an unwillingness to accept the package as it stood and negotiations continued. On 6 May it looked to some of those closest to him as if Cromwell was preparing to accept the title of King but on 8 May he responded with a final refusal. It may have been an interview with Fleetwood, Desborough and Lambert, men close to him and long-time associates, who indicated that they would not serve him under that title, which tipped the balance in his mind, but his own musings on Providence and the pleas of old soldiers, like William Bradford who had followed him from Edge Hill to Dunbar, no doubt played a part.

The process of negotiation had, however, induced greater flexibility. On 25 May the Humble Petition and Advice was offered again to Cromwell with kingship gone and the succession to the position of Protector in his gift. A month later he was installed as Lord Protector under the new constitution with a ceremony that, to some of his old allies, reeked of regal pomp. In the second half of 1657 attention turned to nominating members of the new second chamber. If it was to act effectively as the desired check on the lower house it had to be reliable and of its initial 42 members many were Cromwell's relatives or associates. As a further step towards normality, the members excluded from the lower house in 1656 were readmitted, so that when Parliament reassembled in late January 1658 not only was there a second chamber but the complexion of the Commons had also changed substantially. The new session saw division and acrimonious attacks on the new constitution leading to the abrupt dissolution of Parliament on 4 February. Cromwell now 'ruled by a parliamentary constitution, not an army settlement' but time would be required if it were to prove acceptable, after so many experiments, to the nation at large.

Union with Scotland, based on legislation of 1654, and 'settlement' in Ireland, authorized by an Act of 1652, also required time if their conquest origins were to be overcome. As we have seen, Scotland's military capability was depleted and the exhaustion of war may have made it more compliant. The removal of feudal tenures and greater security for tenants was designed to undermine the power of the great Scots landlords. At the same time, commerce with England was encouraged and there were signs that prosperity was returning at least in the lowlands. In Ireland, the government was committed to wholesale confiscations; some 1000 'Adventurers' had claims on the strength of loans made against promises of Irish land and about 30,000 soldiers could claim entitlement to Irish lands in lieu of pay. The plans to confiscate the lands of Catholics in Ireland and forcibly transport them to Connaught were on a scale and of an inhumanity which make chilling reading. The full implementation of the scheme was well beyond the administrative capability and resources of the English government. Nevertheless, huge misery was caused as it was by the attempt to force all Catholics out of Irish towns. The proportion of Irish land held by Catholics is estimated to have fallen from over 70 per cent to under 20 per cent. Henry Cromwell, Oliver's younger son, who was in effect ruling Ireland from September 1655 rapidly adopted more pragmatic policies. He tacitly dropped the policy of wholesale transportation and set about looking for ways to reconcile traditional interests to the rule of the Protectorate.

Apart from the Hispaniola débâcle, Cromwell had experienced success in the Caribbean and the Mediterranean. Whether Protectoral foreign policy was misguided in identifying Spain as *the* national enemy and ignoring the latent and nascent power of France is open to debate. But, compared with the nation's international standing in the 1620s and 1630s or the 1660s and 1670s, England under Cromwell commanded a respect which it would not do again until the early eighteenth century. Victory at the battle of the Dunes in June 1658 and the acquisition of Dunkirk in alliance with the French symbolized the continued vigour of the regime in foreign affairs. But, as the summer of 1658 wore on, Cromwell's health deteriorated. The agonizing death from cancer of his beloved daughter, Elizabeth, on 6 August left him depressed and he was himself seriously ill from 19 August. Despite some periods of remission he died on that auspicious day 3 September, the anniversary of Dunbar and Worcester. The office of Lord Protector was transmitted peacefully to his son, Richard. Cromwell's body, or rather its effigy, lay in state, in a manner modelled on the funeral rites of James I, at Somerset House from 20 September until 23 November when there was a state funeral of truly regal display. But the stability which so dismayed exiled Royalists in the autumn of 1658 was more apparent than real. Just over two years after his stately funeral, on the anniversary of Charles I's execution, the royal 'martyrdom', on 30 January 1661 Cromwell's corpse was swinging at Tyburn. The Stuarts were restored and Cavalier vindictiveness was having its day.[18]

3

The cat's paw of history
Cromwell's reputation through time

Everyone knows – and is especially blessed with clarity of vision if they have made no serious study of them – the virtues and vices of historical figures like Henry VIII and Elizabeth I. The popular constructions of their reputations are absorbed by us as part of the popular culture of our time. Cromwell is a figure of this type. There is a popular image of him which runs alongside and, to a large extent, independently of the scholarly study and reconstruction of his historical image. The latter is easier to recover because it has a self-conscious literary tradition. We can read the books, articles and essays which successive generations of authors have contributed to the corpus of literature on Cromwell and, on this basis, we can map the changes in that literature over time. The popular reputation is more difficult to chart since it is so much more a matter of oral traditions and features in social rites, gestures and symbols which may often remain unselfconscious and unrecorded. This chapter is more concerned with Cromwell's formal or scholarly reputation, with the literary tradition of Cromwell's meaning. Our interest is in the interplay between record and reputation, between research and judgement, but we will occasionally glance at the issue of Cromwell's popular reputation.[1]

In many cases, contemporaries had their own eyes and ears to rely on in making their assessments of Cromwell. From the start, extremes were in operation. On the one hand he was the chosen instrument of God, a Moses, a Gideon. On the other, he was in league with the Devil. The most familiar form of this was the story that on the day of his victory at Worcester, 3 September 1651, the Devil agreed to give him power for seven years, reclaiming the Lord Protector's soul punctually on the day of his death, 3 September 1658, an event heralded by impressive diabolical storms.[2] It was common for contemporaries to see Cromwell's actions, victories and rise to power as God's will, Providentially determined,[3] as he did himself.[4] English Protestants admired his role as the champion of European Protestantism. Europeans – even Dutchmen – admired England's relative religious freedom under his rule.[5] Others, the disappointed of all shades of opinion, were quick to see perfidy, betrayal, deceit and ambition as the hallmark of his words and deeds. For William Prynne he was already, by January 1648, the epitome of a new kind of politician, the 'Machiavellian Cromwellist', a 'Hypocritical perfidious New Statist'.[6] A month later, an anonymous author portrayed him as 'the very abstract of sedition' in the tragicomedy of current politics, already bent on becoming King Oliver.[7] Soon after, those wishing to go body and soul to Satan were invited to apply to 'the red-nos'd Rebell, Thieftenant Oliver'.[8] In August of 1648, John Lilburne, appalled by his one-time allies' establishment of what seemed to him a military tyranny and their failure to endorse the Leveller programme, issued *An Impeachment of High Treason Against Oliver Cromwell and his son in law Henry Ireton*. They were the principal agents of the army's apostasy and it might be better to join the Royalists than to submit to such people.[9] The bitterness of old allies fallen out complemented the vicious personal attacks and abuse of old enemies.[10] Naturally, the regicide and Cromwell's part in it excited much of the latter. But, on the other side, a growing catalogue of God's judgements on the field of battle, down to Cromwell's final victory at Worcester were used to vindicate Cromwell as acting with divine approval.[11] Like Moses, his authority came directly from God.[12]

But after Worcester, there were to be no further appeals to the God of battles, at least as far as Cromwell was directly concerned and the political dramas in which he was involved were always open to conflicting interpretations. The expulsion of the Rump, for republicans like Hutchinson, Vane and Ludlow, was a disastrous abandonment of principle in the pursuit of personal ambition. For the godly, Fifth Monarchists and other enthusiasts, it was a saintly act, giving priority to religious over civil liberty and opening the door to a truly godly reformation.[13] By the end of December 1653, their perspective too had undergone a radical transformation as the Nominated Assembly was dispersed and the Protectorate inaugurated. From that date Cromwell was frequently depicted as not only the instrument of the downfall of King Charles but also as the usurper of King Jesus. John Spittlehouse, in late 1654, was at pains to point out the divergence between the Lord Protector's disparagement of the Nominated Assembly in his opening speech to the first Protectoral Parliament and his millennial enthusiasm at the opening of the earlier assembly in July 1653. He appealed still to Cromwell not to usurp the authority of Christ.[14] Colonel Edward Lane found a biblical parallel for Cromwell's apostacy in the Old Testament figure of Jehu (2 Kings 9–10). Like Cromwell, Jehu was a regicide and a reformer. Like Cromwell, he was, for a time, God's chosen instrument. But, also like Cromwell, he pretended humility, kept tight control of the army, ingratiated himself with the saints and played the hypocrite. His sin was in giving primacy to the rules of 'State-policy' over the promptings of God. 'Police doth ruine true *Religion*.'[15] In 1655, George Fox, the Quaker leader who claimed to have supported Cromwell for 'betwixt eight and nine years' urged him to lay down all his worldly authority at the feet of the Lord.[16] Rather more harshly, Christopher Feake, the Fifth Monarchist, looked back in 1659 over the last 20 years and saw Cromwell, who had once been the leader and liberator of the godly, as the great turncoat. What required explanation was how Cromwell had been able to sustain the Protectorate in defiance of God and his true saints. 'The Instruments used by him ... were multitudes of Pursevants, Catchpoles, Spies, Spirits, Trapanners, and such like Base Vermin, that use to creep and sneak in every corner, for the service of usurping upstarts in all Generations.'[17]

The 'usurping upstart' and his Protectorate were, however, not without their defenders. A very early attempt at a contemporary history, *Britannia Triumphalis* (1654), portrayed the Rump as corrupt; the Nominated Assembly as confused. The Instrument of Government was both justified and full of promise. Cromwell was 'a man as it were by Divine appointment set apart for great enterprises'.[18] Other defences of the Protectorate argued that it did not prevent the rule of Christ, since Christ's Kingdom was not of this world. But it did preserve godliness and when saints were imprisoned it was to preserve civil peace not to persecute their religion.[19] In a defence of the Protectorate – and the Protector – against the infamous *Killing Noe Murder* (1657) which called for the assassination of Cromwell, the author compared the nation to a sick man and Cromwell to its physician or support. 'We have long been sick, and our disease was well nigh grown to a habit, and now that we are gotten again upon our legs, and able to walk by the help of a staff, what desperate confidence were it, to throw away that supporter . . . ?'[20] Support for Cromwell, even as a transitional ruler whose authority might be justified by divine sanction or by personal attributes such as courage, wisdom and integrity, could come from a wide variety of quarters, including Anglican, Royalist and millennialist.[21]

One of the earliest attempts to reach a balanced assessment of Cromwell was William Sedgewick's *Animadersions upon A Letter and Paper* (1656) replying to *A Word for God* which was a call for saintly violence against the Protectoral regime. Cromwell, Sedgewick argued, had risen from a low and afflicted condition. Submission to the will of God had been hammered into him by suffering and 'publike work' seemed natural to him. To his attributes of vigour, constancy and integrity, providential success had added confidence. But Cromwell's weaknesses – rash passion, want of foresight and 'violent strains and leaps which have stretched conscience and credit' – were equally apparent. Still, he was the one person who, in the eyes of Providence and men, could unite the three kingdoms and keep civil and military power in some balance. In December 1653 he had had unlimited power in his hands but had shown sufficient humility to seek its limitation through the Instrument of Government. Sedgewick acknowledged that there had been apostasy on the part of both the nation at large and the government, and for the second of these Cromwell had to bear the responsibility. The key question was whether his government would have the backing of Providence for the future or not, and, in the end, this came back to the question of Cromwell's providential status.

> I have heard some that have been his servants, near to him and *strict observers* of him report, that his frequent Praying, Fasting, Watching, with other conscientious and strict Observances, shew'd him inclin'd rather to turn Quaker, then to looseness.

It was inconceivable that it would ever be the Protector's intention 'to carry us back to Egypt'. Sedgewick's preferred parallel for Cromwell was with Elijah, the Old Testament prophet who rescued Israel from apostasy by paying attention not to the earthquake, nor to the fire but to the still, small voice of the Lord

(1 Kings 19).[22] Those preoccupied with the European position of Protestantism had even less reservation in justifying Cromwell's rule. He had taken up the mantle of Elizabeth I in countering the Roman Catholic–Imperial–Spanish threat.[23]

The immediate post-mortem and obituary assessments of 1658 and 1659 were, almost inevitably, laudatory. God's blessing on the nation, an example to all other Christian princes, a Gideon, a Josiah, comparable to the heroes of Rome, had gone. No ordinary pen could set forth an adequate assessment of his achievements. Henry Dawbeney did his best by drawing 30 parallels between Moses and Cromwell but it was a pedestrian, if exhaustive, effort.[24] Possibly the first attempt at anything like a full biography, advertised as being translated into five languages, was Samuel Carrington's *The History of the Life and Death of His most serene Highness Oliver Late Lord Protector* (1659).[25] Cromwell, according to Carrington, had been 'a Modell of all kinde of Vertues and Perfections', 'who in the space of ten years time, did accomplish the work of a whole Age: nay more, he perfected the work of future Ages'. History could surely ask no more, but a reckoning from a different quarter, Scotland, was not so forgiving. Robert Pitilloh argued that, to stabilize Protectoral rule in Scotland, Cromwell had ingratiated himself so far with the Presbyterians as to allow them to persecute the godly of other persuasions.[26]

With the Restoration, of course, criticism became harsher. Not only were Cromwell's mortal remains exhumed and subject to such indignities as could be inflicted upon them but so too was his reputation. The most notorious vilification, surprisingly influential in view of its crudity, was James Heath's *Flagellum* (1665), an exhaustive and inventive revival of the satanic Cromwell. Cromwell as monster was certainly the dominant image of him through the later seventeenth and on into the eighteenth century. The Church of England's new Prayer Book of 1662 included a service annually commemorating Charles the Martyr on 30 January, the anniversary of the regicide. This meant obligatory sermons which, in order to extol the virtues of Charles invariably found it instructive to compare them with the vices of his usurper and murderer. For William Winstanley, Cromwell was simply the 'England monster'.[27] But elsewhere, this picture was often qualified by acknowledging either virtue amidst the vice or viciousness on a scale equivalent to grandeur. John Davies in 1661 observed a certain spirit and magnanimity in the prevailing blackness and

10 years later, in an otherwise condemnatory piece, Thomas Gumble saw 'something generous in him'.[28] John Hacket's demonic portrait found it impossible not to concede an element of the heroic:

> That imp of Satan, compounded of all vice and violence, and the Titan-like courage, devoid of all pity and conscience, the greatest of all soldiery, and by his arts greater than them all, waxen to be a Colossus, between whose strides the seas flowed. . . .[29]

However black the picture of the usurper and regicide must be once the legitimate succession had been re-established, it was never quite an unrelieved blackness. The 'Person of Honour' who, in the wake of the Exclusion Crisis (1679–81) found that Cromwell was a valuable exemplar of the ills of usurpation, portrayed him as 'the subtil Fox', 'the *Lucifer* of the rest, who outwitted them all, and ruled by himself, with great Power, and more absolute Sway, than ever any Monarch of England did'. But as he wrote on we can witness the struggle to acknowledge something of the more positive attributes of Cromwell without conceding too much. He was

> a man . . . of many Vices, of deep Dissimulation and Hypocrisie, and tho no great Schollar, of great improved Parts; of a strong, robust Constitution, and naturally, Martiall, of deep reach and a great Politician, after he had conversed with *Ireton* his Son-in-law who taught him his Art. He had some spice of Generosity in him, which he shewed on some occasions. . . . But for his Courage and Resolution, and skill in Martiall Discipline, that is not to be questioned and tho I cannot think he really embraced any religion, as his particular Judgement, yet he embraced all that he found subservient to his Ends.

Had he not been a usurper, he would have been outstanding in his generation.[30]

Two legacies of the Glorious Revolution were the publication of the first edited documents of the mid-seventeenth century and the eventual emergence of a nonconformist historiography. The former – frequently distorted by highly interventionist editors – on balance darkened the image of Cromwell partly because so often they seemed to be based on the observations of those close to him, partly because they spoke of the betrayal of old allies.

Richard Baxter's *Reliquiae Baxterianae*, first published in 1696, told the story of a Cromwell once possessed of the Lord's favour but corrupted by worldly ambition. Edmund Ludlow's *Memoirs*, aggressively edited by John Toland, first appeared in 1698 and presented Cromwell as a man who sacrificed the republician cause, country, conscience and honour on the altar of personal pride.[31] Clarendon's enormously influential *History of the Rebellion and Civil Wars in England*, first published in 1702, told the story from a different perspective; that of a cultivated and moderate Royalist who was a senior figure in the counsels of the Stuarts from 1641 until 1667. Clarendon's Cromwell was certainly an ambitious schemer in a manner familiar from most hostile accounts of him. But Clarendon's knowledge of the workings of contemporary politics was reflected in a more subtle portrait which even went further than subtlety in two respects. The first was to concede that the emergence of the Protectorate, the rule of Oliver as the single person within a balanced constitution, was necessary if chaos and vulnerability – 'such a confusion as would rather have exposed them as a prey to foreigners' – were to be avoided. The second was to admit that Cromwell had great qualities: 'for he could never have done half that mischieve without great parts of courage and industry and judgement'. His understanding of men was 'wonderful'; his dexterity in dealing with them 'great'. He possessed 'a great spirit, an admirable circumspection and sagacity, and a most magnanimous resolution'; 'when he was to act the part of a great man, he did it without any indecency through the want of custom.' He could show great reverence for the law and 'a wonderful civility, generosity and bounty'. In subduing three nations he showed 'a very prodigious address'. 'But his greatness at home was but a shadow of the glory he had abroad. It was hard to discover which feared him most, France, Spain or the Low Countries.' It is hard to resist, as one reads this assessment by a constitutional Royalist who believed that his cause was good but his royal masters were weak, the conclusion that here is the monarch, who, 'had his cause been good',[32] Clarendon would have preferred. His final summation on Cromwell is even more striking. 'He was not a man of blood, and totally declined Machiavelli's method, which prescribes upon any alteration of a government, as a thing absolutely necessary, to cut off all the heads of those . . . who are friends of the old.' A bulwark of order, he was also, Clarendon thought, a staunch defender of ex-Royalists against proposals for

their general massacre. In short, his wickedness was much qualified by great virtues. He was, and posterity would so regard him,
'a brave bad man'.[33]

The negative image of Cromwell which prevailed for over a
century and three-quarters after his death, was then seldom an
unqualified one. The Protector had been, at the least, brave as
well as bad. His international standing was recalled as a source of
national pride, as evidence of national potential and even as a
rebuke to more internationally supine English governments. The
view of Samuel Pepys, that there was something disquieting or
embarrassing about indignities heaped on a great man, persisted.[34] Both those who prized political stability and legitimate
hereditary succession, or at least the sanctity of monarchy, and
those who, from a more republican perspective, despised it were
unlikely to embrace Cromwell warmly. Ideology and party affiliation continued to influence the shaping of his reputation but, as
the example of Clarendon illustrates, while political persuasion
predisposed it never entirely determined the final assessment.
More perceptive, or more honest, commentators could and did
acknowledge aspects of his record which ran against the grain of
prejudice.

Following the Hanoverian succession in 1714 and the defeat of
the first Jacobite rebellion in 1715 the picture of the bad man
with some redeeming features persisted[35] but there also began to
emerge a tradition of almost positive Cromwellian historiography. Isaac Kimber's *Life of Oliver Cromwell* (1725), which went
through six editions by 1728, had Cromwell as driven by ambition but ambitious for the public good. A similarly popular life
by John Banks published in 1739 found more to praise than to
blame – particularly when comparing Cromwell with Charles I.[36]
Both Kimber and Banks were dissenters. The *Biographica
Britannica* of 1750 attempted to sort the facts from the fiction,
dismissing, for example, the fabulous anecdotes of his childhood
adventures and dissipated youth. Objectivity was a problem

> because, through envy on the one side, flattery on the other,
> and strong prejudices upon both, it may be truly said, that
> more of the falsehood and fable is to be met with in the
> accounts of him ... than of almost any other person living
> so near our own times.

Looked at more dispassionately the author claimed that there
were many proofs of his sincerity. He had, as Protector, a

commendable record of moderation in church and state; was 'very honourably descended' and was 'equally remarkable' as soldier and statesman.[37]

Ideology and evidence continued to wrestle. Writing as one committed to government founded on liberty and sympathetic to the republican ideal, Catherine Macaulay writing in the 1760s, saw Cromwell's usurpation of the Rump as evidence of the corrupt baseness of the English people who allowed it to happen; it testified to their unfitness for republican liberty.[38] Driven by 'the most sordid principles of self-interest, with their concomitant vices, envy, hatred, and malice', Cromwell's 'rank hypocrisy' was without political talent or vision. His success depended purely on his vigour and military abilities.[39] With Ludlow as her guide, she came to an assessment convergent with that of the most ardent Royalist and Stuart sympathizer. Her namesake Thomas Babington Macaulay, writing from a far from republican perspective, was more positive about Cromwell's abilities. In his review of Hallam's *Constitutional History* (1821) Macaulay took issue with the view that Cromwell's rise to tyrannical power was by accident and deceit. Whatever the virtues or vices of his rule, his rise was the product of vigour, 'the best qualities of the middling orders', shaped by a 'strong sympathy with the feelings and interests of his people . . . he had a high, stout, honest English heart'.[40]

One of the issues over which Macaulay took Hallam most vigoriously to task was the latter's comparison of Cromwell and Napoleon Bonaparte. The revolutions of the later eighteenth century naturally excited comparison with those of seventeenth-century England. For Americans in the revolutionary decades it was common to identify John Hampden and Algernon Sidney as exemplary champions of liberty with Cromwell as a warning of the dangers inherent in a revolution run out of control. George Washington was a preferable 'patriot-hero' precisely because he resisted the temptations to tyranny to which Oliver had succumbed.[41] English radical writers of the 1790s frequently domesticated their observations of events across the Channel by calling on the events of the 1640s and 1650s in England. Their principal sources were Clarendon and Burnet with assistance from Toland's Ludlow. Principled republicans, Milton, Harrington and Sidney were for a time preferred by Wordsworth and Coleridge. Southey praised Henry Marten as an unflinching regicide. John Thelwall, the English Jacobin, preferred John

Lilburne. Cromwell continued to be portrayed as the ambitious, fanatical usurper, detested by republicans. It was in this context that the comparison between Cromwell and Bonaparte could have its uses. Both were seen as taking advantage of a situation where the love of liberty was firmly established only with a minority and shallowly rooted, at best, with the masses.[42] The Romantics' interest in Cromwell thus began to concern itself with the problem of the corruption of revolutionary idealism. In an article reviewing recent biographies of Cromwell, which he published in 1821, Robert Southey argued that the Lord Protector's imperishable name was 'stained with reproach'. Usurpation required the pragmatic skills of the dissembler and hypocrite, but it also obliged Cromwell to rule tyrannically and destroyed his peace of mind.[43] Out of such themes a tragic drama might be construed. In 1834, after troubles with the censor because it dealt with the regicide, Mary Russell Mitford's play *Charles the First* was staged at the Victoria Theatre, London. Despite its title, Cromwell was the central figure, the character of Henrietta Maria describing him as 'the monster-spirit of the time'. He was a democrat tempted by power and the regicide is the moment when he succumbed to that temptation.[44] William Godwin's *History of the Commonwealth of England* (1824–8) cast the dilemma in a different form. Cromwell was trapped because it was clear from the later 1640s that free elections would have meant a Royalist political victory and Restoration. In his devotion to religion and morality Cromwell was sincere but, from Worcester onwards, the temptation to escape the political cul-de-sac by exploiting his personal position in pursuit of the crown was too great. Throughout Godwin's four volumes Cromwell was contrasted with John Lilburne, the free spirit who retained his democratic integrity because he was never directly involved in the coils of power.[45]

The idea that Thomas Carlyle's famous edition of *Oliver Cromwell's Letters and Speeches*, first published in 1845, transformed the reputation of Cromwell, rescued it from obloquy and disseminated a new heroic version of the Protector cannot be sustained. As we have seen, Cromwell's reputation before Carlyle was more shaded and there had been positive historical assessments of him since at least the early eighteenth century. In particular, the writings of Robert Vaughan and John Robertson had elevated the value of seventeenth-century Puritanism and of Cromwell as its exemplar.[46] In some senses, the attempt to make the record speak for itself had reached its highest level to date in Mark Noble's *Memoirs of the Protectoral House of Cromwell* (1787). An Anglican clergyman, Noble attempted to survey comprehensively all the evidence extant relating to Cromwell, his ancestors and descendants. But the justification for all this effort was Noble's belief that his central figure 'was one of the greatest men, this or any other nation ever produced'.[47] Despite its antiquarian flavour, the positive evaluations of work of this kind were not uninfluential. The 1840s saw a sustained effort to mark the bicentenary of the 1640s by re-evaluating their importance, an effort which had as one of its culminations the controversial, and ultimately unsuccessful, campaign to have a statue of Cromwell erected at Westminister. Hitherto, the events of the Puritan Revolution, epitomized by what were seen as the bloody fanaticism of extra-constitutional excesses of the 1640s and 1650s, had been down-played in favour of the respectable and relatively bloodless events of the Glorious Revolution. But the frustrations of electoral and constitutional reform following the first Reform Act of 1832 and the rise of new 'Victorian' attitudes to religious seriousness and commitment coincided powerfully with the revival of interest in the 1640s and 1650s. The re-examination of Britain's imperial role also placed Cromwell in the 'founders of Empire' pantheon while the apparent instability of many European societies in the 1830s and 1840s magnified his status as a statesman who could bring order out of such chronic instability. It was in this context that Carlyle's work, while not rescuing Cromwell from obscurity or total ignominy, had a major transformative impact and created what has been called the Victorian 'cult of Cromwell'.[48]

Carlyle's progress to his great edition was painful, tortuous and slow. He had begun as a subscriber to the negative view of Cromwell and the Protectorate. They were 'like a pack of fanatical knaves'. Cromwell himself was 'your true enthusiastic hypocrite ... a knave and a demigod'. When he began to read Oliver's own words, Carlyle was frequently appalled.

> What a grunting semi-articulate, phlegmatic, confused, inexplicable abortive rubbish heap is that! Sentences begin but involve themselves in parentheses, lose their way and never end. A vortex, circle wheeling within circle, in complexity and perplexity, in confusion worse confounded. The effect of the whole is a low infinite croak of expostulation,

complaint and angry rebuke. Daedalean art is simple to this
mighty maze without a plan.

But, as he read on, the awkwardness of Cromwell's prose began
to seem a virtue, the lack of artifice a mark of sincerity. From 1838
Carlyle had it in mind to write a major work on Cromwell and
the English Commonwealth but he agonized over what form this
work should take and what increasingly to him seemed to be the
impossibility of a biography. Finally, in 1842 or 1843 he came to
the decision that Cromwell should speak for himself – with some
assistance to the readers from the editor – in an edition of his letters and speeches. On its appearance in November 1845 the first
edition rapidly sold out. The multi-volume work had to be repeatedly reprinted to meet demand and as information about omissions poured in to Carlyle he had to produce successive new
editions (a process carried on by C.L. Stainer and S.C. Lomas after
his death). Carlyle's *Cromwell* became one of the great landmarks
on the cultural and intellectual map of Victorian Britain. It was
also a considerable literary achievement.[49] The Cromwell who,
with Carlyle's assistance, emerged was a rough-hewn individual;
flawed but, in the final analysis, a man of integrity; almost
painfully sincere in his pursuit of God's will but with a largeness
of heart which offset any narrow puritan tendency to bigotry.
However, Carlyle also set Oliver's personal greatness in a wider
frame, invoking the editor's philosophy of history. 'All History'
was, Carlyle proclaimed, 'an inarticulate Bible' since 'the revelation of the Divine Plan' was most fully given to us through history. In the story that made up that revelation there were certain
individuals, heroes, who came closest to embodying God's will for
their own time. Cromwell fitted this bill not only because of his
achievements but because of his own sense of being an instrument
of the divine will. 'History', in Carlyle's sense, could speak
through him. The achievement of the *Letters and Speeches* rested
on both the immediacy with which Cromwell's image and self-
image are projected to the reader but also, for the Victorian reader,
the sense of coming close to 'History' in its largest, Carlylean –
almost Miltonic – sense. The power of the convergence between
Carlyle's God-centred view of 'History' and Cromwell's God-centred view of the events of his own life is perhaps attested to by the
perception shared by many historians, from W.C. Abbott to Blair
Worden, that Carlyle came closer to capturing the essential
Cromwell than any other scholar has done.

Nevertheless, by modern standards of historical scholarship, Carlyle's edition was seriously deficient. Much of the work was slipshod and heavily reliant on secondary works of sometimes dubious reliability. There was a gullibility about Carlyle's willingness to accept material which reached an almost farcical level with his long endorsement of the forged Squire letters.[50] Above all, his interpolations as editor are too obtrusive, and more than occasionally crass, for modern tastes. The kindest verdict is that he was too much of a poet to make a good editor.[51] A number of his reviewers pointed out that Carlyle's image of Cromwell was by no means original. Others, like Richard Cobden, remained sceptical about the work as a whole.[52] Still, Carlyle had launched a cult, if not a craze, for Cromwell. Under his influence, the first American biography, by J.T. Headley, appeared in 1848. In the same year Friedrich Engels was longing for a German Cromwell to bring an end to the Frankfort Assembly.[53] In 1852 the Mutual Improvement society of Watlington, Oxfordshire, after a debate spanning seven consecutive evenings, voted that 'with the exception of sometimes allowing his religion to degenerate into enthusiasm and consenting to the death of the King ... a better Christian, a more noble-minded spirit, a greater warrior, a more constant man has scarcely ever appeared on the face of the earth'.[54] An age of self-conscious improvement, which saw the replacement of effete aristocratic codes by sturdy middle-class values as a sign of progress, began to evoke Cromwell as a symbol of the potential of the English/British race. And the raising of nonconformist self-confidence, as the century wore on, accelerated the process. Cromwell could be at once both an anti-establishment figure, a symbol of religious respectability, a man of action and a source of order.

These positive attributes were also on display in the popular vogue for historical paintings and, from the early nineteenth century, the significance of seventeenth-century subjects in that genre was on the rise. Between 1820 and 1900, it has been estimated,

> something like a hundred and seventy-five paintings appeared on the walls of the Royal Academy connected with Charles I and his family, Oliver Cromwell and the Civil War. No other period could match this for intensity of public interest.[55]

Cromwell's appeal lay in his prefiguring of the new self-made man and the tension between his moral seriousness, his intensity of spiritual introspection and his capacity for explosive action. Between 1853 and 1874, Ford Madox Brown worked on a major study, 'St Ives AD 1630: Cromwell on his Farm'. It depicted Cromwell riding about his tenant farm in melancholic mood, passing through a crisis of faith. Lassitude still holds the man of action in its grip. In 1879 the same artist painted 'Cromwell discussing the Protection of the Vaudois with Milton and Andrew Marvell'. So strong was Brown's identification with Cromwell – Carlyle's Cromwell – that he named his son Oliver. But perhaps the most extraordinary Victorian painting of Cromwell was Augustus Egg's 1859 picture of Cromwell praying on the eve of Naseby. It deliberately evoked conventional images of Christ in agonized prayer in the garden of Gethsemane and its parallels with Christ challenged the iconography of Charles the Martyr.[56]

Self-reliance, moral seriousness and resolute action were all aspects of Cromwell which many Victorians could admire. They were more ambiguous about his status as an anti-establishment figure. In 1849, in an article on the repeal of the Corn Laws, the *Bradford Observer* compared Cobden with Cromwell. They represented 'the incarnate genius of genuine Saxon liberty'.[57] On 14 June 1875, the 230th anniversary of the famous battle, 2000 agricultural labourers assembled at the Cromwell obelisk at Naseby to hear speakers call for better wages, an extended franchise and the reform of the game laws. In the same year, the controversial gift of a statue of Cromwell to the city of Manchester prompted an estimated 50,000 trade unionists to march in support of its erection.[58] But Cromwell's willingness to use armed force against elected assemblies and his ultimately ruthless way with radicals were also themes which concerned the anti-establishment activists of the nineteenth and indeed twentieth centuries. As, towards the last quarter of the nineteenth century, interest in the Levellers and other radicals of the seventeenth century grew, so did this darker assessment of Cromwell. At a more popular level he could still be invoked, at least as late as the 1880s, as a bogeyman to frighten small children into obedience.[59]

In Irish historiography, somewhat surprisingly, Cromwell's most fearsome reputation only emerged in the later nineteenth century. Earlier, his campaign of 1649 and the Cromwellian settlement of the 1650s had been subsumed into a long story of English ignorance of and brutality in Ireland. The events of 1641, the 1660s and the 1690s tended to overshadow the Cromwellian intervention and it was more likely with respect to that, that the bloody nose given to the great commander at Clonmel would be dwelt on rather than Drogheda and Wexford. The vilification of him, in this context, had tended to be perfunctory; the 1650s merely another stage in the long history of legalized robbery by the English.[60] Ironically, Carlyle's elevation of the moral and historical status of Cromwell played a part in generating a re-assessment of the significance of his role in Ireland. A key text here was John P. Prendergast's *The Cromwellian Settlement of Ireland*, first published in 1865. It was based on documents, relating to the confiscation of land and transportation of Irish populations, which Prendergast had discovered in Dublin Castle in 1848. But his study of the documents was also informed by two broad assumptions. One, a Harringtonian one, was that 'the balance of power in a state rests with the class that was the balance of Land'. The other was that there were fundamental ethnic and cultural differences between the Irish and their neighbours across the Irish sea. 'Free by nature, the Irish were followers of nature and freedom in all things.' Their contentment went with a relaxed and communal attitude towards property in land, a contentment rudely shattered by Anglo-Saxon individualism, obsession with private property and legal title, and violence in expropriating Irish communities. The Cromwellian conquest was central to the tragedy of Ireland because it was England's most systematic and brutal attempt to sweep away the communal ethos of the Irish and its material underpinnings. Prendergast's story was a horrifying one and there was plenty of anecdotal – as well as statistical – material in the documents to give it compelling impact. He was aware that the Protectorate, now a name assuming ironic connotations in an Irish context, had neither the administrative ability nor the resources to carry out its plans for Ireland in full. Nevertheless, he claimed that by 1657 perhaps five out of six of the native Irish had perished and the associated devastation left Ireland haunted by three problems: wolves, priests and banditry.[61] Thanks to Cromwellian policies the worst horrors of the Thirty Years War had found a home in Ireland. Astonishingly, the English historian J.A. Froude, one of Carlyle's principal disciples, replied in his *The English in Ireland* (1872–4) by accepting the factual accuracy of Prendergast's account but drawing another conclusion about the 'benefits' of English rule. The Irish, he claimed, 'respect a master hand, though it be a hard and cruel one', and Cromwell had provided an exemplary version of such rule.[62] The crudity and nationalist arrogance of

Froude's response strengthened Irish nationalist interest in Prendergast's findings. W.E.H. Lecky's *A History of Ireland in the Eighteenth Century*, the first volume of which was published in 1878, summarized Cromwell's legacy in Ireland in a way which was to shape his reputation for the next century and a quarter: horror at the massacres of Drogheda and Wexford; a hatred of the English, which lasted down to the present; and a pattern of landownership which would continue to bedevil Anglo-Irish relationships. By the later 1880s both Prendergast and Lecky were growing concerned about the uses to which their views on Cromwellian Ireland were being put by the more extreme nationalists.[63]

Some of the tensions surrounding Cromwell as a highly ambiguous figure in Anglo-Irish history surfaced in the protracted struggle to find a place for him in the pantheon of national heroes in and around the Palace of Westminister. In the 1840s, when the arts of sculpture and painting were enlisted to celebrate the nation's history in Pugin's new Parliament buildings, Cromwell was effectively excluded. As the tercentenary of his birth, in 1899, approached, Lord Rosebery – onetime Prime Minister and leader of the Liberal Party – sought to persuade Parliament that this was the occasion for them to have a statue to one of their great past members. Support from nonconformists was strong; from Irish members, for obvious reasons, not forthcoming. The outcome was a fiasco. Rosebery was allowed to erect a statue – at his own expense. Thorneycroft's fine representation of the Puritan hero with Bible in one hand, sword in the other, was confined to an obscure site, a sunken green. It was unveiled on 14 November 1899, a date of no particular significance, without ceremony and – for fear of disturbances – at 7.30 in the morning.[64]

As the nineteenth century closed, there was no consensus on Cromwell's historical standing. The champion of civil and religious liberty against an oppressive establishment, the protagonist of constitutional reform, jostled with the tyrant, given to arbitrary disruptions of representative and civilian government; the founder of Empire rubbed shoulders with the conqueror bent on the destruction of a people. The 'professionalization of history', growing in strength through the last quarter of the nineteenth century, produced historians capable of puncturing much of the mythology surrounding Cromwell's reputation[65] but not of breaking free of its contested status. This was partly because these historians too had ideological preconceptions underlying their archival zeal. J.R. Seeley, like Froude an imperialist and defender of union with Ireland, believed that, if Britain was to survive in an age of great powers, it must build on its empire. Cromwell's key decision from this perspective was not the regicide but the acquisition of Jamaica and with it the foundation of the British Empire. A strong, forcefully led Britain with a consistent foreign policy was what had to be admired in Cromwell's record.[66] The doyen of late Victorian professional historians, S.R. Gardiner, rejected Cromwell's imperialism, which, along with his defiance of representative institutions, he saw as a stain on his reputation. His stand for freedom of religion was admirable but his Puritanism was too narrowly based to command the support of the nation. It was dependent on a godly minority which in turn made Cromwell, in his darker moments, dependent on military force and coercion. His imperialism and his policy in Ireland, which was cruel but typical of the English in Ireland, reinforced that tendency. It was in his superiority to the Stuarts, his genuine attempt to see beyond the dynastic to the national interest, to reach beyond sectarian interests to religious freedom, above all, in his attempt to establish and maintain English independence, that Cromwell, in Gardiner's view, commanded respect. Despite the pressures on him, he remained essentially a moderate – the would-be successor to John Pym – whose political career was a struggle to keep the Puritan Revolution on moderate lines. But, in this and other respects, he was for Gardiner 'the typical Englishman of the modern world'. In him the English could see their own strengths and weaknesses.[67] But, in the last decades of the nineteenth and the first of the twentieth centuries, it was strength rather than moderation which was the quality most admired in the Lord Protector. In a world of competing Empires, of rapid social and political change, of revolution and war, Cromwell began to take on the mantle of the exemplary strong man. Rosebery himself was an imperialist, an admirer of vigorous political action, and he took Cromwell to be 'the raiser and maintainer of the power of the Empire of England'. The 'strong men' of the Boer War, Kruger and Joseph Chamberlain, were compared to Cromwell and Lloyd George in 1899 was heard longing for a Cromwell – 'worth a wagonload of bishops' – to settle the House of Lords.[68] The theme of the iron man exercised a particular appeal for turn of the century politicians like Rosebery, Lloyd George and Bonar Law, who admired

Cromwell's 'firmness' in Ireland. It was fully expressed in Theodore Roosevelt's 1901 biography of him. Roosevelt strove to express the qualities of leadership, power and action in his American presidential campaigns and subsequent presidency and these were exactly the qualities he found in his hero.[69] The forcefulness of Cromwell was something with wide appeal to early twentieth-century politicians with a mission. Trotsky invoked him to attack the moderation of the English Labour Party; Stalin to demonstrate to H.G. Wells the necessity for force in overthrowing a rotten social order. In a famous interview with *The New York Times* in July 1933, Hitler used the parallel of Cromwell to justify his overthrow of the Weimar constitution to an Anglo-Saxon audience: 'Cromwell ... secured England in a crisis similar to ours, and he saved it by obliterating Parliament and uniting the nation.' Both Hitler and Mussolini were alleged to have portraits of Cromwell in their offices.[70] Interest in Cromwell as the iron man, a dictator, was not, however, confined to the politicians. In Nazi Germany historians in the 1930s rapidly produced studies of the 'fascist' Cromwell. The idea that Britain's rise to greatness might, at least in part, be based on a figure comparable to the Führer was useful propaganda. It was a theme which had, in any case, already been picked up by English-speaking historians. In 1925 Andrew Daker's *Oliver Cromwell* drew the comparison with Mussolini, both had retrieved order from anarchy. Ten years later Sir George MacMunn's study of leadership in history depicted Cromwell as the defender of England from the 'Bolshevist creed' of the Levellers, providing a necessary, if temporary, dictatorship.[71] Maurice Ashley's *Oliver Cromwell: The Conservative Dictator* (1937) drew similar parallels while urging caution in extending them.[72] W.C. Abbott, the editor of what remains the standard edition of Cromwell's letters and speeches, had no hesitation about the value of comparisons between the Protectorate – 'the earliest of modern experiments in dictatorship' – and the fascist dictatorships of twentieth-century Europe.[73] Not everyone, of course, accepted these comparisons. Sir Ernest Barker, in a courageous lecture given in Berlin in December 1936 and expanded into a book the following year, argued that, unlike Hitler, Cromwell was never the sole and undisputed leader of his country, was not a nationalist, did not think of himself as a hero and did not insist on political or religious uniformity.[74] Both John Buchan and Winston Churchill, the latter in his *A History of the English-speaking Peoples*, denied the validity of the comparison. The image of Cromwell the dictator was kept alive into the later twentieth century by writers from the left of centre like H.N. Brailsford who saw Cromwell's crushing of radical alternatives to his rule as the actions of 'a police state' 'as highly centralised as any of the totalitarian regimes of our own century'. But the parallel was always strained and anachronistic and professional historians increasingly pointed this out.[75]

An alternative approach to seizing Cromwell in the round and identifying his consistency in the context of his times was offered by Hilaire Belloc in a trenchant study (1934), written, not unsympathetically, from a Catholic point of view. Belloc rightly saw that part of the appeal of Carlyle's *Cromwell* lay in its anti-Catholic subtext and claimed that this reduced Cromwell to a one-dimensional figure. Ironically, Belloc's own approach was to place Cromwell in a material and cultural milieu which explained a deep-seated hatred and fear of Catholicism. The Cromwells were part of a social stratum which Belloc called 'the new millionaires', those who had grown rich on the plunder of the old church. This was what the Cromwells, Whalleys, Ingolsbys, Barringtons, Hampdens and many others had in common: a vested interest in the continuance of the Protestant settlement. This inheritance drove Cromwell both spiritually and materially and gave his character its underlying integration. The other formative influence was the sense that in the seventeenth century, as Cromwell and his contemporaries observed it, Protestantism was in near-catastrophic retreat in the face of a resurgent Catholicism. Belloc's Cromwell was haunted by 'the apprehension of renewed Catholic power'. It was the element in Royalism and the King's politics which appeared willing to compromise with this threat which led to the regicide. Cromwell's Irish campaign was driven by fear as much as by vengeance, and its lack of creativity meant that one of his most permanent legacies was the ruin of Ireland. The key to Cromwell's rise and rule was a combination of military genius and godly anti-Catholicism but, as the Protectorate demonstrated, he was fundamentally unfitted for civilian rule.[76] For all its exaggerations, Belloc's account is interesting for its anticipation of a theme which was of growing importance for historians in the last quarter of the twentieth century: the fear of popery as a principal feature of the political culture of seventeenth-century England. Puritanism, which was once seen as almost a synonym for progressive, assertive, self-confidence has come to seem much more complex and shaded. Indeed, research into both new and well-worked areas of early modern society and politics has tended, in the last 30 years, to increase the sense of complexity in the forces shaping lives such as Cromwell's. The rise of Cromwell the paradox may well be a response to this complexity.

One result has been that scholars are more inclined to cautious and qualified assessments. The Cromwell who emerges is less of either the clear-cut hero or villain. Historians have become more sceptical of simple affiliations – be they to religious groupings (Puritans) or political parties (Independents) or social classes. The heroic – all-seeing, all-knowing, all-commanding – personality is much less likely to be invoked. Above all, the attempt to recreate the context in which Cromwell operated, and to recreate it ever more elaborately and comprehensively, has led to an emphasis less on the transcendant hero and more on the man of his time. In the 1950s Hugh Trevor-Roger argued that Cromwell failed with his parliaments as Protector because he was the inveterate backbencher and incapable of managing them. In the late 1980s Roger Howell showed that such a judgement could only be based on a misreading of the political context of the 1650s and that the concept of 'parliamentary management' was an anachronism when applied to that period.[77] Similarly the psycho-historical attempts to explain Cromwell, which enjoyed a certain vogue from the 1940s to the 1970s, began to seem inappropriate when it was shown that their evidence was flawed, their findings reductionist and their assumptions anachronistic.[78] Our understanding of Cromwell's relatively relaxed attitude towards a plurality of Protestant religious forms has moved away from an explanation in terms of liberal tolerance, and has been enhanced by a more complete recovery of the seventeenth-century language of liberty of conscience and its implications. Similarly, our grasp of Cromwell's religion has been aided by putting aside the traditional labels – 'Puritan', 'Independent' – and reconstructing his providentialism and antiformalism.[79] Two of the best of the recent biographies have argued that the myth of the all-pervading Cromwell must go. Peter Gaunt, in particular, has shown that the Protectorate was not a 'one-man-show' but a 'coordinated government' in which Cromwell accepted, sometimes severe, constraints upon his freedom of action.[80] As we begin to understand the workings of politics at the centre of the Cromwellian regime, so the more intensive study of regional politics and administration has opened another dimension of the context for assessing

Cromwell's achievements and relative success.[81] One of the most interesting examples of the intensive study of local archives and a concern with appropriate historical context leading to revisionist views has been that of Irish local historians, particularly the work of what have been called the 'Drogheda revisionists'.[82] Awareness too that in the end Cromwell's character and reputation is a construct – something we make – rather than a given has influenced more recent approaches to his assessment.[83]

Nevertheless, outside of the academic study, Cromwell's reputation has remained controversial. That George V could veto Winston Churchill's proposal to name a British battleship 'Cromwell' may amuse us, but 40 years later similar opposition obliged Durham University to abandon plans to name one of its colleges after the Lord Protector who first gave Durham University status.[84] Ten years later an Oxfordshire borough council found itself in a storm of protest over a proposal to name a street after him,[85] and in 1999 the idea of a Roman Catholic historian preaching at a commemorative service as part of the 400th anniversary aroused indignation. Away from the serious study of the seventeenth century, old images of Cromwell and his reputation continue to be recycled. In a highly regarded general history, published on the eve of a new millennium, Cromwell was still moving towards a dictatorship. He was still the man of destiny, the strong man whose qualities we needed now; still 'a horrible great man'; still the 'brave bad man' Clarendon described him as 300 years ago.[86]

In the early 1970s, in an essay reviewing the reputation and bewildering array of assessments of Cromwell, Donald Pennington concluded, somewhat pessimistically, that there was not much hope of a final answer. Consensus, across all levels of discourse about Cromwell, is certainly unlikely in the near future. Yet there is cause for a modest degree of confidence. Provided that we acknowledge the limitations of the available evidence, that we endeavour to place Oliver in the context of his own times and not ours, that we recognize that his received reputation, rather like an archaeological site, is a construct of many layers laid down over time, we can make progress.[87]

|4|

The self-made man risen from obscurity

In many of the stories of great historical figures a recurrent theme has been that of a movement from powerlessness to power, from marginality to centrality, from darkness and disadvantage to light and superiority; or, as it might be put in an American context, from log-cabin to White House. The reputation of Oliver Cromwell has been powerfully shaped by the appearance of such a trajectory.

Born in provincial obscurity into a junior branch of a family whose social and material standing was slipping from a position of regional dominance, Cromwell was without the advantages of great wealth, and lacked any training or worthwhile experience in the law, politics or arms. By his mid-thirties he looked as if his greatest social aspiration might be to prevent his own growing family from slipping below the ranks of gentility. Prone to melancholia and to rash outbursts in what, to a more prudent mind, might have looked like ill-judged causes, the prospects of even maintaining his status cannot have looked secure, at least before 1636. And yet by his mid-fifties this apparently unpromising man had established himself as an outstanding soldier, politician, leader, symbol of godliness, arbiter of national destinies and ruler of Britain. Explaining his rise to power, prestige and achievement from comparatively humble, if not disadvantaged, beginnings is a task that has shaped the presentation of both Cromwell's personality and his reputation. On the one hand, the 'self' of the self-made man has been portrayed as naturally talented, a born military genius; a man of such commitment, resolution, compassion, courage and vigour as to inspire others to follow where he led; or of such saintliness as to be chosen by God as an instrument and accorded the visible signs – in battle at least – of divine approval. The Cromwell of this explanation is a man of great and meritorious natural abilities. His talents, latent until the circumstances in which they could be exercised and fully developed arose, were in this view, both refined and humanized by the disadvantages under which he suffered in his early life. On the other hand, a darker view has been taken of those same abilities and the manner in which they propelled him from obscurity to eminence. His supreme talent, in this less favourable account, was that of a machiavellian schemer, pursuing personal advantage, exploiting such 'genuine' talents as he may have possessed (military ability is generally conceded) and pretending to those qualities which he did not (sincerity, public spirit). What is striking in both the positive and negative stereotypes described here are these shared assumptions: the wondrous nature of his rise from obscurity and the self-propelled nature of that rise, its dependence on Cromwell's own efforts and abilities, be they meritorious or dishonourable.

From a very early date Cromwell's career came to epitomize an openness to social promotion; or, to put it more positively, to the idea of a 'career open to talents'. But it was always possible to view such openness, encouraged as well as exemplified by Cromwell, with disdain and as reflecting a more sinister perception of his rise. The Earl of Manchester, with not unexpected animus, noted that the officers chosen by Cromwell to serve under him were 'not such as were soldiers or men of estate, but such as were common men, poor and of mean parentage, only he would give them the title of godly, precious men'. Rising from obscurity himself, Cromwell was a patron of obscure men – 'such as have filled dung carts before they were captains and since'. In Manchester's account the subversion of hierarchy and the implied exploitation of religious piety ran together. Cromwell's rise was a harbinger of social disorder.[1] Indeed it was common for Cromwell's 'lowly' origins to be mocked in the hostile accounts of him published in the seventeenth and eighteenth centuries. Elevation from such 'dishonourable' status predisposed commentators to see such abilities as Cromwell did possess, and his exploitation of them, as also dishonourable. By contrast, the sea-change in attitudes towards Cromwell in the nineteenth century is associated with more approving views of the 'self-made man' and the 'career-open-to-talents'. Many of his Victorian admirers saw his virtues as the precursors of the ones they associated with the vigorous middle class of their own day.

> In Cromwell, the Chartists and other reformers saw their historic sanction for the new self-made man; they presented him as the hero of the common people, a man of deep Christian morality, a man of resolution, courage and decision, even if it meant the destruction of the *ancien regime*.[2]

His rise from obscurity, in this scenario, foreshadowed the rise of Great Britain for he embodied the qualities necessary for national achievement and its maintenance: the casting aside of effete aristocratic codes and lassitude in favour of middle-class self-reliance, vigour and purpose; a willingness to embrace popular sovereignty or at least to work in alliance with the common people; and a moral seriousness which led to the ethical exercise of power both at home and abroad.[3] What to David Hume, in the later eighteenth century, had appeared to be 'puritanical absurdities' became, in the nineteenth, the ethical values of national greatness and a new, progressive social order.[4]

The image of Cromwell as the self-made man, meritoriously risen from obscurity, has shown considerable persistence. For Antonia Fraser he still demonstrates 'how a man could rise from a modest inheritance and by his own extraordinary qualities live to defy the greatest in the world'. He remains 'an extreme example of the man who made his own destiny and so affected for better or for worse the destiny of his whole country'.[5] More recently, Peter Gaunt made a similar observation. 'An obscure and minor country gentleman in 1640, Cromwell rose rapidly as a brilliant and naturally gifted soldier and more steadily as a politician of influence and real skill.'[6] This interweaving of the rise from obscurity and the attribution of natural ability and skill has remained a constant element in the construction of Cromwell's reputation and greatness. It is a combination which we are told should still evoke wonder. 'That such a man with little rank or standing would rise to the historical prominence that he later occupied is, even to the jaundiced, secular eye of much modern historiography, nothing short of amazing.'[7] There are three key elements in this story, elements which underpin its power to shape Cromwell's reputation. They are: the context of obscurity out of which Cromwell rose; the self-reliance of Cromwell's propulsion upwards, his rise as a self-made man; and, finally, the positive or negative assessment that is made of that process. In this chapter we will examine the first two of these elements by looking again at what we know of the context of Cromwell's early life and of the processes by which his rise to prominence began. It will be argued as a result that the transition from obscurity to spotlight, from marginality to centrality needs to be rethought as not so much a matter of individual, heroic ability – although this undoubtedly played a part – as of social and political connections and their dynamic in an unfolding crisis.

To begin with we need to ask what the most recent research can tell us about Cromwell's background, the social context of his early life. For that we must turn to Professor John Morrill's brilliant reappraisal of the records which might cast light into that period of obscurity. He sees Cromwell's life as falling into three sections or phases: the first four decades, 'his forty years of obscurity in East Anglia' (1599–1640); 13 years as an MP and an officer in the parliamentary and republican armies (1640–53); and five years as the Lord Protector (1653–8). The first phase did not provide an adequate platform for Cromwell's later achievements which 'cannot be predicated upon his training as a man of action and administration in his prime years'; 'in all respects but one', the first 40 years 'were a poor preparation for a public career'. The exception, according to Morrill, was the spiritual crisis and refashioning through which Cromwell passed, probably in the St Ives years, coming away with the enduring conviction that life should be lived in total reliance on a God who could remodel all things.[8] Essentially, Morrill retains the two traditional features of accounts of Cromwell's early life: its obscurity and its lack of preparation for the career which followed. In fact Morrill's researches, and the insights they bring, lead him to deepen the contrast between the younger Cromwell and the great figure he so dramatically became. Until his late thirties 'he was a man in humbler circumstances, a meaner man, that has usually been allowed'; 'his social status was very ill-defined and his economic situation precarious'. The subsidy rolls of the 1620s show an income closer to £100 than the £300 per annum which his father had enjoyed. In other words, Cromwell was, until the mid-1630s, bringing up his family on the lower margins of gentility, in circumstances materially poorer than those of his own upbringing.[9]

Demographic vagaries, for example the survival of a larger number of children for whom provision had to be made, longevity or mortality amongst those from whom an inheritance might be expected, all played a part in the steady turnover of families on the lower edges of gentry status.[10] Social mobility was partly determined by such contingencies and they were clearly a factor in Cromwell's case. He was born into a large family which, no doubt, stretched patrimonial resources and he himself fathered a similarly large family. Equally, as we shall see, his fortunes and social status were to be considerably restored by the fortuitous death of an uncle in 1636. But reliance on the contingencies of family life was not the most advisable course to prevent the consequences of downward social mobility and what is intriguing in these early years is Cromwell's failure to take any of the alternative and accepted routes to protecting, or restoring, his family's fortunes. Provided with the basics of a gentleman's education he chose not to build on those foundations. Whether he attended the Inns of Court or not, and we have seen that the evidence for such attendance is lacking, he appears to have made no serious attempt to equip himself for the law. It is doubtful whether, given his lack of interest in or involvement with local military matters, he even thought seriously of making a career, like some of his future comrades-in-arms, in military service on the continent. Again the evidence, or rather the lack of it, is unhelpful but there is nothing on which to build an alternative case. Emigration may have offered another prospect of escaping from the gravitational pull of downward social mobility but yet again there is no evidence to confirm that Cromwell at any time had advanced or serious plans to forsake East Anglia and start afresh in New England. So the story of the 1620s, the first decade of his marriage to Elizabeth Bourchier and of the birth of six children to them, is one of growing discomfort in terms of social status and material prospects for the immediate future. It was, moreover, a situation in which evidence for the dynamic responsiveness of the self-made man is singularly lacking or, where there are forays into activity, they seem to have been dogged by failure and frustration.

The dominance of the Cromwells in the Huntingdon area was coming to an end, a process symbolized in the sale of the great house, Hinchingbrook, to the Montagu family in 1627. The substance of that bruising decline was probably more painfully apparent in the humiliations Cromwell suffered in the microcosm of Huntingdon town politics in the later 1620s. In disputes over endowments, for example the Fishbourne bequest, he was outmanoeuvred. More significantly in protesting against the remodelling of the town's charter in 1630 he ended up struggling against powers too great for him, in trouble with the Privy Council and forced into a humiliating apology. Not only was the new charter confirmed but Cromwell found himself effectively excluded from the government of the town. In the small-town politics of Huntingdon he looked like a loser and his move to the nearby town of St Ives in 1631 may have been something of a retreat. It was also, according to Morrill, a further step downwards in Cromwell's declining social status. For the five years (1631–6) in which he was a resident of St Ives, Cromwell was a modest tenant farmer. He had moved down from the gentry to the 'middling sort'.[11] It was the death of Thomas Steward, his uncle, in 1636 which saw the restoration of his fortunes. By Steward's will, Oliver as the main beneficiary acquired a reversionary interest in leases from the Dean and chapter of Ely Cathedral, became the leaseholder of the manor of Stuntney, south of Ely, and succeeded his uncle as the administrator of church lands and tithes in the extensive parish of Ely. In the later 1630s we can see him consolidating this position and working on various urban and cathedral trusts. By 1641, Morrill estimates, his income may have been about £300 per annum, the equivalent of the income of the home in which he was himself brought up. He had become one of the more substantial, but not one of the pre-eminent, citizens of a small, provincial, cathedral town. Despite his recent good fortune, he remained on the margins between the urban middling sort and the gentry.[12]

The initial impact of John Morrill's findings is therefore to deepen the problem of Cromwell's rise. A member of a declining family, Cromwell's trajectory, even in the obscure backwaters of Huntingdon and St Ives, is downward, at least until 1636. The recovery he is fortunate enough to make after 1636 is hardly self-made and does not seem sufficient to provide the springboard for national greatness. As he turned 40 in 1639, Cromwell might be thought of as absorbed in juggling his limited fortunes amongst his growing family to provide for as many of them as possible to remain on the right side of the margins of gentility. The last 18 years of his life, the years of achievement and greatness, can therefore become so radically dissociated from the first 40, the years of obscurity, for the two phases to lose explanatory meaning in terms of each other. But Morrill is too sophisticated an historian to leave it at this black and white contrast. Having restated the problem – how might we explain Cromwell's rise to greatness – he then shades its contours.

As the 1620s turned into the 1630s Cromwell may have looked like a man crossing the threshold of gentility into the ranks of the yeomanry but to some extent this is an impression which depends on seeing him in isolation and almost entirely in terms of economic fortunes and borough politics. As Morrill points out there are indicators running in other directions. The grandson and nephew of knights, Cromwell had married the daughter of a substantial fur trader and leather dresser who was establishing himself as a landowner in Essex. Cromwell's cousinage and network of in-laws was impressive and included John Hampden, Oliver St John and links with the Barringtons, Mashams and Richs. Cambridge gave him the symbolic, if not substantial, education of a gentleman and his own sons were educated at Felsted School in Essex, founded and patronized by the Richs, Earls of Warwick and Holland. He had been MP for Huntingdon in 1628 (following his father who had represented the borough in 1593) and was to be an MP again, this time for Cambridge, in the elections of 1640. While the earlier occasion suggested the residual influence of the declining Cromwells, the later suggested that Cromwell had secured alternative patrons.[13] His social status, at least until 1636, might have remained ambiguous, even precarious, 'brittle'. 'His cousinage' may, as Morrill suggests, have 'flattered to deceive' – but it did exist. There were social resources, networks, connections which could be advantageous to him. There was a context there for the recovery of his fortunes. What was required to make it happen, to effectively activate that context in a helpful direction?

Before turning to look again at that context and what might be said about its specific possibilities for Cromwell it is worth glancing at two approaches to a general explanation of how this struggling Cromwell of the 1620s and 1630s could be transformed into the meteorically rising great man. Both modify the view that Cromwell's rise was self-propelled and both developed as features of the nineteenth-century re-evaluation of him. The first of them saw him as the representative of a class, the middle class, which in the mid-seventeenth century was seizing power in bourgeois revolution. The second depicted him as representative of a religious and constitutional movement, Puritanism, which seized power in a Puritan Revolution. Naturally, it was possible to coalesce the two explanations into a middle-class revolution with a

Puritan ideology but in both of them, as in the merged version, Cromwell rose on the back of a great movement. His own efforts were effective on the path to greatness because they embodied the values and aspirations of the movement on whose tidal flow he rose.

The class explanation has taken two forms. Either Cromwell epitomized the rising middle class or he rose by virtue of the socio-political backlash of a declining section of the gentry to which he belonged. In view of Morrill's work it might be thought that Cromwell offered a better fit with the second.[14] The most recent exposition of the class argument has favoured the idea that Cromwell not only rose with a rising, revolutionary middle class but that many of the paradoxes associated with him could be explained in terms of such class affiliation. At exactly the time when Victorian reassessments of Cromwell as an outstanding representative of a new and progressive social order, the middle class, began to take hold, Marx and Engels were formulating the view that class and class conflict were the dynamic and shaping forces of all history. Their thesis in respect to the English Revolution, that it was a crisis precipitated by the attempt of a new bourgeois or middle-class society to break out of the constraints of an old feudal, aristocratic order, commanded attention and great influence for a century and a half. A recent attempt to restate the case has been made by a leading Russian historian, Professor M.A. Barg. His study focused on three key figures in the English Revolution – Cromwell, John Lilburne and Gerrard Winstanley – and explored the social basis from which each of them operated.[15] For Barg, Cromwell's career was to be explained by the meshing of his personal characteristics and changes in the social structure of early modern England, in particular 'the birth of a new, bourgeois civilization'. The two key characteristics of his personal background were a marked Protestant anti-Catholicism (appropriate to one whose family fortunes had been shaped by the confiscation of the property of the pre-Reformation church) and, secondly, a 'poverty complex' or sense of wounded pride at the decline of those fortunes. Like many others in the class to which he belonged by birth, position and outlook, 'the middle provincial gentry', Cromwell saw the policies of the crown in the 1630s as inimical to his beliefs and the interests of the class which he represented. Dissatisfied with the position which had been reached by way of a rapprochement with the crown by 1642, he was prepared to go to war to defend those beliefs and interests. What distinguished him from many other representatives of the provincial gentry was the breadth of vision which he brought to the fighting of what he recognized must be a 'revolutionary war'. Such a war had to be based on a tactical alliance between the middling gentry and the lower orders. To make that alliance work Cromwell appreciated that military command would have to be socially inclusive, rather than exclusive, and that the cause had to embrace some of the aspirations of the lower orders; political, legal and religious liberties. The New Model Army was an expression of this revolutionary alliance. In 1647, with the first civil war won, Cromwell's attention was forcibly redirected to the problem of controlling his lower-class allies, since they were developing radical agendas of their own. The second civil war saw the repatching of that alliance but again victory and the necessity to set aside the old King and the constitution opened up the disparity of aspiration between the allies. Cromwell's great achievement of 1648–9 and thereafter was to keep his one-time popular ally under control and to refine the New Model Army as the main instrument of a purely bourgeois coup.

With the Rump, power shifted to a narrower class base; a base consolidated in the franchise and constituency redistribution arrangements of the Instrument of Government. The lower orders, mutinous in the army, rebellious in the Levellers, subversive in the Diggers and distracting in the more extreme sects, were suppressed and a retreat towards autocracy, narrow class rule, followed. Cromwell's paradoxes, inconsistencies and apparent apostacies were to be explained in terms of the tactical nature of his alliances and his willingness to turn against old allies when the fundamental interests of his class were threatened; 'sharing all the illusions of his day, he nevertheless remained from start to finish the embodiment of the interests of those very social forces in the name of which the bourgeois revolutions occurred'.[16]

The problem of Cromwell's rise from obscurity is then resolved in Professor Barg's view by a combination of changing class fortunes and the distinctiveness of Cromwell's insight into the tactics required to serve the interests of his class effectively. A rising middle class was the escalator, carrying him and his kind upwards, but there was a self-made element in the shrewdness and energy with which he saw and pursued the best means forward for his class. Brilliant, and influential, as expositions like Barg's have frequently been, there remain three problems with this form of analysis and explanation and they all reflect the difficulties of accommodating the conceptual framework of 'class' to the context of seventeenth-century social relationships and perceptions as we have come to understand them over the last 40 or so years. The first is the adequacy of class terminology as a means of describing the social reality inhabited by Cromwell. To a marked degree this problem is reflected in the uneasy shifts of Barg's own terminology. Sometimes he talks about a bourgeois class, sometimes about the gentry, the provincial gentry or the middling gentry. Equally, Barg invokes a class alliance as the key element in the revolutionary struggle as well as in Cromwell's own distinctive leadership. But this immediately raises the question of how important, *and typical*, such alliances might be. Ought we to think of the basic socio-political building blocks of early modern society as ones of discrete class or ones of transclass alliances and networks? If the latter, does this not drastically reduce the relevance of class in itself for historical explanation? Behind all of this is the problem of whether it is best to envisage the basic blocks of seventeenth-century society as horizontally bonded entities (classes) potentially in conflict with similarly bonded entities above or below them in the social scale. Cutting across this are issues of regional, urban/rural, gender and age variation. Can class be a constant regardless of geography, age and gender? A second tier of problems relate to how people saw their own social affiliations. Cromwell never, of course, talked of himself as a member of a bourgeois class. He tended to emphasize ambiguity in describing his own social status and origins ('by birth a gentleman, living neither in any considerable height, nor yet in obscurity') and to stress the value of an ordered social hierarchy ('A nobleman, a gentleman, a yeoman, that is a good interest of the nation and a great one') rather than the interests of a particular class. Furthermore, his affiliations were most frequently with kinship groups, with the 'godly' or with the defenders of civil liberty, with his military colleagues of all ranks rather than with groupings defined in primarily socio-economic terms. If people living in the past did not see themselves as belonging to class affiliations, what kind of reality are we ascribing to them when we insist on their class identity? The third problem relates to the mobilization of social groups in the early modern period. The more that we have studied the social background of active movements, like the Levellers or Diggers, the less confident we have become òf any simple correlation between these coalitions and a single class.[17] Groups of people, small or large, were not effectively mobilized under labels of class affiliation but rather under slogans referring to religion, customary rights, local privileges or identity, or more abstract concepts like justice, legality, loyalty or freedom. The ability of 'class' to explain events such as these can only be rescued by assuming that the people of the past did not express themselves as accurately as we would like; that we know better than they what their true interests were and how they might be best expressed. The logical consequences of this are that either we ignore what they have to say as unhelpful or we must endeavour to explain why they wandered in a maze of false consciousness while we see things so much more clearly. In other words, there is a potential condescension towards the past here which most historians would now reject in favour of trying to understand the past in its own terms.

If explaining Cromwell's rise in terms of social transition, at least in class terms, has proven unsatisfactory, an alternative has been to explain his rise in terms of religious movements and their political and constitutional impacts. At its simplest, if the Civil War was England's war of religion, then religious warriors, of whom Cromwell could, *par excellence*, be seen to be one, would be at a premium.[18] When the assumption was that Puritanism was a combative, militant, even revolutionary, force, then the godly warrior could be borne up by such a force. Accounts based on this assumption, whether they linked it to a rising middle class or not, stressed the progressive, revolutionary nature of Puritanism. Either as a steadily rising movement uniting magistrates and ministers in an alliance against the threats of popery and superstition, or as a counter-revolutionary alliance against the Laudian policies of the 1630s, Puritanism was seen as one of the principal ideological glues binding the forces which were to bring down the administration of the Personal Rule.[19] In this scenario, Cromwell – God's Englishman – emerged as an archetype of the Puritan ideal, even down to the perceived tension within his personality between hesitant, agonizing introspection and explosive action. Cromwell, the Puritan hero of the Puritan Revolution, who rose with the forces which underpinned the revolutionary breakthrough of Puritanism, was a common feature of the historiography of the later nineteenth and earlier twentieth centuries.

The second half of the twentieth century, however, saw the structure of explanation associated with the rise of Puritanism undermined to the point of untenability. In the first place, Puritanism (like many '-isms') began to be seen as a reification, a thing in itself, more or less detached from individuals who were alleged to be Puritans. The generalizations made about Puritanism – theological, ecclesiological, social and political – seemed less and less related to specific individuals or groups. Puritanism, in origin a term of abuse, had always been a contested term. That contestation now came to haunt historical scholarship. What did the term mean? How could Puritans be identified and distinguished from others? The 1960s and 1970s saw historians struggling with definitions.[20] To no avail. There were calls to abandon the term altogether.[21] Studies of individuals, of their beliefs and controversies, of groups and of local communities began to emphasize diversity rather than cohesion. 'Puritanism' was in danger of disintegrating or of losing identity in a bland, undifferentiated, anti-Catholic, Protestant piety. At the same time, the links between Puritanism and 'progressive' or revolutionary forces came into question. The hotter sort of Protestants of the early seventeenth century were shown to be often authoritarian rather than libertarian, defenders of the divinity of monarchy and advocates of non-resistance. This was hardly the basis of a revolutionary ideology. Despite the shock of Laudianism, many 'Puritans' were shown to view rebellion with alarm. Not all 'Puritans' fought for Parliament and many who did were able to do so only by subscribing to the fiction that they were fighting to liberate the King from his evil advisers. The fall of the Church of England and the problem of re-establishing ecclesiastical order exposed diversity and division. 'Puritanism' was, if anything, a house of many mansions and competing ones at that. Moreover, it was difficult to fit Cromwell into any one of them. William Lamont, the historian who has made the shrewdest and subtlest case for retaining the concept of Puritanism, makes his case by working from individuals rather than abstractions. For him 'three representative puritans' are William Prynne, Richard Baxter and Lodowicke Muggleton. The point here must be that each of them viewed Cromwell with unease if not hostility.[22]

The abstraction, instability and, in the end, limited usefulness of the term has made historians cautious about, even resistant to, subscribing to phrases like the 'Puritan Revolution' or the 'rise of Puritanism'. Accordingly, explaining Cromwell's rise in such terms has also tended to fall out of favour. But an alternative, accepting the diversity within Puritanism, might be to identify him as the leader or champion of a group within that coalition. In this way, Cromwell has been seen as the political and military leader of the Independents. Emerging as a movement resistant to the Presbyterianism advocated by the Scots and embraced in a lame, Erastian form by the Westminster Assembly, the Independents, a minority at Westminister, were alleged to have established a powerful base in the New Model Army. Cromwell, as a leading and successful Independent in arms, rose with that force. If Puritanism could no longer do the job of explaining Cromwell's rise, might not a subset of it, Independency, be more satisfactory?[23] An American historian, Sarah Gibbard Cook, took this approach to its most developed form in arguing that Cromwell was not merely an Independent but a particular kind of Independent, a Congregational Independent. This ecclesiastical party wanted a loose but nationally provided and funded church based on the existing parish structure and congregations operating within it. They were anti-episcopalian but willing to tolerate churches of orthodox Protestant persuasion outside of the parish system.[24] Theirs, in other words, was the policy of the Protectorate church settlement of the Triers and Ejectors. There can be no doubt that such a policy existed and that it was politically backed by a group working with Cromwell but the first problem is that to call them 'Congregational Independents' and to describe them as a party is to adduce an identity for them rather than to discover an identity which they gave themselves. Moreover, while it may say something about the politics of the Protectoral church settlement, it does little to explain Cromwell's rise to power. In fact, Cromwell had been, at various times, willing to contemplate the restoration of a form of episcopacy (as, for example, in The Heads of Proposals) and to endorse a Presbyterian settlement. What in practice Independency meant to him is very difficult to determine. We know too little about his own religious practice, on the one hand, and on the other, he repeatedly resisted the notion that the essence of religion was bound up with forms of worship or church government.[25] Such cohesion as there had been amongst those still referred to as political Independents had fractured in the face of the revolutionary events of 1648–9.[26] The terminology of 'party', in any case, suggests too great a degree of cohesion and consistency to be readily accommodated to the twists and turns of Cromwell's reactions to events from 1647 until his death. It is better, as I argue in more detail below, to see him as belonging to and attempting to hold together a number of overlapping networks. Less formal and requiring less cohesion and consistency than the name 'party' suggests, these networks are nevertheless important resources linking Cromwell to sources of power, support and collaboration which were to be vital in his rise to eminence from 1640. To scme extent, it is also the case that his inconsistencies, his paradoxes, may be explained in terms of the strains of the recurrent exercises in network repair and rebuilding which successive crises made necessary, just as, on occasion they exacerbated the difficulties of such reconciliations.

The problem of Cromwell's rise from obscurity therefore needs to be re-examined. The escalators of class, Puritanism, even of Independency have proved unsatisfactory. Some of the basic assumptions underpinning the portrait of the self-made man risen, without preparation, to greatness from obscurity ought to be revisited. How obscure was his background and early life? Was a rise to prominence from such a background so untypical as to require us to presuppose the support of social change or the rise of a party to enable it? How *self-made* was his rise? To what degree was it a matter of his own, individual, unaided effort?

In an age when everybody is potentially famous for 15 minutes we may view anything short of front-page tabloid status as obscurity. To look back to a world without a predatory and insatiable, personality-driven, national mass media is to require a different perception of what obscurity was and meant. Cromwell's most protracted reflection on his own rise is in his speech of 12 September 1654 to the first Protectoral Parliament. Here he made the famous statement about his origins: 'I was by birth a gentleman, living neither in any considerable height, nor yet in obscurity.'[27] 'Obscurity' was not, for him, an appropriate description of his background but, in this context, it meant lowliness of birth and Cromwell's self-description is in this sense accurate. He did not think of himself as a lowly or isolated individual struggling unaided to make his way in the world. He repeatedly identified himself with networks and informal associations, connections, and throughout his life and career sought to build, maintain and develop such networks. His military and political career is incomprehensible unless we think in terms of them. '[N]or yet in obscurity' is a useful self-description, even for someone slipping dangerously on the margins of gentility, because it reminds us that Cromwell saw himself and his family as extensively connected to social, religious and political networks of which he may have been a minor member but which were perceived of as of regional, national and even of cosmic significance. He belonged. The Cromwells of the East Midlands/East Anglia may have been declining materially but they were well and powerfully connected. Interrelationship with Barringtons, Hampdens, Whalleys, Mashams, Stewards, Bourchiers, St Johns, Ingolsbys and Knightleys were carefully maintained, established or extended. Oliver's education at Sidney Sussex may have been partly determined by links with the Montagus, possible rivals but also godly neighbours. His marriage to Elizabeth Bourchier seems to have hinged on the intermediary connection of the Barringtons who were related to both the Cromwells and the Bourchiers.[28] A gentle education was therefore followed by an advantageous marriage. Bourchier was an upwardly mobile Jacobean merchant, knighted by James I in 1610, an investor in property in Essex and owner of a fine country house, Little Standbridge Hall near Felsted. Cromwell's own sons were educated at Felsted School, very much the centre of the godly patronage network of Robert Rich, Earl of Warwick, and close to the residences of the Bourchiers and Barringtons.[29] When he was chosen as MP for Huntingdon in 1628 it may have owed something to the residual influence of the Cromwells in decline and to the willingness of the Montagus (who commanded both seats in 1640) to compromise. Cromwell and James Montagu, the third son of the Earl of Manchester, represented the borough between them. But Oliver found himself with several kinsmen in the House of Commons including John Hampden, Oliver St John, Sir Francis Barrington, Edmund Dench, Richard Knightly and Sir Miles Hobart. His election as MP for Cambridge to both the Short and Long Parliaments suggests significant connections working to that end. The records are frustratingly sparse and unhelpful but John Morrill has suggested that Cromwell's link to the Rich family may have influenced the electors in his favour.[30] In terms of the major political themes of the 1630s Cromwell may look marginal. His intemperance in local, urban disputes in the later 1620s had landed him in trouble. In the 1630s he kept a low profile but, by his own standards, he was justified in repudiating the description of himself as 'obscure'. He was of gentle background and education, well married and, after 1636, established in modest comfort as head of a growing family whose prospects he now looked able to protect. Those facts may have owed little to individual effort and almost everything to kinship and wider connections but those connections were what gave him, and his family, opportunities for education and political involvement. When he joined the Long Parliament in late 1640 it was the third parliament of which he had been a member. Almost two thirds of his colleagues had never sat in a Parliament before.[31] There were over 15 of his kinsmen in the Commons and he possessed powerful connections in the Lords.[32]

Rather than seeing him before 1640 as an obscure and isolated individual we need to recognize his membership of three overlapping networks: his kindred, the godly and the patriots or defenders of civil liberty. An early study of his kindred probably exaggerated when Cromwell is described as having 'a large and almost abnormal number of relations and connections',[33] nevertheless, his dependence on his kinship network should already be clear. His identification with godly networks was growing in the 1630s possibly following a conversion experience early in that decade.[34] It is his membership of the political networks of the 1630s, in which his cousins Oliver St John and John Hampden were prominent, and the extent of his own ambitions in relation to them which are so poorly documented as to convey a sense of marginality, if not obscurity. The networks of kin, religion and politics do not neatly coincide but there is substantial shared membership. Many of Cromwell's kin were readily identified politically.[35] They also shared godly experiences and aspirations.

To look at even a couple of his early letters is to glimpse the significance of his membership of these networks and their interlocking nature. Writing to his 'beloved Cousin', the wife of Oliver St John (who was twice married to cousins of Cromwell), on 13 October 1638, Cromwell writes as one of the godly to another and speaks enthusiastically, if conventionally, about his own conversion.

To my beloved Cousin Mrs St Johns, at Sir William Masham his House called Oates, in Essex: Present these

Dear Cousin,

I thankfully acknowledge your love in your kind remembrance of me upon this opportunity. Alas, you do too highly prize my lines, and my company. I may be ashamed to own your expressions, considering how unprofitable I am, and the mean improving of my talent.

Yet to honour my God by declaring what he hath done for my soul, in this I am confident, and I will be so. Truly, then, this I find: That He giveth springs in a dry and barren wilderness where no water is. I live (you know where) in Meshek, which they say signifies *Prolonging*; in Kedar, which signifieth *Blackness*: yet the Lord forsaketh me not. Though He do prolong, yet He will (I trust) bring me to His tabernacle, to His resting place. My soul is with the congregation of the firstborn, my body rests in hope, and if here I may honour my God either by doing or by suffering, I shall be most glad.

Truly no poor creature hath more cause to put forth himself in the cause of his God than I. I have had plentiful wages beforehand, and I am sure I shall never earn the least mite. The Lord accept me in His Son, and give me to walk in the light, as He is the light. He it is that enlighteneth our blackness, our darkness. I dare not say, He hideth His face from me. He giveth me to see the light in His light. One beam in a dark place hath exceeding much refreshment in it. Blessed be His name for shining upon so dark a heart as mine! You know what my manner of life hath been. Oh, I have lived and loved darkness, and hated the light. I was a chief, the chief of sinners. This is true: I hated godliness, yet God had mercy on me. O the riches of His mercy! Praise Him for me, pray for me, that He who hath begun a good work would perfect it to the day of Christ.

Salute all my good friends in that family whereof you are yet a member. I am much bound to them for their love. I bless the Lord for them; and that my son, by their procurement, is so well. Let him have your prayers, your counsel; let me have them. Salute your husband and sister from me. He is not a man of his word! He promised to write about Mr Wrath of Epping; but as yet I received no letters. Put him in mind to do what with conveniency may be done for the poor cousin I did solicit him about.

Once more farewell. The Lord be with you; so prayeth.
Your truly loving cousin,
Oliver Cromwell

Ely
October 13th, 1638
[P.S.] My wife's service and love presented to all her friends.[36]

Alongside the godly network, 'the congregation of the first born', Cromwell evokes a number of familial connections. Mrs St John is currently at the house of Sir William Masham in Kent. She is asked to pass on Elizabeth Cromwell's greetings to all her family and friends in the neighbourhood. Thanks are expressed for the favours that have been done by them on behalf of Oliver's son. A teasing reference is made to Mrs St John's husband, Oliver St John who, the previous year, had defended another cousin, John Hampden, in the case brought against him for non-payment of shipmoney. Cousinage, godly networks and potential political connections all here interlock. Five years later we can see the same overlapping of connections. In September 1643, struggling to maintain his forces in the field, Cromwell wrote to Oliver St John as a man able to bring pressure from Westminster on those who control the pursestrings. It is the mobilization of networks – 'Remember who tells you' – simultaneously based on kin, political sympathy and godliness, for, as Cromwell points out, St John would respect the 'sober Christians' under his command if he knew them.[37] A month later it was another cousin, Sir Thomas Barrington, to whom, as Deputy Lieutenant for Essex, he appealed for support for his 'honest', 'faithful' men.[38]

Let us take one last letter as illustrative of this theme. It is a justly famous letter written to Cromwell's brother-in-law, Valentine Walton, to inform him of the death of his son on the field of Marston Moor. The battle fought three days earlier had been a notable victory for the combined forces of Parliament and their Scots allies and one in which Cromwell's cavalry had played a decisive role.

To Colonel Valentine Walton

Dear Sir,

It's our duty to sympathise in all mercies; that we may praise the Lord together in chastisements or trials, that so we may sorrow together.

Truly England and the Church of God hath had a great favour from the Lord, in this great victory given unto us, such as the like never was since this war began. It had all the evidences of an absolute victory obtained by the Lord's blessing upon the godly party principally. We never charged but we routed the enemy. The left wing, which I commanded, being our own horse, saving a few Scots in our rear, beat all the Prince's horse. God made them as stubble to our swords, we charged their regiments of foot with our horse, routed all we charged. The particulars I cannot relate now, but I believe, of twenty-thousand the Prince hath not four-thousand left. Give glory, all the glory, to God.

Sir, God hath taken away your eldest son by a cannon-shot. It brake his leg. We were necessitated to have it cut off, whereof he died.

Sir, you know my trials this way: but the Lord supported me with this: that the Lord took him into the happiness we all pant after and live for. There is your precious child full of glory, to know sin nor sorrow any more. He was a gallant young man, exceeding gracious. God give you His comfort. Before his death he was so full of comfort that to Frank Russel and myself he could not express it, it was so great above his pain. This he said to us. Indeed it was admirable. A little after, he said one thing lay upon his spirit. I asked him what it was. He told me that it was, that God had not suffered him to be no more the executioner of His enemies. At his fall, his horse being killed with the bullet, and as I am informed three horses more, I am told he bid them open to the right and left, that he might see the rogues run. Truly he was exceedingly beloved in the Army, of all that knew him. But few knew him, for he was a precious young man, fit for God. You have cause to bless the Lord. He is a glorious saint in Heaven, wherein you ought exceedingly to rejoice. Let this drink up your sorrow; seeing these are not feigned words to comfort you, but the thing is so real and undoubted a truth. You may do all things by the strength of Christ. Seek that, and you shall easily bear your trial. Let this public mercy to the Church of God make you to forget your private sorrow. The Lord be your strength; so prays

Your truly faithful and loving brother,

OLIVER CROMWELL

July 5th, 1644.

[P.S.] My love to your daughter, and to my Cousin Percevall, Sister Desbrowe and all friends with you.[39]

Often read as a model of sympathetic, sentimental condolence, one ought rather to recognize within this letter the tough and unsentimental attitude of the godly towards death and, in particular the death of the enemies of God and His cause. Uncontrolled grief is not allowed. Excessive sorrow would show lack of faith in the Lord. When things go well the saints should be sober; when 'chastisements or trials' befall them they must 'praise the Lord'. Informed of the death of his son, Walton is told that he has 'cause to bless the Lord'; that he 'ought exceedingly to rejoice'. The image of Cromwell and of the young, fatally wounded Walton is of men who relish the slaughter of their enemies. In a chillingly famous phrase: 'God made them as stubble to our swords'. For the butchery of 3500 Royalist troops or, as Cromwell appears to have thought, 16,000 out of 20,000, 'Give glory, all the glory, to God'. The young man's one regret, as he lay dying, was that he was not going to be able to kill more of God's enemies. His last wish was to see the enemy still in flight for their lives. This is the godly warrior, both in Cromwell's and the younger Walton's attitudes, at his least sentimental.

Written to a kinsman about the death of a nephew it is also a communication between members of a godly network and it assumes a mutual understanding of values and beliefs in respect to death, grief and the providential determination of events by God. The victory itself was 'obtained by the Lord's blessing upon the godly partly principally'. It is a 'public mercy to the Church of God', that invisible congregation of the true saints, to which both Cromwell and Walton belong, and which should enable Walton to forget his private sorrow. But Cromwell also reminds Walton as a 'loving brother' of the bonds of kinship, of how his own son, Oliver, died of illness while on active service earlier in the same year. The postscript underlines that this is a family letter by embracing a niece, cousin and sister. We need not assume that these are self-conscious stratagems. Indeed, their unselfconsciousness is part of the point. Cromwell belonged to kinship, religious and political networks which it was natural for him to call upon, to maintain assiduously and to engage with in a mutually understood discourse which interpreted the events and struggles of the time as happenings under the dispensation of a providentially active God.

To think of Cromwell before 1640 as an isolated, obscure individual, whose advancement, if it was to come at all, had to be self-made, is then to miss the context of the networks to which he belonged and in which it was natural for him to move and think. Both his subsequent military and political careers are, it will be argued, best understood by seeing him as operating within established networks, extending them and building new ones, seeking coalitions with other networks and attempting to rebuild or realign them when the networks of which he was a member were ruptured by the pressure of events and crisis. We can distinguish the nature of Cromwell's networking at various stages of his life and use those distinctions to explain some of the features of his rise. Before 1640, for example, he appears as a largely passive, somewhat ineffective, minor member of some kinship/godly networks. But what also needs to be taken into account is the functioning of those networks in the decade of the 1630s. Excluded from Court in a period of non-parliamentary rule, their leaders were virtually excluded from national politics. Their legal challenges to the system – as, for example, in the shipmoney case – were defeats. They had no political dynamic at a national level and Cromwell's passivity may be explained in those terms. The leaders of his networks were going nowhere or were contemplating colonial ventures. The débâcle of the Bishops' Wars and the Parliaments of 1640 transformed the situation. The networks to which Cromwell had some affiliation were galvanized. By 1641 the ministry which had excluded them at the national level from influence in church and state was in collapse, imprisoned or in flight. In Parliament alone there was a deluge of work to be taken on – impeachments, prosecutions, enquiries, committees, legislation, measures for security. Tasks multiplied. Men were in short supply. The networks at Westminister needed to use all available resources. Cromwell was given his opportunity to learn. Mistakes were made but he did learn and when war came after 20 months of intensive activity his apprenticeship was over and the bonds of his political networks had been extended, tempered and refined. Military activity, into which he threw himself with an alacrity verging on abandon, was no different. It was his connections, his networks on which he relied and which made things possible. Prominent amongst his allies were his kindred, cousins like Edward Whalley, brothers-in-law like John Desborough or those who were recruited to the ranks of kinship, like his future sons-in-law Henry Ireton and Charles Fleetwood. Others were deliberately recruited because of their godliness, their informal membership of the 'godly party'. We will need to take stock of this when we look at Cromwell's military and political careers and their associated reputations, but it is also very important, at this point, to stress that, while we find it convenient to distinguish the political, the military and the religious, such differentiation hardly occurred to and would scarcely have had meaning for Cromwell's contemporaries. Politics, religion and war were, from 1642, a seamless web and the networks with which Cromwell engaged, although in some respects separable, were similarly entangled one with another. Disengaging military action from politics is only perceived as a problem from about 1647 and it is a problem still nagging at Cromwell in 1657. So, while we may find it useful to make some separation in the chapters that follow, it is as well to remember that what is helpful for purposes of explanation does not necessarily mirror past reality. In emphasizing networking as the context for Cromwell's rise and achievement we also need to acknowledge the rupturing of those networks under the pressure of events. At various times Cromwell parted company with Vane, St John, Ludlow, and Hutchinson over issues relating to civil and religious liberty; with members of the sects over issues of godly rule; and almost with the military in February 1657 and the months following over the nature of a possible constitutional settlement. Not only should this remind us that networks are fluid but not infinitely elastic sets of relationships but it also goes some way to explaining the sharpness of Cromwell's early reputation as expounded by some of his one-time allies. The bitterest disagreements are sometimes those between old allies and associates.

Describing Cromwell as a self-made man risen from obscurity, then, does not get things quite right. It misleads both as to the distance travelled and in respect to the social context of the process, the degree of self-reliance involved. Of course, without his particular combination of abilities and sensibilities – military, political and religious – Cromwell would not have achieved greatness in the eyes of his contemporaries and posterity but the rise to eminence from humble circumstances was not unknown in his time. William Laud, Archbishop of Canterbury (1633–45), was born the son of a Reading draper, albeit a prosperous one. One of his successors, William Sancroft (Archbishop of Canterbury 1677–90) was born of yeoman stock. Philip Skippon, another distinguished parliamentary commander, was born in much greater obscurity than Cromwell and from the age of 18 saw long years of military service on the continent. Later in the century, another great military commander, John Churchill, rose to become the first Duke of Marlborough, having been born into 'an obscure family of minor provincial gentry impoverished by the Civil Wars'.[40] What distinguishes Cromwell is not the rise to great place but his simultaneous pre-eminence in military prestige, political influence and godly status. In respect to all three, he rose with the networks of which he was a member. In our secular eyes, his pre-eminence also appears to owe much to a combination of ability and good luck, fortune. To Cromwell and his colleagues, the last suggestion would have been shocking in its impiety, its paganism and its derogation of the majesty of Almighty God. Cromwell rehearsed the details of his rise in his speech to Parliament on 12 September 1654 precisely in order to show that it was not his doing but God's.[41] To such a God, his brother-in-law, John Desborough, reminded him, after his victory at Dunbar, Cromwell owed everything: 'he alone is the Lord of Hosts, your victories have been given you of himself; it is himselfe that hath raised you up amongst men, and hath called you to high imployments'.[42]

|5|

Swordsman

When war came in mid-1642 Cromwell was 43 with a family of seven children and complex management responsibilities in and around Ely. Yet he did not hesitate to commit himself to active service. Of over 55 members of the Long Parliament who fought, he was the most successful and his advancement was rapid. In August 1642 he was captain of a troop of cavalry which he and others had mustered at Huntingdon. By February 1643 he was colonel of a regiment in the Eastern Association. At the beginning of the following year he was Lieutenant-General, second in command to the Earl of Manchester and in charge of the cavalry of the Eastern Association. In 1645 he became Lieutenant-General of the horse in the New Model Army. In March 1649 he was named as Commander-in-Chief for the expedition to Ireland. Just over a year later, in June 1650, he was appointed Captain General and led the New Model's campaigns in Scotland and England. Within eight years he had risen from military novice, whose main asset appeared to be enthusiasm, to sole commander of England's armies and architect of their victories in Ireland, Scotland and England. This is the record of achievement which made his eventual political pre-eminence possible. Moreover, it provided him with the power base which in a very tangible sense made that pre-eminence almost irresistible.

In many ways this has been the least controversial aspect of Cromwell's reputation. Given the evidence of his victories, it is hard to deny him some, at least, of the aspects of military greatness and few, even of those most hostile to him, have tried. He is generally acknowledged to have possessed great aptitude for warfare and for the leadership of men, often in situations of extreme difficulty. The more contentious questions relate to the nature of that aptitude, the uses to which it was put and its part in Cromwell's overall achievement. To what extent was Cromwell a solo-player, self-servingly ambitious and determined to use military success to climb ever upwards? Were the attack on his commander, the Earl of Manchester, in 1644, the Self-Denying Ordinance and his own evasion of it, and the setting aside of Fairfax in 1650, illustrations of exactly this process? Was he one of the long line of military commanders who became impatient with their political masters and used their military capacity to seize political power, ruling, however velvet the glove, with the mailed fist thereafter?

Three things seem to be critical in Cromwell's rapid establishment of himself as a commander of considerable military potential. The first is the nature of the civil war especially in its first 18 months. The English by 1640 had generally little aptitude for fighting as their performance against the Scots in the Bishops' Wars had demonstrated. When civil war broke out in the late summer of 1642 it began as a war fought predominantly by amateurs, assisted by a small number of commanders with some experience. William Waller, almost an exact contemporary of Cromwell's, had briefly been a gentleman volunteer with the militia of the republic of Venice when a young man, and had served, equally briefly, as a member of the lifeguard of Queen Elizabeth of Bohemia. His experience of active service appears to have been limited to attendance at one siege and yet he was regarded by his contemporaries as an experienced commander.[1] Almost all of those involved in the early days of the war had to learn the arts of war as they went along. In such company, Cromwell was at no disadvantage. Given the nature of logistical and other forms of support for the armies in 1642, the military arts necessarily involved a great deal of extemporization. Actual fighting with the enemy was the tip of an iceberg beneath which an unremitting and potentially exhausting struggle against desertion, sickness, lack of supplies of all kinds (but especially money), lack of discipline and the poor quality and preparation of the troops, had to be waged. Cromwell's lack of military training, and therefore of expectations, may ironically have been an advantage. The fact that he was also a politician, with connections at Westminster, certainly was. The second factor critical to Cromwell's establishment of himself as a military presence to be reckoned with was that he was a learner. He came to the experience of war with an open mind and a willingness to learn, not just on the technical front of warfare itself but on the broader basis of the links between warfare, logistics and politics. That broader awareness was something which he never lost and was, as we shall see, an awareness which stood him in good stead. The third factor was that he showed himself from the first to be team player. The army became another aspect of his networking, intimately related to his other networks of kindred, godliness and political affiliations. This aspect of Cromwell's military career has frequently been overlooked or reduced to the one-dimensional ability to lead. But Cromwell showed himself to be an effective collaborator and subordinate, as well as a leader. Indeed his success as a commander is, in large part, a reflection of the strength of the team which he led but it was a team very largely of his creating. The initial, and somewhat precipitate, actions of July and August 1642, seizing the plate of the Cambridge colleges and raising a troop in Huntingdon, were not undertaken alone but in collaboration with his brothers-in-law, John Desborough and Valentine Walton (senior).[2] Indeed, Cromwell's approach to recruiting an effective force was to build on his existing networks both familial and religious. As his first regiment of 'Ironsides' emerged, the original troop captains included his son, Oliver, his nephew, Valentine Walton (junior), his cousin, Edward Whalley, his brother-in-law, John Desborough, and his future son-in-law Henry Ireton.[3] The preference for 'men of spirit' was frequently seen as socially subversive. In fact, Cromwell's preference was clearly for 'men of honour and birth' but, given that they did not appear in sufficient numbers, he had to seek out others. 'But seeing that it was necessary the work must go on, better plain men than none, but best to have men patient of wants, faithful and conscientious in the employment . . . .' Such men were more readily recruited amongst the godly, regardless of their specific persuasion.[4]

Cromwell could accept a subordinate role and work well within it. In early 1645 he served under William Waller whose recollection was that 'although he was blunt he did not bear himself with pride or disdaine. As an officer he was obedient and did never dispute my orders nor argue upon them'.[5] He served under Sir Thomas Fairfax for five years and, although their politics and religious persuasion differed, it was a partnership never questioned by Cromwell. The notion that Fairfax was a cipher, while real power was exercised by Cromwell, will not stand scrutiny. It does a disservice to Fairfax' considerable abilities and achievements as a general and misrepresents his relationship with Cromwell. In the early summer of 1650, when Fairfax was considering resigning his commission rather than lead an invasion of Scotland, Cromwell was amongst those attempting to persuade him to stay on. The burden of contemporary opinion was that Cromwell was sincere in these attempts. He even suggested that the model of the Irish expedition be followed: he, Cromwell, would be sent as Lieutenant-General to Scotland, while Fairfax retained overall command of English forces. It was Cromwell who proposed that a committee of five (himself, Oliver St John, Bulstrode Whitelocke, Lambert and Harrison) be appointed to attempt to dissuade Fairfax from resignation.[6] None of this looks like a man of an ambition which bridles at serving under a superior officer. The incident which reads the other way is, of course, Cromwell's quarrel with the Earl of Manchester, a quarrel which led to the Self-Denying Ordinance and the formation of the New Model Army

Manchester and Cromwell had, in fact, worked well together in the early months of 1644, as commander and deputy of the forces of the Eastern Association. A basis of that cooperation was a shared approach to the development of a godly army. It was Manchester's policy to appoint godly officers and Cromwell was a key agent in implementing that policy.[7] But their agreement was to support and promote godliness irrespective of the particular form which individual's Protestant godliness took. So that, over the winter of 1643–4, Cromwell backed Colonel Edward King, a Presbyterian, as commander of the Eastern Association's forces in Lincolnshire and in his struggle with the county committee of that county. Similarly, when Lieutenant-Colonel William Dodson, another Presbyterian, found service with a growing number of Independents intolerable, it was Cromwell who repeatedly attempted to persuade Dodson to stay on.[8] The attitudes of both Cromwell and Manchester seem to have changed substantially as a result of their experiences in the Marston Moor campaign and its aftermath. Cromwell, who had been anxious about Scots' demands for religious uniformity since the early days of the Long Parliament, was for the first time exposed to their views on *iure divino* Presbyterianism and their demand that the full Scots system be adopted in England. His anxieties about Scots religious imperialism were exacerbated by friction with the Scots over credit for the allies' victory at Marston Moor and growing resentment at the aggressiveness of Presbyterian officers towards Independents in the army. Manchester, on the other hand, appears to have been appalled at the divisions which he

saw opening beneath the surface of allied co-operation and victory. His reaction was to think of ending the war by means of a
negotiated peace as soon as practicable. Herein lay the seeds of
the lacklustre follow-up to the parliamentary victories at
Marston Moor (July 1644) and the second battle of Newbury
(October 1644).[9] Seeing, as he thought, an ecumenical policy of
recruitment and promotion being wrecked by Presbyterian intolerance and intransigence, Cromwell now sought to exclude
Presbyterians such as Colonel King.[10] In the autumn of 1644, the
army of the Eastern Association was beginning to polarize
around factions led by Major-General Lawrence Crawford and
Cromwell, a process which only deepened Manchester's gloom
and led to his ordering both men to appear before the Committee
of Both Kingdoms in an unavailing attempt to resolve the
dispute.

After the victory of Marston Moor, the allies' forces dispersed:
Leven and the Scots to the Newcastle area, Fairfax to Yorkshire,
and Manchester back to the territory of the Eastern Association.
For those, like Cromwell, who saw the victory as a God-given
turning point in the war this was an exceedingly frustrating
relapse into passivity at the strategic level. It was not until
October that the opportunity to re-engage the King's main forces
came at the second battle of Newbury. Parliament had already
shown its concern about the feuds within Manchester's army.
Newbury raised the question of its operational effectiveness for,
not only was there a failure to follow up the victory and make
full use of the parliamentary army's superior numbers, but the
King was allowed, in the aftermath of a defeat, to relieve and
secure Donnington Castle, an important strategic fortress which
commanded the Great Bath Road from London to the West. On
13 November the Commons ordered those MPs who were members of the Committee of Both Kingdoms (which, of course,
included Cromwell) to report on how this disaster could have
occurred. Nine days later they ordered two of their number,
William Waller and Oliver Cromwell, to report specifically on
the conduct of the army. At the same time, on 23 November,
Parliament instructed the Committee of Both Kingdoms to consider the wholesale reorganization of its armies. It may have been
this and the prospect that the Earl of Essex, trying to secure his
own future as overall commander of the parliamentary war
effort, would condemn them all for faction and incompetence,
which triggered Cromwell's attack on Manchester.[11]

However partisan Cromwell's charges against Manchester may have looked, they were substantially backed by a number of other witnesses including Hesilrigg and Waller, men who did not share Oliver's political and religious outlook. On 25 November, when he reported as instructed to the Commons, Cromwell alleged that Manchester was 'backward to all engagements' and had failed to follow up the advantages of Marston Moor and Newbury. When remonstrated with after the fall of Donington Castle, Manchester's response had been that 'if we beat the King ninety-nine times, he would be King still, and his posterity, and we subjects still; but, if he beat us but once, we should be hanged, and our posterity be undone'. As Cromwell and others pointed out, the logic of this was to relinquish the struggle.[12] As in most quarrels between those who have been close associates and collaborators, countercharges of a very similar character were soon forthcoming. Cromwell was accused of being uncooperative and of disparaging the Scots and the peerage generally as well as the Earl of Manchester.[13] The Commons set up a committee under the chairmanship of Zouch Tate, himself a Presbyterian, to investigate the various charges and this committee began its deliberations almost immediately. Both Cromwell and Manchester must eventually have come to realize that an all-out quarrel of this type could end up destroying them both and that, in the meantime, it could only damage Parliament's position in the negotiations currently in train for a settlement with the King. When Tate came to the House on 9 December with an interim report a series of events, which look as if they were pre-arranged, was triggered. Rather than identify blameworthy individuals, Tate identified 'pride and covetousness' as the sources of the problem. Cromwell rose and seized on that keynote. In a short, conciliatory speech he declared that it would now be wise

> Not to insist upon any complaint or oversight of any Commander-in-chief upon any occasion whatsoever; for as I must acknowledge myself guilty of oversights, so I know they can rarely be avoided in military matters. . . . I am far from reflecting on any. I know the worth of those commanders. Members of both houses, who are yet in power. . . . Therefore, waiving a strict enquiry into the cause of these things, let us apply ourselves to the remedy; which is most necessary.

Cromwell, in other words, was recommending that the Commons drop its enquiry and proceed to solutions. They were:

'a more speedy, vigorous and effectual prosecution of the War'; a reorganization of the army such as the Committee of Both Kingdoms had been considering since 23 November; and, more radically, that members of both Houses would withdraw – 'deny themselves' – from military service and so end the suspicion that they were greedy for place and willing to prolong the war. It was an extraordinary speech: at once cutting the ground from under the quarrel; offering an even-handed approach to separating politics and military activity; appealing over the heads of the politicians to the general interest of a nation in an 'almost dying condition' in a speedy resolution of the war; but at the same time backing proposals for wholesale military reorganization and a more vigorous prosecution of the war. Its combination of conciliation and boldness took many by surprise and carried the day.[14] Tate moved a resolution that was effectively to exclude any member of either House from 'any office or command, military or civil'. The same motion was introduced into the Lords by Viscount Saye and Sele that very day. Ten days later the draft of the Self-Denying Ordinance was sent from the Commons to the Lords. After some to-ing and fro-ing, not only the Ordinance but the reorganization of the military effort and the formation of a New Model Army had been agreed. Sir Thomas Fairfax had been appointed Lord General. Philip Skippon was Major-General of the infantry. The corresponding post for the cavalry was, for the moment, unfilled.[15]

Cromwell's action in speaking as he did in the Commons on 9 December showed him, for the first time, as a potential political leader. The timing of his initiative was exemplary and the blend of conciliation and firmness was masterly. He not only escaped a personally difficult situation but he secured the reform of both the structure of the army and its command which he had come to believe essential. Of course, there was a price to pay and the majority in Parliament began to push through the legislation for a Presbyterian church which was designed to restore, in society at large, the religious uniformity which Cromwell had found so difficult to accept within the army. There remains the question of premeditation. Was there a deep-laid scheme to oust the old commanders while enabling Cromwell to escape the provisions of the Self-Denying Ordinance? There are three main reasons for thinking such premeditation improbable. The first is that, while concerted action on 9 December appears likely, no one could have foreseen the outcome which was something of a battle of wills between the Lords and the Commons. In particular, the final version of the Self-Denying Ordinance was substantially different to the resolution proposed by Tate and Vane on that day. It allowed specifically for those who had resigned their commissions to be reappointed at a future date.[16] The decision of the New Model's Council of War to request an extension of Cromwell's commission was by no means a foregone conclusion and there was powerful opposition to it within the Council.[17] A second reason for discarding the notion of Cromwell's evasion of the Self-Denying Ordinance as premeditated is that the initiative was endorsed by Parliament which was not a body controlled by his friends. His commission should have lapsed on 12 May 1645 but the military situation and especially the Royalists' sack of Leicester on 1 May, which seemed to herald a more brutal phase of the fighting, persuaded Parliament to extend his commission for a further 40 days. On 10 June they again extended his commission and at Fairfax' request appointed him to the vacant post of Lieutenant-General of the horse. Four days later the wisdom of that decision appeared to be vindicated by the outcome of the battle of Naseby and Cromwell's part in that victory. One of the consequences of the sack of Leicester was that Parliament had given Fairfax a much freer hand than any field commander had previously enjoyed. This did not, however, extend to the employment of Cromwell whose commission was subject to periodical review and renewal by Parliament. This is the third reason for regarding the outcome of the Self-Denying Ordinance as beyond his control and planning. One of its results was that he became the most scrutinized and reviewed officer in the army. Indeed one of the questions which needs to be considered is why Cromwell stayed so long with the army. Between Naseby (June 1645) and the surrender of Oxford (June 1646) the war was increasingly a mopping-up operation. Attention was turning to the issues of political and religious settlement consequent upon a parliamentary victory. As a politician-soldier Cromwell might well have thought that the most pressing priorities were now political, at Westminster rather than in the field. Yet he remained with the army until midsummer 1646. The best answer to this puzzle is that he continued to regard himself as a member of the military team, in for the duration. The convulsion of late 1644, to which his attack on the Earl of Manchester was central, was very much the exception rather than the rule. Galled by a combination of loss of military initiative and internal bickering which, as he saw it, was the product of Presbyterian intolerance, he spoke the blunt truth, again as he saw it, to a parliamentary enquiry.[18] Once the conflict was in the open, Cromwell was ready to assume his share of responsibility, to look for reconciliation and to propose a compromise way forward. These were the responses of a team player to things gone wrong and they were to be amongst the hallmarks of Cromwell's politics for the rest of his life. In his management of the New Model Army, Fairfax established processes of consultation with his senior officers over all major military decisions and Cromwell continued the practice within his own command.[19]

It has often been suggested that Cromwell made an early impact in the war by modelling himself on the great Swedish commander and protestant hero of the Thirty Years War, King Gustavus Adolphus. It is also presumed that he studied the Swedish King's tactics by reading such popular accounts of his battles as those in *The Swedish Intelligencer* or *The Swedish Soldier*.[20] To go back to those sources is to be disappointed. Like other, best-selling battle reportage of the period, they are strong on narrative but weak on analysis and the detail of troop dispositions and tactics.[21] It is much more likely that Cromwell learned by observation and by trial and error. Prince Rupert brought with him to the Royalist war effort cavalry innovations modelled on those of the Swedes in the Thirty Years War. Principal amongst these were the arrangement of cavalry on the field (in three ranks rather than five) and using the weight of a more rapid charge to penetrate enemy ranks rather than wheeling before them to discharge pistols. Cromwell, in what for him was a somewhat indecisive action, would have seen Rupert employing these innovations at the battle of Edgehill (October 1642). He copied them but he also learned from Rupert's mistakes, for the lack of discipline amongst the Royalist horsemen meant that the impetus of the charge carried them off the field and rendered them inoperative for much, if not all, of the rest of the battle. Cromwell's cavalry were soon distinguished by their capacity to charge, regroup and be redeployed. Again, such discipline, reflected both off and on the field, was part of an awareness of functioning within a greater whole, of being part of a larger team and a wider strategy. But field battles, where these skills could be deployed and displayed, were few and far between. The battle of Winceby, in October, was an important, if relatively small-scale, engagement but it was the only set-piece confrontation with the enemy that Cromwell experienced in 1643. His time was taken up with sieges, the occupation of territory rather than with confronting the massed forces of the enemy, and with the desperate struggle to get the sinews of war, men and money, together in sufficient quantity. And yet by the end of 1643, as far as the London newsbooks were concerned, he was already an identifiable military figure, a hero in the making.[22] Why was this so?

Partly it must be attributed to his relative success in what, by the end of 1643, looked like a bleak picture for the parliamentary side. By then all of the west, except Gloucester and Plymouth, was in the King's hands; the north with the exception of Hull and Lancashire, was effectively under royal control and, in the Midlands, Parliament was holding its own with great difficulty. By contrast, the eastern counties appeared to be reasonably well secured.[23] As recruiters and motivators of men, Cromwell and his team stood out. From barely a troop in December 1642, they had expanded to five troops (300 men) by March 1643 and doubled in size again by the autumn of that year. What was equally noteworthy was the quality, men of spirit, and the discipline of the units thus established. Offences against property and the person were punished severely. Desertion, again running against the norm, was uncommon. The troops were drilled, exercised and trained in the care of their horses. In return for their commitment, Cromwell took their needs, in terms of food, clothing, pay and spiritual sustenance, seriously.[24] That he was not always successful, especially with regard to pay and provisions, is borne out by his letters of 1643 which are sometimes pre-emptory, sometimes near to panic exhortations to the civil authorities to respond to his and his troops' needs. This too was part of the learning process and Cromwell learned two lessons which were reflected in his attitudes from this time onwards. One was the need to liberate the military effort from local provision of resources if it was to be effective. The other was a recognition of the burden which the military represented for local communities as well as taxpayers and the political price which might have to be paid for the alienating effect of these burdens. In his mind the two lessons came together. As he told the House of Commons on 9 December 1644, 'if the Army be not put into another method, and the war more vigorously prosecuted, the people can bear the war no longer, and will enforce you to a dishonourable peace'.[25]

To a considerable degree, his reputation by the end of 1643 can be explained in terms of his style of leadership and a string,

although a not unbroken one, of successes. His close relationship
with his men, the combination of firm discipline and provision
for their welfare, his selective recruiting and habitual attribution
of success to Providence, were all features of that reputation.
Like shafts of light in the prevailing gloom, a string of successes,
however minor and temporary, stood out: Peterborough,
Crowland Abbey and Burghley House secured in April 1643,
Belton in May, Gainsborough in July and victory, with Fairfax,
against a menacing Royalist threat in Lincolnshire at the battle of
Winceby in October. But listing the triumphs does not tell the
whole story. It is often suggested that Cromwell's strategic sense
came late in his military career but a closer examination of his
activity in 1643 reveals a much surer grasp of strategy than has
often been acknowledged.[26] If parliamentary forces were to control the counties of East Anglia, they had to prevent the divided
loyalties of the area from being inflamed into conflict by incur-
sions of Royalist forces. Cromwell's responsibility in 1643 was
for the north-western boundaries of the region. Having secured
the line of the Great Ouse from King's Lynn, through Ely, St Ives
and Huntingdon, his strategy was to push forward to the next
defensible line, that of the River Nene by occupying
Peterborough and Wisbech. Such security enabled him to con-
solidate the territory behind his line and, when the occasion
warranted it, to sally out beyond it, sometimes with limited
success as at Gainsborough, sometimes more decisively as in the
cooperative effort with Fairfax at Winceby. The limitations on
more adventurous activity like that were ones of supply, regional-
mindedness and cooperation between parliamentary forces: all
problems which Cromwell the politician was campaigning to
overcome by late 1644. But there is impressive evidence of a
grasp of strategy and strategic limitations in his thinking by
1643. It was this, alongside his image of success and the play of
politics, which meant that he was not an altogether implausible
appointment to the Committee of Both Kingdoms in February
1644.

It remains true, nevertheless, that the first phase of his military
career was built on tactical, rather than strategic, capability. It
could hardly be otherwise since most of the time he functioned in
a subordinate role and had responsibility for only one arm of the
military effort, that of the cavalry. The incorporation of much of
the Eastern Association's cavalry, the Ironsides, into the New
Model Army must have made him seem like the natural but (after

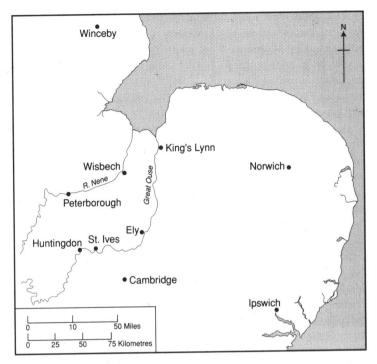

Cromwell's East Anglia

Parliament's refusal on 17 December 1644 to exempt the Earl of Essex from the Self-Denying Ordinance) unlikely future commander of them. The New Model was in fact a worryingly scratch force. What amounted to a purge of officers had taken place. Disease was rife, desertions commonplace. Even in mid-1645 many regiments were under strength and verging on mutiny. It is largely to the credit of Fairfax and Skippon, rather than Cromwell, that a high-quality fighting machine was built out of such initially unpromising materials. But the New Model, or 'new noddle' as it was mockingly called by some, was, to begin with, regarded with contempt by its enemies and concern by its friends. It was an untried force: 'a company of young Tyroes, or fresh-water soldiers'.[27] Cromwell himself was later to describe them as 'a company of poor, ignorant men'. One Londoner, with some military experience, who supported the idea of a military reorganization remembered it in June 1645 as 'an army ...

looked upon with scorn as wholly inexpert'.[28] On 1 May 1645 Royalist forces had sacked Leicester. In Scotland, the King's supporters led by Montrose were resurgent and Parliament became desperate to engage the Royalists' main field force in the English midlands before the King could develop a wider and even more menacing strategy. It was against this background that Fairfax was given a freer hand and that Parliament acceded to his request to be allowed to appoint Cromwell the cavalry commander of the New Model. When the anticipated engagement took place on 14 June at Naseby there can have been little confidence of a parliamentary victory. Numerical superiority lay with the New Model Army but the qualitative advantage and, on the day, the strategic disposition favoured the Royalists. Prince Rupert's cavalry on the Royalist right swept through the left wing of Parliament's forces in what should have been the decisive breakthrough. Unfortunately, but typically, they ended up by losing contact with the battle. Cromwell's cavalry on the right wing of the New Model also advanced but, operating under tighter discipline, was able to sweep into the flank of the Royalist infantry, thus tipping the balance in favour of Skippon's foot soldiers. By the end of the day, perhaps as many as 1000 of the King's men were dead, 4500 taken prisoner, as opposed to 150 of the New Model slain; 'the things that are not' had, in the Biblical phrases Cromwell used to describe the crushing victory, brought 'to naught the things that are'. What divine providence had also delivered was the political bonus of the King's incriminating correspondence with foreign powers as a result of the capture of his baggage train. Naseby was a dramatic triumph both in its scale and its unexpectedness. It vindicated the military reforms which had created the New Model and the retention of Oliver Cromwell in military service. As at Marston Moor, the discipline of the cavalry and his tactical insight and effectiveness had been decisive contributions to victory. The mood of military elation was confirmed a month later at Langport in Somerset when the Royalists were beaten out of a commanding position and defeated in the last major engagement of the first civil war. 'To see this,' asked Cromwell, 'is it not to see the face of God?'[29] For many it was, and it is from this time that the reputation of the New Model Army and of Cromwell as the master of cavalry tactics in battle took hold.

It was the second civil war and, in particular, the campaign leading up to the battle of Preston which provided the opportunity for his strategic grasp to be displayed again. Rebellion in

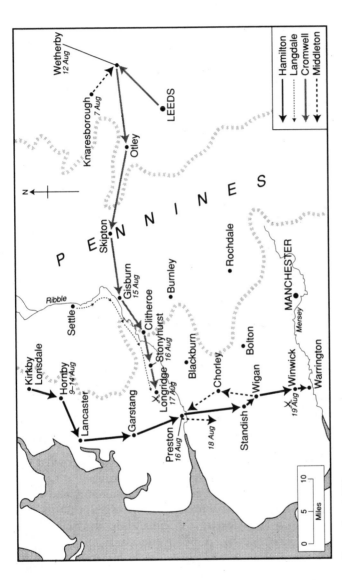

The Preston Campaign 1648.
Source: Peter Young, *The English Civil War: A Military History of the Three Civil Wars 1642–1651* (London, 1974)

South Wales and in the Home Counties simultaneously stretched Fairfax' resources and, for the first time, Cromwell was given command of a substantial army (6500 men) to put down the insurrection in Wales. When, having signed an engagement with the King, the Scots sent an army of invasion across the border into England on 8 July 1648, Fairfax was still wrestling with the problems of order and rebellion in south-eastern England. Cromwell was therefore sent with 9000 men at his disposal to deal with the new menace. The Scots had decided to strike south through Lancashire hoping to pick up more recruits on the way. Cromwell had to cross the Pennines in order to intercept the Scots. The crucial question was whether to block their path by intercepting them from the south or to cut off their line of supply and retreat from the north. Cromell's strategic decision was to opt for the second and bolder course. It was a decision driven by the wider situation in England. A speedy and decisive victory was necessary if disorder in England itself was not to spread. By cutting off the Scots' retreat, Cromwell committed both armies to a decisive engagement. It was a gamble but a calculated one. While marching over the Pennines, Cromwell had sent scouting parties ahead and he knew that the Scots, in their advance, had become very strung out, dispersed at some points over a 14-mile stretch. By striking hard and quickly, using to the full the advantages of surprise and superior intelligence, Cromwell was able to devastate a numerically superior force. But it was strategic considerations which fuelled his boldness. Once, in the first shock of the engagement, the infantry had given him the initiative, he never let go of it and over the next few days he turned the Scots' defeat into a rout. So overwhelming was the defeat that in England Royalist resistance virtually collapsed and in Scotland political crisis ensued.

It is worth noting that, on his march north towards what was to be the Preston campaign, Cromwell had stopped at Leicester to re-equip his troops with shoes from Northampton and stockings from Coventry. That eye for the welfare of his men was what kept them with him despite the exhausting demands of his approach to campaigning. A wider concern with logistics and thorough preparation is well borne out in his approach to the Irish campaign in 1649. Named as commander-in-chief for the expedition as early as 15 March it was to be exactly five months later, on 15 August, that Cromwell landed in Ireland. The time between was not wasted. He was well aware that Ireland had proved an intractable military challenge for many before him. He knew that an army in hostile territory required adequate and continuing supplies and pay; and that distance from Westminister all too readily translated into neglect of both. He saw, too, that occupying Ireland would mean a war of sieges and that siege warfare could only be expedited by good artillery. He therefore had a list of essentials and the months between March and August 1649 were devoted to seeing that they were delivered.[30] It was, nevertheless, a struggle. The effort of getting the necessary supplies in place must have made him sceptical about their renewal and so have reinforced his desire for a rapid result in Ireland. But meeting the logistical requirements of campaigning was not the only form his preparations took. Persuading John Owen to accompany his forces as chaplain and provide for their spiritual welfare was clearly important. He also prepared the ground by lining up political allies who might be useful. The key figure here was Robert Boyle, Lord Broghill, the second son of the Earl of Cork, who was intercepted on his way to join the Stuart court in exile and persuaded to work with Cromwell in Ireland. Broghill was to prove invaluable in winning over Protestant Royalists in southern Ireland to the Cromwellian campaign and he remained a staunch supporter of Cromwell's throughout the 1650s. Knowing that the enemy in Ireland were deeply divided and potentially in conflict one with another, Cromwell and his subordinate officers did all they could to foment those divisions and a paper war in which Cromwell himself was involved was largely directed to that end. Equally, much time was spent in the last weeks before departure for Ireland, as the troops assembled at Milford Haven, with Cromwell personally overseeing final arrangements in Swansea, Tenby and Milford Haven. This attention to detail and adequate preparation reminds us that effective campaigning was built on competent administration and, since war is politics by other means, on shrewd politics. Cromwell is an interesting example of a commander willing to give attention to both.

The apogee of his attainment as a commander, as strategist, tactician and leader of men, came in the Scots campaign of 1650 to 1651 culminating in the 'crowning mercy' of victory at Worcester.[31] Cromwell returned from Ireland in May 1650. The following month, on Fairfax' resignation, he was appointed Captain-General and almost immediately left for Scotland. On 5 February 1649, six days after the execution of Charles I, the

Scots had provocatively proclaimed Charles II not only King of
Scotland but of 'Great Britain, France and Ireland'. Their earlier
defeat in the Preston campaign of August 1648 had led to a political transformation in Scotland. The Kirk party, whose political
leader was the Earl of Argylle, seized power and, for a time, it
looked as if a rapprochement between Protestant Scotland and
republican England might be possible. But Cromwell's success in
Ireland meant that, if the Stuarts were ever to be restored it
would have to be as Protestant monarchs, whatever their personal predilections. It was against this background that, despite
their mutual distrust, negotiations began between Charles Stuart
and the Kirk party. Charles' objective was the re-establishment of
his dynasty on the thrones of three kingdoms. The Kirk, insisting
that he subscribe the Covenant and conduct himself in conformity with it, had still the same goal as in 1640 and 1643: to
secure Presbyterianism in Scotland by its adoption in England.
Charles landed in Scotland on 24 June 1650.

The English republic's Council of State favoured a pre-emptive
strike. Fairfax, unwilling to lead an aggressive war against a
Protestant nation, was eventually replaced by Cromwell. David
Leslie's preparation for an English invasion involved denuding
the area between Berwick and Leith which forced Cromwell to
rely on sea-borne provisioning through the port of Dunbar. This
involved Cromwell in a major logistics operation and, at one
point, 140 ships were involved.[32] Given the standard problem of
attrition by sickness in campaigning armies, the English commander's objective had to be to draw the Scots out of their defensive strongholds to as early an engagement as possible. He tested
their position in two ways. In a pamphlet campaign, he asked the
Scots whether they were not flying in the face of Providence by
supporting a dynasty against which God appeared to have turned
His face. The other approach was to offer the Scots a series of
tempting targets to draw them out of their lines. In one manoeuvre, he advanced west of Edinburgh and gave every appearance
of moving north. The opportunity was there for Leslie to desert
his defensive position and cut Cromwell off from the south. But
the Scots' commander was too wary to fall into the trap and he
knew that delay was doing his work for him. By August 1650
sickness had reduced Cromwell's effective force by about 25 per
cent. Leslie's vulnerability was the eagerness of the Kirk party to
intervene in his running of the campaign. In early August they
purged Leslie's army of about 3000 soldiers considered by them

to be insufficiently godly. Cromwell's taunts about Providence also rattled them. They became increasingly dissatisfied with Leslie's defensive tactics because they were not trusting enough in the Lord. When Cromwell, with a depleted army, moved south towards Dunbar, Leslie appeared able to reconcile tactical advantage with the political pressure on him. With the advantage of superior numbers he managed to surround the English forces, trapping them between himself and the sea at Dunbar. Cromwell's genius was, in consultation with his senior officers, to spot the one weakness of disposition in the Scots' position. Redeploying his own troops under cover of darkness, he managed to seize the initiative in what had looked like a hopelessly defensive situation and to neutralize any numerical superiority the Scots enjoyed by maximizing the element of surprise and the concentration of his forces. The result was an overwhelming victory. Three to four thousand Scots were killed; 10,000 were taken prisoner and English casualties were minimal, possibly as few as 20 dead.

On 4 September 1650, the day after the battle, Cromwell, ever the professional, wrote seven letters following up the propaganda advantage which victory had given him. He naturally did not fail to point out that the God of battles had adjudicated and had found the Scots, under the Kirk, wanting. And indeed the defeat at Dunbar, followed by Cromwell's occupation of Edinburgh and Lambert's defeat of the Scots' forces of the Western Association, left Charles Stuart as the only figure who could rally Scottish opposition to the English invasion. The winter of 1650–1 gave that opposition some breathing space. Cromwell himself was ill for much of the period from February to May 1651. This gave Charles time to show the value of his name as a recruiting asset and in May 1651 he was strong enough to seize effective control of Scottish resistance. By midsummer, Cromwell had an emergent strategy. His forces probed north and east, taking Perth and Dundee, and obliging the Scots' army under Charles to move south for fear of being cut off from the north. The door to England down the west coast was deliberately left open and there were those in the Royalist camp who believed that an early strike for London was the best hope for eventual success in Scotland as well as in England. Leslie, still nominally in command of the Scots army, preferred to fight on known, friendly ground where Cromwell's supply problems were at their greatest but he was overruled.

When the Scots' army entered England at the end of July 1651, Cromwell's generals showed a composure which suggests that the eventuality had been foreseen and the response preplanned. Without further orders, Thomas Harrison and his forces set off south from Leith to shadow Leslie's march south on the other side of the Pennines. Cromwell split his main force in two, taking half of it off in pursuit of the invading Scots. The other half under the command of George Monck, instead of assuming a defensive role, went immediately on to the offensive, thus preventing reinforcements from Scotland being sent in support of Leslie. Once the trained bands were assembled in the south to block Charles' path to London and it was obvious that Royalist support in England would be severely limited, it became dispiritingly clear to Charles' supporters that his army was being driven into a cul-de-sac. Politically the invasion of a Scots army did much to unite the English around what had become a generally unpopular government. Finally trapped in Worcester and confronting a force of about 28,000 (possibly double his own resources) under Cromwell, Charles had little option but surrender or defeat. What impresses is that, even in this situation of numerical superiority, Cromwell looked for a solution by guile rather than by way of a frontal assault which would have been expensive in terms of casualties amongst his troops. He feinted across the bridges to the east of the city in order to draw the Royalists out, then doubled back and attacked them in the flank. The result was a crushing victory, delivered on 3 September 1651, the anniversary of Dunbar. None but a handful of Scots made it back to their native land. By the end of the year, from being an independent state, with their own King, their own government and their own army, Scotland was reduced to being a satellite state with all its cities under enemy occupation, its army destroyed and its one-time King in flight. The poets and pamphleteers of the English republic could contrast this with monarchical England's vulnerability to Scots invasion in 1640 and 1644 and trumpet a triumph for republican arms. But there was no doubt that its accomplishment owed most to Oliver Cromwell and the team of generals and officers he had built around him.

The Scots war from June 1650 to September 1651 was Cromwell's final military campaign and his culminating achievement as a soldier. From a cold start in the summer of 1642 he had learned to be the complete soldier, skilled in the preparation, motivation and leadership of men, in tactics and strategy;

economical of the lives of those under his command, ruthless in the destruction of the enemy; with a command of the logistical and political sides of warfare and an outstanding record of success in both siege and set piece battle warfare. He knew the political price of an enormously costly and destructive civil conflict and sought overwhelming victory as the route to ending it. The potential stain on his military reputation relates to the quality of ruthlessness and the morality of war. Above all, it relates to the massacres of Drogheda and Wexford.

As we have seen, Cromwell arrived in Ireland in August 1649 and, in the wake of Jones' victory at Rathmines, to a campaign which he knew would be one of sieges. Siege warfare could be long and slow. The confused situation of shifting alliances, with four separate armies opposing him, the uncertainty of adequate future supplies from England and the risk of support from Scotland for the Stuarts, all made Cromwell determined to bring the Irish campaign to as rapid a conclusion as possible. One line of assessment here might be that sieges had to be concluded swiftly and that, where there was resistance, the punishment should be exemplary. Under the existing rules of war a besieged town or fortress, which had been offered terms of surrender, forfeited the right of exemption from slaughter, or quarter, if it refused those terms and continued to resist. While acknowledging these factors, many historians have found it hard to reconcile Cromwell's actions with honourable conduct under these conditions. We might take as illustration the verdict of Barry Coward, author of a fine, and generally very sympathetic, short biography of Cromwell, on his conduct in the Irish campaigns.

> The brutal behaviour of his troops towards soldiers and civilians alike – for which he was personally responsible – at the first engagement of the war, the siege of Drogheda (3–10 September 1649), and that he sanctioned at the siege of Wexford (2–10 October 1649), was not extraordinary in the context of the punitive treatment meted out to civilians by European armies in the Thirty Years' War and by other commanders in Ireland. But Cromwell had never before initiated or approved massacres like those committed by his troops at Drogheda and Wexford. At Wexford alone at least 2000 people, including civilians, were killed.

In Coward's view, Cromwell treated all opponents in Ireland, including civilians, as war criminals, implicated in what he believed to be the wholesale massacres of Protestants in the Irish insurrection of 1641; war criminals upon whom vengeance was wreaked by divine providence.[33] He wrote of Wexford

> we intending better to this place, than so great a ruin, hoping the town might be of more use to you and your army, yet God would not have it so; but, by an unexpected providence, in His righteous justice, brought a just judgement upon them, causing them to become a prey to the soldier.[34]

At Drogheda, it is generally argued, Cromwell, by the rules of war of his own time, put a garrison, which had been offered terms and refused them, to the sword. The crime was to extend the slaughter to civilians, innocent non-combatants. At Wexford, the standard view is that he lost control of his troops and an 'unexpected' but indiscriminate slaughter followed which Cromwell justified as Providential.[35] He also hoped that the example of these atrocities would 'tend to prevent the effusion of blood for the future' by frightening other besieged strongholds into early submission.[36]

Until recently the view that indiscriminate massacres took place in Ireland under Cromwell was one widely held and not only by Irish nationalist historians.[37] A challenge to this view has recently been made by an Irish local historian, Tom Reilly, working on local Irish sources. Reilly claims that the townspeople of Drogheda, which was predominantly an English, Royalist, garrison town, were not indiscriminately massacred; that civilian volunteers in Wexford were killed but that Cromwell cannot be held fully responsible, since the English troops had slipped out of his control; that Cromwell fought, on a military basis, in accordance with the rules of war and that his opposition to Catholicism was political rather than religious. He never, according to this view, ordered the indiscriminate slaughter of civilians.[38] Reilly insists that part of Cromwell's discipline in respect to his troops in Ireland was that they should respect Irish civilians and cites the case of his sentencing two soldiers, who stole from a local woman, to be hanged.[39] On 10 September 1649, Drogheda was summoned to surrender and refused. An artillery bombardment commenced immediately and early the following morning an assault began in which Cromwell's troops soon gained entry to the town. Two questions are critical. Was quarter at any time offered to the defenders in the heat of the battle? Was there indiscriminate slaughter of non-combatants? Reilly finds the evidence inconclusive on the first question. On the second, he argues that the casualty statistics will not bear out the notion of a wholesale slaughter of civilians and that the ease with which the local administration of the town was recommenced suggests otherwise.[40]

On 2 October Cromwell moved his troops on to the hills overlooking Wexford and sealed off the port, which had become a centre of privateering activity, from the sea. The weather was atrocious; almost continuous rain which soaked his troops who were already ravaged by dysentery. On 3 October he summoned the town to surrender. The local commander, Colonel David Sinnott, prevaricated, stringing out the negotiations in the hope of the arrival of a relieving Royalist force under the Earl of Castlehaven. On 11 October, finally frustrated, Cromwell began a bombardment of the town. Sinnott sought to reopen negotiations and Cromwell offered what were intended to be final terms. While these were under consideration, the governor of the castle on the outskirts of the town surrendered. Having taken the castle, there was nothing to stop the English from swarming into the town. In the process, the angry troops, now out of control, killed some 1500 occupants of the town. Confusion obviously played a part in this outcome, but again Reilly claims that the first-hand evidence will not support the idea of an indiscriminate slaughter of civilians. The statistics suggest, in his view, that the number of innocent civilians killed must have been small and their deaths were not premeditated.[41]

Reilly is right to question the uncritical ease with which the allegations of indiscriminate slaughter have been repeated by historians. The statistics and the continuities of life in the communities involved bear this out. But the degree to which this evidence should lead to an adjustment of the received picture is a matter which can only be resolved by putting it in the contemporary context. The refusal of quarter to the besieged who continued to resist after being offered terms was commonplace. On 14 October 1645 Basing House in Hampshire was refused quarter on these grounds and about 300 were killed, perhaps a quarter of the garrison. Some contemporary accounts claimed that civilians were amongst the slain.[42] The scale is, obviously, much smaller but Basing House, although an important and stubborn Royalist stronghold, was treated with a fury seldom allowed by Cromwell whose deployment of artillery on this and other occasions tended to bring a speedier end to sieges. The key as to why Cromwell could report this untypical behaviour as an illustration that 'God exceedingly abounds in His goodness to us' was surely that Basing House was the home of the Marquis of Winchester, a prominent Catholic and the house had many Catholics in it. The night before the assault Cromwell had spent in prayer and he had no doubt in his mind that he had acted as a servant of God and that 'He hath brought forth a glorious work'.[43] Cromwell could draw a distinction between the poor, deluded people of Ireland, who were Catholic because they knew no better, and those who led or maintained them in delusion. To fight for God's cause was his vocation. Those who fought for a false God were idolators and blasphemers. Their cause was wicked. They could expect the harsh formalities of war and no more. In the case of a holy war against militant and hostile Catholicism there could be no give in the steel of Cromwell's avenging sword.

The additional context for Cromwell's conduct, or at least the conduct he sanctioned and justified, has to be the secondary purpose of the Irish expedition. If its primary purpose was to secure Ireland, its secondary one was to open it up for a renewed wave of settlement and the compensation of those who, like Cromwell, had advanced money to the English Parliament on the security of Irish land as long ago as 1641–2. The transplantation, transportation and expropriation of an Irish Catholic population were implicit in the operation from the start and, without doubt, informed the participants' attitudes towards it. We can observe the absence of normal restraints in a report by the commander of the new, Cromwellian garrison at Wexford:

> In searching the woods and bogs, we found great store of corn, which we burnt, also all the houses and cabins we could find: in all which we found great plenty of corn. We continued burning and destroying for four days: in which time we wanted no provision for horse or man, finding housing enough to lie in; though we burnt our quarters every morning, and continued burning all day.[44]

Of course, Cromwell must be judged in the context of his own times and there were those who expected him to be much harsher in Ireland than he was. On 16 November 1650, William Hickman wrote to Cromwell, then campaigning in Scotland, to complain that although he had been chosen by God to fight His and His people's battles he had been too sparing in Ireland since

'God hath marked out that people for destruction'.[45] We need to remember that the God, whose servant Cromwell saw himself as, could be an implacable God, sometimes harsh in his chastisement of his servants, relentless to his enemies. Nevertheless, as some historians have observed, there is a note of unease in Cromwell's reports to the Rump which suggests that, even by these standards, things had gone too far. They would have preserved Wexford but God would not allow it. Nevertheless, reflecting on the soldiers' conduct he 'could have wished for their own good and the good of the garrison, they had been more moderate'.[46] In his report on Drogheda there is a strained fiction, which Cromwell must have known did not square with the facts, that this essentially English Royalist garrison was somehow implicated in and punished for the native Irish risings of 1641. God had 'manifested his severity and justice' and his servant, somewhat uncomfortably, adjusted himself to that fact. There were, he reassured himself, 'satisfactory grounds to such actions, *which otherwise cannot but work remorse and regret*'.[47] Drogheda and Wexford can be assessed in terms of the contemporary rules of war but they should also be seen in the context of a ruthless imperialism about which perhaps Cromwell, and certainly his son Henry, had qualms.[48]

Cromwell's ability to learn 'on the job' and to become an outstanding military leader, who distinguished himself in all aspects of contemporary military life, is dramatic and a key element in his reputation for greatness. But what, above all, distinguished him from other successful contemporary commanders like David Leslie, Thomas Fairfax, William Waller and even John Lambert was the fact that his military activity was always subordinate to the claims of religion and politics and that in both of these spheres he also established claims to pre-eminence. Indeed, the interplay between the three is essentially the story of his career from 1642 onwards. War remained, for Cromwell, politics, and we might say, religion by other means. Both politics and religion could sanction the vigorous, even ruthless, pursuit of military ends. But they could also call for the arts of the peacemaker. Cromwell never expressed any sense that this was contradictory or paradoxical. If he did feel some unease after Drogheda and Wexford, it did not permanently disturb his sense of consistency. To understand that we must turn to the examination of two sides of the one whole: his religion and his politics.

|6|

Man of God

Thomas Carlyle saw Cromwell as a rough-hewn, semi-articulate but essentially sincere man of God. As the nineteenth century wore on, the central place of religion in this assessment of Oliver's reputation was confirmed by the nonconformist writers who consolidated Carlyle's endorsement. If sincerity and the matching of practice to precept were at the heart of any reputation for genuine faith, then Cromwell's credentials as a, sometimes painfully, God-driven Englishman seemed clear. But, just as his military ability, even greatness, have barely been disputed, so religion has been one of the most controversial areas of his reputation. A glance at a report by the diplomat, Giovanni Sagredo, to his Venetian masters, after an audience with Cromwell in late 1655, reveals a more sceptical appraisal. Sagredo wrote:

> he makes a great show of his zeal. . . . and even goes every Sunday to preach to the soldiers and exhort them to live after the Divine law. He does this with fervour, even to tears, which he has ready at a moment's notice, and this way he stimulates the troops to second his designs.[1]

Sagredo may have been writing in a mood of frustration and disappointment at the Lord Protector's evasive response to an invitation to join the Venetian republic in a crusade against the Ottoman Empire but his hostile view of Cromwell's religion as both a pretence and a manipulative tool was typical of more sceptical appraisals. The profession of godliness, this version alleged, was a means to the achievement of his personal ends. Two periods, in particular, are associated with this reputation for hypocrisy. In the first, from the spring of 1647 to early 1649, his godliness was allegedly instrumental in enabling him to control the New Model Army, the sects and the radicals, to carry through the coup of 1648–9 before turning to discipline the army and the radicals. The second period is that associated with his apostacy of 1653. Having inaugurated the Nominated Assembly in an invocation of saintly, millennial purpose, Cromwell allowed it to collapse six months later, usurping King Jesus to make himself Lord Protector. Saints joined republicans in finding not only that the man of God had feet of clay but that they have been duped by a master dissembler.

Of course, these are judgements as much of Cromwell's politics as of his religion. They illustrate once again the inextricably interwined nature of the two. The secular, pluralistic society in which we live inevitably compartmentalizes religion and insulates much of its mainstream activities from direct religious influence. The practice, in this chapter and the next, of treating politics and religion separately serves our convenience and comprehension rather than mirroring the realities of the past and we must remind ourselves of this repeatedly. An associated problem for us is that of assessing sincerity and godliness. Sincerity has come to mean some form of personal authenticity; being true to oneself. But the self was regarded with deep suspicion by the godly of seventeenth-century England. Flawed by an inborn, original sin it had to be curbed so that the sinner could become an instrument of God's will. Not only must proud flesh be humbled but the spirit must be broken, as Christ was broken on the cross, if the assurance of grace was to be experienced. When we think of godliness it is more often as observers rather than practitioners. It has become a matter of following certain codes and practices, in the end of adhering to certain forms, rather than a matter of spiritual engagement which, in a New Age way, we have to a large extent divorced from godliness and redeveloped as self-fulfillment. Cromwell's religion has accordingly tended to be assessed in terms of his fulfillment of formal requirements and his personal authenticity in respect to those requirements. Was he a good and genuine Puritan or Independent? Only comparatively recently have we begun to ask questions about what kind of God, rather than what form of religion, it was that Cromwell claimed to serve and what such service might involve. With this, and an openness to what his attitudes and experience might tell us about religion in the early modern world, we must begin.

Ironically, the nonconformist historians who seized on Cromwell as *the* illustration of what nonconformity had contributed to British history, on Cromwell as the nonconformist hero, while emphasizing his anti-establishment nonconformism, also wanted to identify him with alternative forms: Puritan, Independent, Congregational-Independent. In this view, he may have opposed the establishment, including the established church, but he was a great churchman. In large part, this reflected nonconformity's own history. Escaping the seemingly anarchistic potential of the sectarian religious flux of the mid-seventeenth century and confronting the repressive attitudes and policies of post-Restoration England, the nonconformist had to organize in order to survive. Institutionalization led them to subscribe to articles of belief, forms of practice, structures of self-management and to attach identifying labels to themselves and to others. As denominationalism sharpened the boundaries between nonconformist groups (and in some cases exacerbated their mutual hostility), nonconformity became conformist. This was a process begun in the later 1650s but accelerated in the later seventeenth and eighteenth centuries. The good nonconformist became one who subscribed faithfully to the articles of belief of a particular denomination and whose religious practice was in strict conformity with the rules and practises of that denomination. Nonconformist historians, frequently writing the history of their own denomination, tended to write those ideals back into the past. So Cromwell's godliness became identified with a particular way, Independency or Congregational Independency. His sincerity was, in large part, assessed against the standards of consistency and faithful conformity to a particular denomination or religious order.

The problem with this is that we know so little, have such sparse evidence, for Cromwell's religious practice. We assume that he was baptized, as were his own children, according to the rites of the Church of England. Similarly, he was most likely married in accordance with the Book of Common Prayer. But we have no evidence of how he regularly worshipped in the 1630s, 1640s and 1650s. We do not know to what extent, or if at all, he used the Presbyterian Directory of Worship once the Prayer Book was declared illegal in the mid-1640s. We know a good deal about the chaplains of the New Model Amy, about Cromwell's personal chaplains and about the sermons they preached, but very little about the actual services they conducted or the liturgies they may have used. At least one of Cromwell's daughters – Mary, on her marriage to Lord Fauconberg at Hampton Court on 18 November 1657 – may have married according to the officially proscribed rites of the Prayer Book. But that possibility leaves us with the problem of how eclectic in his religious practices, how indifferent to forms of worship and church government, Cromwell might have been. In August 1647 The Heads of Proposals allowed for bishops without 'coercive power, authority and jurisdiction'.[2] In October, two months later, Cromwell supported a motion before the House of Commons that a Presbyterian system of church government be established for three years.[3] Such pragmatism about the nature of the ecclesiastical order can be taken as a sign of insincerity but only if we judge it from the standpoint of denominational loyalty. It might rather serve as evidence of a pragmatism about the nature of ecclesiastical forms based on other sincerely held loyalties and priorities. The questions here are whether Cromwell's faith attached greater importance to the practices of piety rather than to ecclesiastical ordinances; whether the substance, as he saw it, of religion was a greater priority than its forms; whether service to a living God, rather than loyalty to a particular church, was the essence of his religion.

In terms of the great authorities of theological systems, the Calvins and the Bezas, it is equally difficult to pin Cromwell down, largely because he left no writings reflecting on such systems. The two authorities which did fundamentally shape his religion and his religious interpretation of his own experience were the Bible and God's providential intervention in the world. Whether or not he was a loyal churchman, Cromwell was an impressive Biblicist, struggling to conform, if to nothing else, to the word of God. His use of Scripture in his letters and speeches is so intensive that it is frequently hard to tell where his prose leaves off and Biblical quotation begins. In chapter two we reproduced his letter of 13 October 1638 to Mrs St John. In two paragraphs of that relatively short letter, Cromwell cites eight psalms from the Old Testament and five epistles from the New. His citations are from both the Geneva and the Authorized Versions of the Bible.[4] In his speech opening the first Protectoral Parliament, on 4 September 1654, as well as quotations from the books of Timothy and Jude and from Psalm 40, Cromwell laid heavy emphasis on the Book of Exodus, 'the only parallel of God's dealing with us that I know in the world'.[5] Dissolving the same Parliament he quoted scripture no less than nine times and to his second Parliament, in a speech on 17 September 1656, he read out Psalm 85 in its entirety.[6] Opening the Nominated Assembly in July 1653, he took time towards the end of a long speech on a very hot day to expound Psalm 68 with its message that God would 'bring His people again from the depths of the sea, as once He led Israel through the Red Sea'.[7] He not only knew the Scriptures with a thoroughness which is hard for us to comprehend, he also saw it as a source of examples to be followed or to be encouraged by, admonitions to take heed of and, above all, of guidance which could be applied to the day-to-day circumstances of personal, military and political life. As we shall see shortly, his God was incessantly intervening in the lives of his saints. These interventions or Providences could be read as guidance, signs of divine approval or of warnings against a particular course of action. But he was well aware of the danger of misreading, of fleshly readings of Providence. At the height of the Kingship crisis of 1657 Cromwell told the parliamentary committee sent to persuade him to take the crown 'I must needs say I have had a great deal of experience of Providence, and though it is no rule without or against the Word, yet it is a very good expositor of the Word in many cases'.[8] Reflecting on God's providence, an almost daily exercise, must be done with Bible in hand. In the case of his decision about Kingship, as in so many other decisions, there is good evidence that these were the twin authorities to which he turned.[9] Nor should we assume that the openness to interpretation of the Bible gave him a free hand. His justification of a course of action by reference to Scripture was frequently met by a barrage of Biblical sources offering an alternative way and delivered by opponents coming to contest his policies also with Bibles to hand. Reliance on scriptural authority, rather than providing the ultimate manipulative tool, represented a double accountability, to God and to the scripturally informed and alert saints. Cromwell's consistent and conscientious attempt to conform to scriptural standards of wisdom and godliness was always a double-edged sword.

In one of the most famous contemporary images of Cromwell, William Faithorne's emblematic print of 1653, the godly soldier, sword in one hand, open Bible in the other, is shown treading down error and anarchy, presiding over peace and plenty and hoisting the crowns of three kingdoms transfixed on his sword. Towards the top left-hand corner of the picture is a representation of Abraham about to sacrifice his son Isaac. To the saints the significance of such an image would have been immediately obvious. It was an evocation of the living God to whom Cromwell

William Faithorne, 'The Emblems of Englands Distractions' (1653).
Source: Maurice Ashley, *Oliver Cromwell and His World* (London, 1972)

was a servant. This God demanded sacrifices and ruled by will rather than law. The birth of Isaac to the centenarian Abraham and his 90-year-old wife, Sarah, was an astonishing fulfillment of God's promise of an heir to Abraham, through whom He would establish an eternal covenant with his chosen people. All the more astonishing then that God should later command Abraham to kill Isaac as a sacrificial offering (Genesis 22). The sacrifice of an only and beloved son is, of course, an Old Testament prefiguring of God's sacrifice of his only son, Jesus, in the New. But it is also an image of a God who could 'tempt' his servants, make them suffer, impose severe tests upon them and appear to break the rules. The God of Moses was the God of the Ten Commandments, a God of rules, including the rule 'Thou shalt not kill'. The God of Abraham was a god of will, of trials and a readiness to put the rules at risk. This was a God who, instead of setting the rules and leaving human beings to exercise their free will in relation to them, constantly intervened in human affairs, a living God who tested, encouraged, warned and chastised his people. The nature of this God obviously had important implications for Cromwell's religion.

Reformation was an aspiration close to the hearts of the godly in Cromwell's England. Re-*form*-ation, however, implied the discarding of old forms, their replacement with new ones and the stabilization of a new order. But, in this respect, as Patrick Collinson has reminded us, the consequences of the English Reformation were those of failure rather than of success.[10] Throughout its slow consolidation the reformed church failed to win universal acceptance. Such acceptance as there was, was a compromise, a subscription of less than the whole heart. It was a compromise grumbled and chafed at by the godly but most determinedly challenged, from a different direction, by Archbishop Laud and his allies in the 1630s. The problem was particularly acute in England since, from 1534, church and state were one, sharing a single head. Monarch and Bible were the dual authorities of the English church-state but to many Protestants the Bible remained the book of a jealous God who made exclusive and uncompromising demands on his followers. The crisis of 1640–1 was then simultaneously a crisis of church and state and the ministries of both collapsed together. These were awesome events and, in seeking for solutions and a way forward, Parliament had recourse not only to law and lawmaking but it also inaugurated a sustained enquiry into God's will for them, into the divine meaning of the events of which they were a part.

From its opening in November 1640 the Long Parliament regularly called days of public humiliation or thanksgiving – the Fast Days – and selected preachers to preach sermons to it, usually one in the morning, another in the afternoon. Again and again, the sermons returned to the theme of an imminent millennium, the struggles of the latter days, the breaking of the day of the Lord, the coming of Christ to rule on earth. Three notes were repeatedly struck. The first is that of an active God whose relationship with his chosen people was highly fluid. Cornelius Burgess and Stephen Marshall preached on 17 November 1640, the first of all the Fast Days. For Burgess the escape from chronic instability might be by means of a covenant with God, but this would be entirely on His terms.

> if he do somewhat to hold us up by the chin that we sink not, yet he will hold us down from the throne, that we reign not, till we come up actually and fully to this point of Covenanting with him.[11]

Marshall reminded his audience that

> if God leave a people, all their strength is gone, as Sampson was when his Lockes were cut off, [and he went on to ask] what is it for a people *to be with God*. [It was] not meerly to draw neer to him in the external performance of certain duties [but] to bee on God's side in all causes [wherever that might lead us].[12]

On a similar occasion, nine months later, Marshall stressed that England could never be assured of God's favour which had to be repeatedly renewed by ceaseless adaptation to God's changing purpose.[13] The terrifying unpredictability of that favour was evoked by Edmund Calamy in *England's Looking-Glass*, a sermon preached shortly before Christmas 1641. 'God hath an independent and illimited Prerogative over all Kingdoms and Nations to build or destroy them as he pleaseth.' Men might deplore the absolutist pretensions of earthly monarchs but, as subjects of a heavenly King, they must submit to the absolute and arbitrary will of their divine sovereign. 'If God's power over Kingdom's be so large, and so absolute; let all the world stand in awe, and not dare to sin against such a mighty and terrible God.'[14]

Cromwell, a listener to some, if not all, of these sermons, was eager to be a servant of this God and we might well pause to ask what service to such a dynamic and apparently wilful God might mean. This second note, that of human instrumentality, emphasized that God's agents possessed no autonomy and were totally dependent on God. It was 'the greatest happiness on earth to be instrumentall for God', preached Jeremiah Burroughs in September 1641.[15] But it was also true that, while divine activity shaped events, human activity achieved nothing. Human instruments were best when most compliant in God's hand, allowing Him to work through them. They could never claim credit. 'This is that day,' proclaimed Burgess in November 1641, 'wherein our God came riding to us in his Chariot of Triumph, and made himself fearful in prayses, by doing wonders and leaving us no more to doe, but to praise his Name. . . .'[16] When it came to civil war, asserted a sermon of 1643, even bullets were directed by God towards or away from their targets.[17] The only possible security was to accept one's total dependence on God and to follow where he led.[18] There would be times when this would be to situations beyond all reason. In 1643 Jeremiah Whittacker could only explain the apparent absurdity of two sides engaging in bloody civil war while proclaiming the same war aims by reference to the living God's willingness to bring calamity down upon a nation of hypocrites. However it might baffle human reason, it was nevertheless God who engineered these calamities. 'It is God that shakes the Nations, for what ever instruments are used, God appears to be the maine agent.'[19]

By late 1648, a few weeks before Pride's Purge and the watershed of the English Revolution, a third note came to predominate. Against the struggle over constitutional forms and governmental structures it set the irrelevance of all human powers, constitutions, institutional arrangements and formalities of all kinds. It is a note sounded in the title of George Cokayn's sermon delivered on 29 November 1648: *Flesh Expiring and Spirit Inspiring in the New Earth: Or God himselfe supplying the room of Withered Powers, judging and inheriting all Nations.* A month earlier Peter Sterry, soon to become chaplain of the republic's Council of State and later chaplain to Oliver Cromwell as Lord Protector, had argued that Heaven changes the face of the earth in ways barely comprehensible to those who pretend to earthly power.

> Who is not amazed to see the changes that are made in the Garment of this earth? One day we see it, as a field

Flourishing with faire Hopes; another Day that Field van-
ish't, and in its Place, as a City on Fire, or a Sea of Blood.
He that now discerns not the Light of Heaven, the
Brightness of the Godhead, which is Christ coming upon
us, and thus changing us; What manner of Night is he in?
Sure a Night, as Black as the Shadow of Death.

Sterry's advice was that Parliament should do nothing to confine
that imminent coming of Christ, and to that end it should avoid
all forms and constitutions.[20] Here then was a key figure arguing,
at a critical moment, that as servants of a living God, his elect,
the English should avoid any kind of formal constitution.

These three notes, the terrifying dynamism of a living God, the
reduction of human beings and institutions to disposable instruments in His hands, and, third, the futility of any reliance on secular forms and powers, each found their echo in Cromwell and
those closest to him. As we have seen, Cromwell saw the devastation of Drogheda and Wexford, as of Basing House before
them, as God's doing. His account of Drogheda was particularly
graphic in this respect:

give me leave to say how it comes to pass that this work is
wrought. It was set upon some of our hearts, That a great
thing should be done, not by power or might, but by the
Spirit of God. And is it not so clear? That which caused
your men to storm so courageously, it was the Spirit of
God, who gave your men courage, and took it away again;
and gave the enemy courage, and took it away again; and
gave your men courage again, and therewith this happy
success. And therefore it is good that God alone have all the
glory.[21]

There were no accidents of war. The ebb and flow of battle were
to be explained as God's almost capricious (although Cromwell
would not have seen them as such) interventions. On 26
September 1650 Oliver St John wrote to Cromwell, from whom
he had been estranged over the regicide, to share his thoughts on
the victory at Dunbar. What was significant to St John was that
both sides were Protestant and both had appealed to God to support their cause. The Lord had judged. 'I beleve that was never
any battayle fought, whearin the honour both of God and man
weare more concerned.' He urged Cromwell, in what must surely
rank in the coals-to-Newcastle category of the superfluous, to

meditate on the Providential meaning of these events and to notice that God mixes water with the wine; He gives and He takes away. Nevertheless His Providential involvement with His people had never been clearer. 'How bare hath the arms of the Lord bin made in these our days; so constante and great have his workes bin for his people.'[22] As Cromwell knew that God gave him victory, so others saw Oliver as the Lord's instrument. Fairfax in 1645 urged Cromwell's retention by the New Model Army in part because he was a known agent of Providence.[23] At the very end of 1650 the 'People of New England' wrote to point out that God had made Cromwell his instrument and asked him to assure them of liberty of religion.[24] Eighteen months later William Erberry urged him on to the work of reformation. 'Greate thinges God has done by you in warr, and good things men expect from you in peace.'[25] Even before he became Lord Protector, Cromwell received a substantial correspondence appealing to him as the Lord's instrument for help and for hope. His answer was enshrined in a letter which he wrote as Lord Protector to his naval commanders, Robert Blake and Edward Montagu, on their way into Spanish waters in April 1656. They should deliver themselves up to 'the disposition of our All-wise Father', reliance on whom was the special obligation of those who were 'children of his begetting through the Spirit'. Since we, by our own efforts, could not turn away evil or attain good, we should follow Solomon's advice: do what we have to do with all of our might, and content ourselves with the outcome God dispenses to us.[26] Similarly, writing to another of his saintly/military network, an old comrade in arms Lieutenant-Colonel Wilks in January 1655, Cromwell denied that anything he had achieved had been by his own strength of will. Even the saints had to be careful not to impugn God's absolute and immediate sovereignty.

> if the work be the Lord's, and that they are His purposes which He hath proposed in his own wisdom, He will make His own councils stand; and therefore let men take heed lest they be found fighters against Him, especially His own people.[27]

The view of contemporary history which Cromwell rehearsed when addressing the Nominated Assembly in July 1653 was one in which the role of human will was negligible. The last few years had witnessed the 'strange windings and turnings of Providence: those very great appearances of God, *in crossing and thwarting the purposes of men*'.[28] It was He who had raised up 'a poor and contemptible company of men, neither versed in military affairs, nor having much natural propensity to them, even in the owning of a principle of godliness and of religion'. But, once they 'owned' religion and gave it priority, God 'by his using of the most improbable and the most contemptible and despicable means' gave them victory. The year 1648, in particular, had been one of divinely wrought wonders: 'so many insurrections, invasions, secret designs, open and public attempts, quashed in so short a time, and this by the very signal appearance of God Himself, which, I hope, we shall never forget'. But then 1649, 1650 and 1651 followed and 'had not God miraculously appeared' all would have been frustrated. Triumph in Ireland and Scotland were God's doing, their culmination 'His marvellous salvation wrought at Worcester'.[29] In this world, as Cromwell reminded the godly of Scotland in the declaration accompanying his invasion of July 1650, human forms, institutions and constitutions had to give way to the living God. Service to the substance ought to triumph over fidelity to the form.[30] His final decision to reject the title of King was set in precisely these terms. It was not simply a dynasty, but an institutional form and title which had been laid aside by Providence: 'God in his severity hath not only eradicated a whole family and thrust them out of the land for reasons best known to himself, [but] has made the issue and close of it to be the very eradication of a name or title.' God had 'not only dealt so with the persons and the family but he hath blasted the title'. Accordingly, Cromwell 'would not seek to set up that that Providence hath destroyed and laid in the dust, and I would not build Jericho again'.[31]

The truly godly were those who submitted themselves to the service of this living God, 'men of honest hearts, engaged to God, strengthened by providence, enlightened in his words to know his word, to which he hath set his deal, sealed with the blood of his son in the blood of his servants'.[32] With them, Cromwell would endeavour to do the Lord's work in peace and war. For them, in this sense, the identity of the formal commander of the Irish expedition of 1649 was an irrelevance. 'It matters not who is our Commander-in-Chief if God be so, and if God be amongst us, and His presence be with us, it matters not who is our Commander-in-Chief.'[33] This God could be a ruthless commander: at Marston Moor reducing the enemy to stubble beneath the swords of an avenging army; in Ireland reducing the garrisons of

Drogheda and Wexford to desolation. But as a God of battles, He had to be acknowledged. To attribute the outcome of battles to men was an impiety; to attribute it to chance or the fortunes of war came close to a denial of the living God, to atheism. Again and again, Cromwell insisted that God was directly the author of Parliament's victories. In April 1645 he complained to the Committee of Both Kingdoms that, in this respect, 'God is not owned enough'. The fall of Bristol, he informed the Speaker of the House of Commons in September of the same year, was the work of God. 'He must be a very atheist that doth not acknowledge it.'[34]

Cromwell was by no means alone in reading contemporary events in the light of the providential interventions of a living God. Indeed his strength and appeal as a perceived instrument of God rested on this shared mentality. After the battle of Dunbar, Henry Vane, who was alleged to make too little of Providences while Cromwell made too much, wrote to inform Cromwell of the reception of news of the victory at Westminster. 'I never knew anything take a deeper and more kindly impression upon the Parliament, who in the generall have good aymes, and are capable of improvement upon such wonderfull deliverances as these vouchsafed to them. You may be sure we will not be wanting. . . .'[35] On hearing of the surrender of Edinburgh Castle to Cromwell's forces, an East Anglian clergyman wrote in his diary, 'nothing can withstand gods purpose'.[36] In June 1655 Sir Edward Nicholas, secretary of state to Charles Stuart's government in exile, received a letter from the Earl of Norwich which explained that the Lord Protector realized the inadequacy of his son Richard as his successor but that he would naturally rely on 'his good God' to compensate for those deficiencies.[37] Indeed Cromwell's providentialism was shared by none other than Charles I. Bleak as his situation was after Naseby and Langport, Charles believed that all was still at the disposing of divine providence. 'God will not suffer rebels to prosper, nor His cause to be overthrown, and whatever personal punishment it shall please Him to inflict on me must not make me repine, much less give over this quarrel.'[38]

Cromwell's belief in a providential God intervening in the lives of individuals, groups and nations is not then something which set him apart from his contemporaries. It was part of a shared *mentalité*, his expression of it part of a shared discourse. Typically, as a believer in a living God guiding the faithful by both his word and by providences which were single events or chains of occurrences, Cromwell had both to read these signals and set them in the context of Scripture.[39] In moments of extreme political crisis, such as that at the end of 1648, when Providence and the dynamism of a living God might rub against respect for custom, the rule of law and loyalty to established institutions, the weight to be given to Providence was put to the test. On 1 September 1648, after the victory at Preston, Cromwell wrote to Oliver St John to make it clear that the long attempt to reach a settlement with Charles I was now, one way or another, coming to an end. Cromwell asked him to 'Remember my love to my dear brother H. V[ane]. I pray he make not too little, nor I too much, of outward dispensations'. There is lightness of touch in this affectionate reference to his difference with Vane over the weight to be given to providential signs – dispensations – of God in the world, but actually it was an issue which cut very deep with both men. In 1656 Vane was imprisoned for his defence, as he saw it, of civil liberty and republican principle in his *Healing Question*. He reminded Cromwell of the message which St John had passed on to him eight years earlier and maintained his dissatisfaction that Cromwell's active interpretations of Providence could jeopardize civil liberty. But for Cromwell the die was cast. Providences, tempered by Scripture, would be his guide, 'God preserve us all,' he went on to say in his letter to St John, 'that we, in the simplicity of our spirits, may patiently attend upon them. Let us all be careful what use men will make of these actings. They shall, will they, nill they, fulfill the pleasure of God, and so shall serve our generation.'[40] Providences had to be read carefully but, in the end, God acted and his instruments had to pick up such clues as He providentially dispensed as to what His intentions were. The following day in another letter to another old political ally, Lord Wharton, and still musing on the challenge of following Providence when it involved hard decisions, Cromwell stressed the way in which this process could perfect the saint's state of inner grace. 'I think through all these outward mercies (as we call them), faith, patience, love, hope, all are exercised and perfected, yes Christ formed, and grows to a perfect man within us.' However painful therefore, the reading and following of Providences was an essential part of religious practice. 'To a worldly man they are outward, to a saint Christian.'[41] It was precisely because God had indicated providentially, through war and in battle, that Royalist victory in the first civil war was not

His will, that the second civil war was an act of impiety, a defiance of God by the King and his supporters, as well as politically unacceptable. Harshness against them, especially against those who had switched sides and deserted God's cause, was justified, 'judging their iniquity double, because they have sinned against so much light, and against so many evidences of Divine Presence going along with and prospering a righteous cause'.[42]

God's providential guidance could clarify the issues but, in a crisis, determining the precise meaning of that guidance was never easy. It was itself a testing process. So we would be wrong to imagine Cromwell as in any simple-minded way reading off a chain of events in a manner to suit himself and then claiming divine sanction for the course of action he wished to pursue. If we stay with the crisis of late 1648 we may see him, as that crisis deepened, writing to his kinsman, Colonel Robert Hammond, governor of the Isle of Wight where Charles I was a prisoner, seeking to persuade Hammond of the necessities that faced them and, at the same time, wrestling with his own conscience and his reading of Providence. In the first of two revealing letters to Hammond, on 6 November 1648, he began with the necessity to wait upon God's guidance.

> Peace is only good when we receive it out of our Father's hand, it's dangerous to snatch it, most dangerous to go against the will of God to attain it. War is good when led to by our Father, most evil when it comes from the lusts that are in our members. We wait upon the Lord, who will teach us and lead us whether to doing or suffering.

The alternatives facing them were 'a hard choice'. But the political crisis was also a crisis of conscience, a spiritual crisis.

> we trust our daily business is to approve our consciences to Godward, and not to shift and shirk, which were in us exceeding baseness so to do, having had such favour from the Lord, and such manifestations of His presence, and I hope the same experience will keep their hearts and hands from him, against whom God hath so witnessed [ie. Charles I], though reason should suggest things never so plausible.[43]

Nearly three weeks later and with the options of either a parliamentary reinstatement of the King or a military coup against Parliament becoming more real, Cromwell wrote again to

Hammond. The latter was deeply troubled at the prospect of a militarily backed minority acting against the parliamentary majority. Cromwell urged him first to see the dilemma as 'being for the exercise of faith and patience, whereby in the end we shall be made perfect (James i)'. The way to meet this test was to seek guidance from the Lord as to his intentions,

> to know the mind of God in all that chain of Providence, whereby God hath brought thee thither, and that person [i.e. Charles I] to thee. . . . I dare be positive to say, it is not that the wicked should be exalted, that God should so appear as indeed He hath done.

Hammond was anxious that Scripture enjoined obedience, either active or passive, to 'authorities and powers' [Romans xiii:l; 1 Peter ii:13–14]. Cromwell agreed but argued that the particular form through which power and authority would be exercised was not divinely ordered but a matter of human choice. The critical issue was whether they were now at a point where that choice should be exercised and a particular form of government be set aside. To answer this he offered three considerations. First, the safety of the people. Second, whether, if they went on with the present institutions, there was a danger that everything they had fought for and promised would be undone. The third consideration was whether the army itself, called by God, was not a lawful power. In the end it was useful to weigh this type of consideration but 'truly these kinds of reasonings may be but fleshly, either with or against'. Much better to look to God's guidance.

> My dear friend, let us look into providences; surely they mean somewhat. They hang so together; have been so constant, so clear and unclouded. . . . What think you of Providence disposing the hearts of so many of God's people this way, especially in this poor Army, wherein the great God has vouchsafed to appear.

If God was guiding His people, whatever the difficulties and however disturbing it might be, towards a particular solution, this must be taken seriously. But in the end Hammond must be guided by his God.

> Dear Robin, beware of men, look up to the Lord. Let him be free to speak and command in thy heart. Take heed of the things I fear thou hast reasoned thyself into, and thou

shalt be able through Him, without consulting flesh and blood, to do valiantly for Him and His people.[44]

Cromwell could, and indeed had to, weigh the secular arguments which humans must rely on when God's guidance is not clear or is withheld. But such divine guidance must be sought and when it could be found Cromwell would follow it. His religion was almost invariably the ultimate determinant of his action.

In a secular age we have come to see the well-springs of human action as arising from the pursuit of interests rather than from religious persuasion or divine promptings. We tend to view moral or religious appeals by politicians with some scepticism and we would be alarmed to hear them lay claim to special insight into God's will. It is perfectly legitimate to ask whether Cromwell was sincere or whether he was exploiting certain common forms of contemporary religious language. There are three arguments for his sincerity. One is his consistency. Whatever the audience and whatever the circumstance, Cromwell was liable to bring in the issue of obedience to God's will and providential direction as to what that might be. Whether the decisions were hard or easy, such guidance was sought. In other words, the mask, if it were a mask, never drops, which, in turn, would presuppose either sincerity or an almost supernatural degree of self-control. Second, there are a number of ways and situations in which it is not obvious that Cromwell's religious attitudes best served his worldly interests. Ascribing triumphs to God involved a degree of self-abasement which, while (as in Ireland) lifting some of the responsibility from his shoulders, also took away the glory. God's instruments were disposable and such service involved not only insecurity but uncomfortable self-scrutiny and openness to criticism. In January 1651 his son-in-law, Henry Ireton, and the Council of Officers in Ireland wrote to Cromwell reviewing the Lord's dealings with them and him and detailing their collective shortcomings: 'too much of a proud, vaine, foolish, worldly spirit is yet amongst the best of us'.[45]

Third, the euphoria of an instrumentality by which the things that are not could set at nought the things that are, could soon be displaced by a sense that God's chosen were once more languishing in the wilderness. The years 1654–6, the years of the consolidation of the Protectorate can also be seen to have been years of a profound spiritual/political crisis. What is impressive about this is the rigour and humility with which that crisis was faced in a process of national and personal self-examination. On 20 March 1654 Cromwell called for a day of national fasting and humiliation to take place in London and Westminster on 24 March and in the rest of the country a fortnight later. It was undeniable that God had delivered the nation from 'bondage and thraldome, both Spiritual and Civil, and Procuring for them a just Liberty by his own People'. Now there was a loss of impetus, backsliding, and the 'Voice of God' was to be seen in the drought currently afflicting the country. The nation was invited to spend the appointed days searching their hearts according 'to their own Light' but were also asked to ponder a variety of questions. They were about worthiness, charity, seriousness, humility. Towards the end of his declaration Cromwell confessed that the reformation of manners, so central to him and his government, was failing. There was widespread

> resistance, hatred and neglect of the gospel ... wickedness, oaths, drunkenness, revellings, and all manner of licentiousness. ... [It was] not only warrantable but a duty, to call upon you, and our selves to set apart time to humble our souls before the Lord, to cry unto him for broken and penitent hearts, and that he would turn away his wrath, and be reconciled to us.[46]

Despite these efforts, the theme of Cromwell's speech opening his first Parliament when it met in September 1654 remained that of a crisis of spiritual motivation. Having escaped Egyptian bondage, the nation repined still in the wilderness. It is as if Cromwell were lamenting his inability to make the whole nation a part of his godly network, and, seen in that light, it is difficult to see what political capital could be gained by communicating and inviting the nation to explore this sense of failure. It was one thing to proclaim divine instrumentality when the saints' efforts were crowned with mercies, another to expose one's failure and loss of Providential status when disaster befell the cause. It is Cromwell's willingness to follow through the logic of Providentialism when things went wrong that most powerfully suggests the sincerity of his religious faith and the Providentialism which was such an important element of it. The most graphic illustration of this came when an English expedition to the Caribbean, undertaken at his personal initiative, was humiliated at Hispaniola. For once the God of battles appeared to have deserted him and when the news of the defeat reached

him, in July 1655, he experienced a deep crisis of self-doubt. He
shut himself in his room for the whole day and inaugurated a
series of exercises in national humiliation and self scrutiny which
went on until September 1656. Perhaps like Achan, the Old
Testament apostate, he had turned away from the path of the
Lord and he and his people were being punished accordingly.
This crisis of 1655 was a political, diplomatic and foreign policy
crisis, but it was also, as Blair Worden has shown, a spiritual
trauma and a crisis of religious prestige.[47] That Cromwell himself
made it the latter is testimony to his religious sincerity.

Two important consequences flowed from his faith in the providential acting of a living God. In the face of this God, reliance on
human institutions, constitutions, on earthly forms be they ecclesiastical or civil, on carnal or fleshly formalities, was a kind of
impiety. The second consequence was a concern to allow the living God to deal with his saints as He wished. This meant granting them the liberty to follow their consciences as they were
prompted by God.

In a letter weighing the consequences of victory at Dunbar,
William Hickman told Cromwell, 'God hath designed your
Excellency to drive Anti-Christ out of all his forms'. Presbytery
had been mortally wounded by Cromwell's victory but he must
not allow himself to be deluded by a new form, Independency or
'Congregational Government by Saints'. His policy should be to
submit to God's providence, not to forms unless they possessed
explicit scriptural warrant.[48] This was not advice uncongenial to
Cromwell. The miraculous year of 1648 had demonstrated to
him that the God he followed was bent on bringing down the
things that are. Writing to the Speaker of the Commons shortly
after the battle of Preston he pointed out that 'wherever anything
in this world is exalted, or exalts itself, God will pull it down, for
this is the day wherein He alone will be exalted'.[49] To Cromwell,
the Scots, in their zeal to have the Presbyterian form guaranteed
in Scotland by its imposition in England, had elevated forms
above Christian charity and their defeat had been the rebuke of
Providence.[50] Likewise, divine providence had brought down the
institution of monarchy in England and in 1657, after careful
deliberation, Cromwell could not persuade himself that it was
God's will that the institution should be revived. Even his own
adoption of the constitutional forms of the Instrument of
Government was an apostasy in the eyes of those saints who saw
it as erecting barriers to the freedom of a living God to determine

the course of events amongst His chosen people.[51] The fluidity of the operation of Providence in the world, the freedom of the living God, explains why Cromwell could never be wedded and glued to forms of civil government, still less to forms of church government and discipline. He was in favour of order but not in defiance of God's freedom to act and to deal with His saints.

If we look at just a few of the men chosen by Cromwell to act as his chaplains we can see this theme illustrated. John Owen, amongst the most famous of them, believed that to place religious forms before Christian substance was to enter 'the confines of self-righteousness, if not hypocrisy'. No form of church government was free from corruption. Church reform should be relaxed on institutional issues and give priority to pastoral care.[52] Peter Sterry believed that 'to be subject to ... the Church in the outward forme for the outward forme's sake is a bondage'. In October 1647, in an important sermon preached to the House of Commons, he compared reliance on human prudence to the Israelite's worship of the golden calf.

> If Christ be risen from the dead, why do you subject him to Ordinances? ... Formes are sweet Helps, but too severe Lords over our Faith. ... When we Consecrate or converse with any Ordinance or Peculiar way of Worship; let us then remember that our Object is the Person of Jesus Christ, that Wisdome of God, whose way is more untrac'd than the Eagle, whose extent is wider than the Earth. The Heaven of Heavens cannot take in All of Him, to containe or confine Him, much lesse any One Ordinance in this World, or Fleshly Fashion. ... Tis in vain to shut up Christ in any Thing.[53] .

Men like Sterry and Owen were an important part of Cromwell's godly entourage, his saintly network, when he was at the height of his power. These were the men with whom he worked in the 1650s for a religious settlement which would constrain formality but encourage godly piety, which could sustain religious harmony without uniformity. Their greatest achievement was to establish the framework of a Cromwellian church settlement at the heart of which were the Protectoral ordinances of March and August 1654. The first of these set up a national commission of 'triers' to screen candidates for the public ministry. The emphasis of the process was on Protestant piety broadly defined rather than on narrow denominational qualifications.

The later ordinance put the disciplining and disqualification of unsuitable ministers in the hands of county commissions of 'ejectors'. There was also an attempt, in an irenic spirit, to clarify the doctrinal fundamentals of the Christian faith but in the end this came to nothing. The intention of Cromwell and his allies was to avoid liturgical and ecclesiastical formalities while trying to guarantee decent and substantial provision for public worship throughout the nation.[54] To many, even of his moderate critics like Richard Baxter, Cromwell came close to succeeding in this aim. The wider purpose was to create a godly nation, flexible and fit enough to serve the purposes of the Lord. In two respects – the achievement of godly unity and the reformation of manners – success was more elusive.

Since there was one God with a single purpose for His creation, the unity of His saints was important. But since God also dealt with them as individuals, in terms of His particular providences, their experience of Him and their insights into His purpose would differ. It would be quite wrong to override those experiences and insights in a drive for conformity. It was God Himself who, in the end, would bring His saints into a oneness of purpose. What should be respected then was that process and the saints obligation to follow their consciences in pursuit of God's purposes. Cromwell believed accordingly in what may appear to be two incompatibles: unity and liberty of conscience. But they only appear incompatible if we do not share his further belief that the living God was perpetually shaping and reshaping human lives and in His good time would bring the godly to unity. It was the function of government not to impede this process, to encourage the godly to open themselves to God's promptings and to give them the freedom to conscientiously follow where those promptings led. Liberty of conscience was essential to Cromwell but it is also important to distinguish it from toleration if we mean by that the willingness to concede the right of others to express beliefs abhorrent to us. There were limits to the liberty of conscience that even Cromwell would concede and the boundaries were those of what he saw as a rightly informed conscience: Protestant, justified by Scripture and Providence, pious and moral. In this respect, his ideal was

> a free and uninterrupted Passage of the Gospel running through the midst of us, and Liberty for all to hold forth and profess with sobriety, their Light and Knowledge

therein, according as the Lord in his rich Grace and Wisdom hath dispensed to every man, and with the same freedom to practice and exercise the Faith of the Gospel, and to lead quiet and peaceable Lives in all Godliness and Honesty, without any Interruption from the Powers God hath set over this Commonwealth.[55]

To coerce the consciences of the godly was to defy God in His dealings with His saints. Such impiety, particularly in the days of the hated Archbishop Laud and his allies, was what had fatally robbed episcopacy of its legitimacy as a means of pastoral supervision in church and society. Cromwell could distinguish those bishops like James Ussher, Archbishop of Armagh, pious men, God-fearing in the true sense, but any system which imposed on the 'tender consciences' of the saints had to be opposed. Many in the godly networks saw the civil war as a war of liberty of conscience, in this sense, as well as one in defence of civil liberty. But not all on the parliamentary side took such a view and, as ecclesiastical control broke down, their priority became the restoration of religious order through a much greater degree of conformity than Cromwell would have conceded. The political importance of this was bound up with Scottish involvement in English affairs and the associated issue of proposals and demands for a Presbyterian system of church government in England. In the first months of the Long Parliament, Cromwell was not only seeking the release of John Lilburne, a prisoner of the bishops' fears of the critics of episcopacy, he was also enquiring as to the Scots' views on religious uniformity.[56] In September 1644, as the process of discussing a Presbyterian church settlement for England got under way, he and St John persuaded the Commons to instruct the Westminister Assembly to

endeavour the finding out some way, how far tender consciences, who cannot in all things submit to the common rule which shall be established, may be borne with according to the word, and as may stand with the public peace.[57]

But Cromwell was to be made directly aware of the continuing politicization of this issue. His letter to the speaker of the House of Commons after the battle of Naseby concluded with a plea for liberty of conscience.

Honest men served you faithfully in this action. Sir, they are trusty; I beseech you in the name of God, not to discourage them. I wish this action may beget thankfulness and humility in all that are concerned in it. He that ventures his life for the liberty of his country, I wish he trust God for the liberty of his conscience, and you for the liberty he fights for.

Two versions of this letter were published. One, on the order of the Commons, excluded this last paragraph; the other, authorized by the Lords, included it.[58] Three months later, reporting the capture of Bristol, Cromwell again ended his letter with a plea for liberty of conscience.

It may be thought that some praises are due to these gallant men of whose valour so much mention is made ... Presbyterians, Independents, all have here the same spirit of faith and prayer; the same pretence and answer; they agree here, know no names of difference: pity it is it should be otherwise anywhere. All that believe, have the real unity, which is the most glorious, because inward and spiritual, in the Body, and to the Head. As for being united in forms, commonly called Uniformity; every Christian will for peace-sake study and do, as far as conscience will permit; and from brethren, in things of the mind we look for no compulsion, but that of light and reason.

Again the version printed by parliamentary authority omitted this and other text but a fuller version was printed without authority and scattered about the streets of the capital.[59]

What is perhaps remarkable is that Cromwell never hit back in kind. On the one hand, he was prepared to compromise with any Protestant ecclesiastical structure provided that it offered some accommodation for tender consciences. On the other hand, he was prepared to indulge many of the scruples of tender consciences, provided they did not threaten civil disorder. On 13 October 1647 he was one of the tellers in the Commons for the ayes on a proposal to establish a Presbyterian system for a three year trial period. In The Heads of Proposals non-coercive episcopacy was offered as a compromise which might win the King to a settlement. In July 1649 he and Ireton were tellers against a motion that, if it had passed the Commons, would have given authority for the silencing of ministers who preached against the existing government. Throughout the Protectorate he struggled with his most recalcitrant godly opponents, insisting that those who were imprisoned were held not for expressing their views but for inciting civil disorder and sedition. The borderline between liberty of conscience and the license to follow one's conscience into civil disobedience has never been easy to draw and it may have been Cromwell's unease over that boundary which drew him repeatedly into bruising and unprofitable verbal encounters with the likes of Christopher Feake, John Simpson, George Fox and John Rogers.

Cromwell clearly had reservations about episcopacy and Presbyterianism as potentially coercive forms, just as he saw the lay/clerical distinction as one undermined by the accessibility of Scripture and God's directness of intervention with his saints. But there were many ways of experiencing the living God and many paths in his service. There should be a *reciprocity* of respect and the granting of liberty between saints working in the service of the Lord. This was an expectation of his brothers and sisters in Christ which was to be bitterly disappointed. At the Putney debates in late October 1647 he grumbled about the lack of such reciprocity:

> They that have stood so much for liberty of conscience, if they will not grant that liberty to every man, but say it is a deserting I know not what – if that be denied me, I think there is not that equality that [is] professed to be amongst us.[60]

This sense of exasperation deepened as time passed. Writing to Charles Fleetwood on 22 August 1653, he recalled the story of Moses who, having led the Hebrews out of slavery to the Egyptians was dismayed to find them fighting amongst themselves and ready to revile him should he seek to maintain the peace (Exodus ii:13–14). Cromwell's sorrow was that the saints were now hostile to one another and his attempts at reconciliation were unacceptable to them. 'Being of different judgements, of each sort most seeking to propagate their own, that spirit of kindness that is to them all, is hardly accepted of any'.[61] Richard Baxter saw Cromwell as the patron of the sects which sprang up in the 1640s but this is surely mistaken. The sects distinguished themselves one from another on the basis of formal distinctions for which Cromwell himself had little time. And he came to associate their mutual acrimony with the 'scatterings, divisions and confusions' which destroyed Christian unity. They would not hesitate to 'cut the throats of one another, should not I keep the peace'. They were willing to demand a liberty for themselves which they denied to others. In March 1654 one of the objectives of the day of national fasting and humiliation was to pray for an end to 'Faction' in 'Profession', for a major effort to overcome the absence of 'Brotherly Love' and a 'Healing Spirit'. Writing a year later and again to Fleetwood, the Lord Protector was close to despair.

> The wretched jealousies that are amongst us, and the spirit of calumny, turns all to gall and wormwood. My heart is for the people of God: that the Lord knows, and I trust in due time will manifest; yet thence are my wounds; which through it grieves me, yet through the Grace of God doth not discourage me totally.[62]

Freed from episcopal oppression of their own consciences, there were too many of the godly who could not resist putting 'their finger upon their brethren's consciences, to pinch theme there'. 'Every sect saith, Oh, Give me liberty. But give him it, and to his power he will not yield it to anybody else. Where is our ingenuity? Truly that's a thing ought to be very reciprocal'.[63] The spirit that was here lacking was shown by Cromwell himself in a variety of ways. He looked for means of working, at the opposite ends of the Protestant spectrum, with Quakers and Anglicans and showed practical sympathy for some Roman Catholics.[64] We may find the breadth of Cromwell's compassion for the godly of many persuasions admirable but we should not mislead ourselves as to its sources. It rested not on a liberal philosophy of a pluralistic society but on faith in a living God who spoke to his saints in many ways but would in the end bring them to unity. His despair was to find so many of the saints unwilling to work towards that end. His vision was not matched by a corresponding response from the elect nation.

Much the same might be said about the desire that an England freed from Babylonish captivity might be a godly nation in the sense of a morally reformed society. Just as an army of godly discipline was more likely to be favoured in battle by Providence, so a morally reformed people were more likely to be protected and blessed by the Almighty. The reformation of manners was thus a question simultaneously of honouring God, cleansing the nation and national security. It was a combination of themes which, for example, the Lord Protector harked back to repeatedly in speeches, proclamations and, in 1655 and 1656, in instructions to his Major-Generals. There were flurries of activity in response but, in the end, a sense of weary compromise with a sinful world prevailed. Partly this was a consequence of a divided and demoralized church establishment which had no consistent approach to the use of the traditional tools of ecclesiastical social discipline.[65] Partly, and this appears to be true even under the Major-Generals, the effort was crippled by the lack of sufficient godly and enthusiastic personnel to man the traditional organs of local government and give sustained impetus to the processes of moral reform.[66] But mainly, perhaps, the failure of the reformation of manners may be attributed to the fact that aspirations for such a cultural revolution were simply too high in the wake of a destructive civil war and too daunting for the sense of the fragility of community which was one of that war's consequences. Nevertheless, many of the godly who, like Richard Baxter, survived into a world without such aspirations to godly nationhood, were able with hindsight to look back on the Protectorate as, if not the promised land realized, a decent ante-chamber to it.

Apart from attempting to achieve that state of grace which gave assurance of Christ's redeeming presence, Cromwell's religious aims were manifold. The objective of godly unity, on a national basis, was always going to be problematic. Either the consensual stretch of a comprehensive unity went too far for the rigours of godliness or godliness was pursued too vigorously and narrowly for unity and ended up pinching men's consciences. Cromwell aimed to end the 'penal statutes that force the conscience of honest conscientious men', to creat an environment of liberty of conscience for all those whom he regarded as 'honest', 'godly' or 'conscientious'.[67] Whether to the satisfaction of his compatriots or not, we may say that he was reasonably successful in this. In regard to the desired reformation of manners, there remained much for the labourers in the vineyard still to do at his death. Living 'at the edge of the promises and prophecies', there were times when he felt obliged to weigh his role as a godly prince preparing the nation for the coming millennium and the return of Christ to rule with his saints.[68] The Jews were readmitted but the God on whom Cromwell waited did not come. In the meantime, he sought to follow the directing force of Providence in the service of the Lord, fearing 'unbelief, self-seeking, confidence in the arm of the flesh, and opinion of any instrument that they are other than as dry bones'.[69] Here, although Cromwell was certainly looking for judgement from another source, we may conclude that, dry as the bones might be, they achieved memorable things in the Lord's service.

|7|

The politician

As in his military career, so in politics Cromwell was a late beginner. When the Long Parliament met in November 1640 he was amongst the minority of MPs who had attended a previous parliament but, beyond some familiarity with the nature and procedures of the Commons, he remained a raw backbencher. Faced with a dramatic increase in the opportunities for political action, he showed a remarkable capacity to learn, to acquire new skills. Most impressively, as he acquired strategic vision in his soldiering he also developed a leading politician's capacity to approach political crises and problems with a rounded view and creative initiative. He became a political actor; not merely one to whom things happened but one who could shape events and their outcomes. Of course, politicians are never entirely in control of events. In unsettled situations, by definition, they are barely in control of them at all. If they have access to coercive means, as Cromwell undoubtedly did, they may use violence to limit the number of options but can never entirely control the outcome of crisis. In these respects, he wrestled with both the politician's sense of contingent events and outcomes and with a demanding God who in some respects offered clear pathways through these complexities, while, in other ways, He rendered them even more tortuous.

In this chapter we shall be looking more closely at Cromwell's politics between 1640 and 1653; in the next, at his rule as Lord Protector and his response to the challenge of statebuilding between 1653 and 1658. Following his rise from backbencher to Lord Protector, in this chapter, we shall focus on his maturation as a politician, the question of ambition and the issue of consistency, or the lack of it, underpinning his politics.

There were three key transitions in Cromwell's maturation as a politician. The first is that from the black-and-white, 'them versus us' perspective of what we might call the holy warrior. In May 1641 he had written to the mayor and aldermen of his constituency, Cambridge, sending them a copy of the Protestation which pledged MPs to a defence of the realm against 'force, practice, counsels, plots, conspiracies', and any other stratagems which would undermine the Protestant religion in favour of Roman Catholicism. His letter urged the civic authorities of Cambridge to endorse the Protestation because 'Combination carries strength with it. It's dreadful to adversaries.'[1] Over 12 months before the civil war broke out, Cromwell was, verbally at least, manning the battlements of a holy war. Even earlier, writing to his friend Mr Storie in January 1635, he had described those responsible for the suppression of lectureships as 'the enemies of God his truth'.[2] It was a drawing of lines of battle around which there could be no compromise. But, as time went on, Cromwell came to stress healing and settling, the challenges of peacemaking and the establishment of a framework within which people of differing persuasions might co-exist. This was, in part, associated with a second transition which was shaped by his experience of the fragmentation of a victorious alliance. Men had fought on the same side only to find that victory exposed the divergence of their objectives, divergence which had hitherto been masked by the blandness of their stated war aims. Victory was not the end of the political struggle but the beginning of its redirection. So the drive to military victory – the destruction of the enemies of God's truth – was gradually displaced, in Cromwell's agenda, by a concern to find political solutions which would embrace as many elements of the political nation as was reasonably possible. Inevitably, those solutions involved a counterpart to military strategy, a political concern with the means by which the frameworks of settlement might be engineered. The third transition in Cromwell's political maturation was his realization that politics is a form of ironics, that political intentions, however good, are likely to be thwarted, the consequences of political action to be largely unintended and that volatile situations therefore called for caution, careful calculation and stamina. Responding to the proposals put before the debates at Putney in October 1647, he observed that 'it is not enough to propose things that are good in the end, but it is our duty as Christians and men to consider consequences and to consider the way'.[3] In other words, Cromwell's practice of politics, and his thinking

about it, began to acquire a degree of sophistication and awareness of difficulties which made him increasingly suspect in the
eyes of more zealous, and sometimes more naïve, compatriots.
This, in turn, fuelled a reputation for political manipulation and
sophistry. Especially in times of political crisis, politicians operate
in a complex and rapidly changing world where consistency may
be an unaffordable luxury, where one may be called upon not
only to reprioritize the desirable but to face the tragedy of choice
between evils. In so far as Cromwell operated in such a context
from the mid-1640s, we must surely adjust our standard of judgement to, at least, acknowledge its constraints upon him. This does
not, of course, preclude judgement. If Cromwell had arrived at a
political/religious irenicism, had he achieved it without losing a
sense of God's purpose or did settlement come to dominate his
priorities at the expense of reformation? Had the process of coali-
tion-building which was integral to his view of the means towards
settlement come to be at the expense of old allies and, as many of
them alleged, the betrayal of the good old cause?

An overview of his maturation as a politician from late 1640
will help us to isolate those issues around which his reputation as
a politician has developed. His conduct in the first 18 months
(November 1640–July 1642) of the Long Parliament has often
been presented as that of a gauche and isolated backbencher who
would require success in war to attract attention and influence.
At best, he is sometimes depicted as on the edges of a coalition
headed by the Earls of Bedford, Warwick and John Pym; as
someone used by them, a kind of expendable, forlorn hope, to
test parliamentary feeling on such issues as the root and branch
abolition of episcopacy. There is something in this but it may easily be overdone. The fragmentary evidence of his political connections, at this time and later, suggests that he was linked,
particularly closely, through Oliver St John, with Viscount Saye
and Sele, Lord Wharton and *via* them with the wider connection
of godly patriots working to re-establish, as they saw it, civil and
religious liberty. It is these connections which explain the large
number of Commons committees, some of them critical ones, to
which the relatively inexperienced MP was rapidly re-appointed
and the growing frequency with which he was used as a
Commons messenger or link with the Lords.[4] Above all, he was
acquiring knowledge and experience. The overwhelming parliamentary majority which had brought down the ministry of the
personal rule was, by late November 1641, deeply divided over

the Grand Remonstrance. His zeal against popery and an oppressive episcopacy may have remained unabated but he was early aware that the Scots allies of the English patriots might eventually offer the prospect of Protestant oppression instead of religious liberty.[5]

Between 1642 and 1644 the war enthusiast became not only a more skilled commander of men but also more aware in his appreciation of the relationship between war and politics. Cromwell came to realize that war was not only a matter of great national causes but of regional and inter-regional political struggles and, increasingly, that there was a direct link between how people believed the war should be fought and what they considered the desirable outcomes of that conflict. The second set of concerns crystallized in the quarrel with Manchester towards the end of 1644. It is clear from Cromwell's conduct in that quarrel that he had realized that uncompromising confrontation would be counterproductive and that a lateral move might be the best way of securing his objectives. The reorganization of war policy and the army followed and it is hard to see how that would have been achieved so decisively without the Self-Denying Ordinance. Of course, this leaves open the question as to whether the manoeuvre was a disinterested one for the public good or a stratagem to take the direction of the war effort out of hands unacceptable to Oliver and to place it under those whom he could manage. At the same time, Cromwell had been a member of the Committee of Both Kingdoms since February 1644 and his thinking must have been influenced by exposure to the issues and problems of national war management. The political economy of the war, its financing through taxation and credit and the political price to be paid for these resources, as well as the politico-religious objectives of the Scots, who were strongly represented on the Committee, would have been borne in on him. In 1645 the political problems of religious settlement must have been focused for him by parliamentary action to remove the pleas for liberty of conscience from their published versions of his despatches after the battle of Naseby and the capture of Bristol.

The virtual termination of the war in June 1646, with the surrender of Oxford, brought Cromwell to the politics of peace and the limits of the possible. He may have been one of the outstanding architects of victory but a settlement still had to be reached with the King and the majority in Parliament were pushing ahead with the abolition of episcopacy and the establishment of a

Presbyterian church. Cromwell was seriously unwell between August 1646 and April 1647 and played only a limited role in Parliament throughout that period and, by the time he recovered, relations between Parliament and the army were deteriorating rapidly. The year of 1647 saw Cromwell trying to reconcile the two. When relations deteriorated to the point where all-out resistance by the army seemed a real prospect, he backed The Heads of Proposals, which was designed to offer a parliamentary settlement which might be acceptable to the King, the army, the godly and those who saw substantial constitutional reform as essential. In the circumstances of 1647, this was always an ambitious scheme and it foundered on the intransigence of the King, whose folly was to believe that time was on his side, and the Levellers, who were looking for more radical solutions. In his continuing search for a formula which could reconcile a divided nation, Cromwell was to return repeatedly to the key elements of The Heads of Proposals. More immediately, the attempt to reconcile the irreconcilable was, to his critics, deeply suspect. The failure of that attempt plunged England and Scotland into the second civil war of 1648 and pushed Cromwell into renewed alliance with those now angry enough to demand justice on 'that man of blood'. Victory and Charles' continued inflexibility led the Council of Officers, on 18 November 1648, to endorse the proposal to try the King. It was clear by early December that this demand could only be met by the overthrow of the parliamentary majority. The purging of Parliament and the revolution of 1648–9 followed. Few historians would now hold to the view that this was all engineered by an exceptionally cunning Cromwell. Rather, they would argue that the regicide and revolution left his attempt to reconcile the army, the godly, the King and Parliament in tragic disarray. That he persisted with the twin aims of preserving social order and preventing further civil war, while trying to rescue something of the moderate strategy of 1647, shows remarkable political endurance and resourcefulness. It was Cromwell who encouraged moderates to return to the Rump after the regicide and who took the lead in suppressing mutiny in the army and in crushing the challenge of the Levellers to the new regime.

If the *annus mirabilis* of March 1648–March 1649 confronted him, in the end, with the choice between two evils, the signs of Providential approval in the victorious Irish and Scots campaigns of 1649–51 had the effect of encouraging him, confirming his identification with God's army and balancing the conservative undertow of his drive for reconciliation with a renewed desire for godly reformation, however vaguely that might be defined. The Rump might pride itself on emulating the martial glories of classical republics and on commissioning a navy adequate to challenge the Dutch but its critics found it wanting in zeal for reformation. In August 1652 it was presented by the officers of the New Model Army with a petition outlining a 14-point reform programme. By April of the following year, not only had progress on this agenda been very limited but the MPs decided not to renew the Commission for the Propagation of the Gospel in Wales, a project dear to the hearts of the saints and godly officers. Irritation between Parliament and army was intense and erupted in what may well have been no more than a muddle over intentions relating to the Bill for a new representative under discussion on 20 April 1653. Cromwell's expulsion of the Rump on that day saw him at his least temperate, the political actor who has thrown caution to the winds and acts without having thought through the consequences.

All the more remarkable is the rapidity with which some Cromwellian political balance was recovered. The Nominated Assembly, was not, as was once thought, an exercise in giving the saints free rein but an attempt to bring together men of approved godliness who, nevertheless, represented the traditional rulers of the regions. Ireland and Scotland were represented for the first time. There seem to have been three political objectives informing the exercise: the avoidance of military rule; the establishment of some form of 'representation' without risking the overthrow of the cause which 'free' elections might have entailed; and the provision of a framework for constitutional solutions to emerge from a 'representative' assembly. Given Cromwell's assumption that it was undesirable to 'manage' such an assembly, what turned out to be unacceptable was the capacity of a minority of members to use the Assembly to push through radical and ill thought through reforms. The moderate majority's decision to hand power and responsibility back to Cromwell in December 1653, led to an attempt to reconcile the nation *via* a constitution echoing The Heads of Proposals. The Instrument of Government offered the traditional ruling classes a restoration of their representation in a unicameral assembly and a single person head of state, in the form of a Lord Protector.[6] He would be accountable to, and to some extent controlled by, a Council in the composition of which the representative would have a say. This was responsible government as had been understood by patriots since the early seventeenth century. At the same time there was provision, within the constitution, for a standing army and national security. Before the first Parliament met under this constitution, a nationally regulated, locally disciplined, ministry was provided for, through a system of Triers and Ejectors established by Protectoral ordinance. On such a basis, Cromwell hoped to reconcile the major elements of the political life of the nation. The problem remained that it was an imposed solution and, while in his speech of 12 September 1654 Cromwell offered the prospect of constitutional revision around four fundamentals, there were too many axes to be ground before consensus, on what constitutional revision might mean, could emerge. The dissolution of Parliament at the earliest conceivable date, on 22 January 1655, was a tacit admission that, however elaborately conceived, imposed solutions to the problem of reconciliation would always find their legitimacy contested.

The problem of those who were irreconcilable and the security concerns they gave rise to were exemplified in 1655 and 1656 by the Penruddock rising, the Venner plot and the prospect, in the winter of 1655–6, of an alliance between Royalists and Fifth Monarchists. The government was also conscious of the heavy financial burden of the army and navy, as well as the problems posed by deteriorating relations with Spain and the consequences of the Hispaniola fiasco. The Major-Generals scheme was a response to most of these concerns: providing for security more cheaply and enabling the New Model to be scaled down. Its disadvantages were its fiscal involvement through the decimation tax and its usurpation of the local magistracy by its intervention in local police functions. Moreover, a naval war with Spain required parliamentary taxation and it was clear that a parliament would be an opportunity for the widespread resentment against the Major-Generals to be expressed. When Cromwell's second protectoral Parliament met in September 1656, he was ready to pre-empt criticism by surrendering the Major-Generals, and by February 1657 he was facing the possibility of a constitutional settlement delivered to him by Parliament and therefore possessed of a legitimacy which an imposed settlement could never have had. He dealt with the officers' resistance to the revision of 'their' constitution, the Instrument, by a display of anger at their obduracy; by highlighting the capacity of a unicameral legislature for intolerance as in the case of James Nayler; and by wearing down Parliament's initial all-or-nothing approach to the point where he could reject kingship without jettisoning the rest of the package. The title of monarch may have been blasted but the trappings of monarchy were more in evidence in the second phase of the Protectorate and this, in itself, represented a conscious attempt at the political reconciliation Cromwell had been seeking since 1647 and the constituent elements of which had been so damagingly exploded by the events of 1648–9.

This brief review of the political features of Cromwell's career from 1640 needs to be supplemented by an understanding of the informal political activity, the building and rebuilding of networks, associations and understandings with other players which was the major part of his political activity throughout his career. In this chapter we will look in more detail at this down to 1653 and it will form a feature of our consideration of Cromwell as a state builder, post-1653, in the next chapter. But much of Cromwell's reputation in the past has hinged upon two considerations as to the purpose behind this activity. Was its ultimate purpose that of self-aggrandizement? Was Cromwell the ambitious, power-hungry politician who cloaked his use of others and his exploitation of situations for personal advancement behind a machiavellian pose of public-spirited self-sacrifice? Second, was there any consistency of purpose discernible behind the extraordinary series of experiments and strategies to which Cromwell was a party from 1640, or were opportunism and the pragmatics of political survival and, where possible, advancement, the only threads connecting his various twists and turns. Since the 1640s the 'Machiavilian Cromwellist' has been set against the high-minded servant of God and it is time for us to look at what his political record may be able to tell us about this aspect of his reputation.

One of the difficulties which the view of Cromwell as driven purely by ambition has to confront is his neglect of the most obvious opportunities to establish and formalize his personal ascendancy. For example, after the victory at Worcester, the 'crowning mercy', he was seen to have achieved unparalleled things. The Rump showed extraordinary generosity in granting him an income of £4000 a year for life and the palace of Hampton Court. For many Royalists in exile the game appeared to be up. Sir Edward Nicholas, Secretary of State in exile, found himself thinking of returning to England to submit to the mercy of 'Cromwell and his masters'.[7] John Buchan believed that, had Cromwell offered himself as monarch on his return to London after Worcester, the nation would have submitted.[8] A similar occasion was presented when Cromwell expelled the Rump.[9] He had the backing of the army. A power vacuum of his creating existed and he was virtually free to fill it as he chose. But he held back from the ultimate self-aggrandizement, the seizure of the title of King or Emperor. Was this the conduct of an ambitious man? As Johann Sommerville has pointed out, both after the expulsion of the Rump and after the Nominated Assembly's surrender of their responsibilities, Cromwell had held arbitrary power: 'on both occasions he had been anxious to give up the power as soon as possible'.[10] On the second occasion, in December 1653, the exiled Royalists expected, and feared, that Cromwell would take on the sovereign power. 'I do with you,' Sir Edward Nicholas wrote to Edward Hyde, 'apprehend nothing more prejudicial or pernicious to his Majesty's interest than that Cromwell should by any title take on himself (as it is evident it his design) the Sovereign power in England.'[11] Certainly, under the title of Lord Protector, he had taken on something approximating to the status of sovereign but what must have puzzled these observers was the degree to which he had accepted that his power should be bound about with constitutional constraints. Cromwell was himself well aware that there were those who saw him as cunningly exploitative of the language of necessity to advance himself and his family while claiming to serve the interest of the nation. Sensitivity to such charges was in evidence in his speech of 22 January 1655, dissolving the first Protectoral Parliament, and it is worth noting the source of his sensitivity.

> But if any man shall object, it is an easy thing to talk of necessities when men create necessities; would not the Lord Protector make himself great, and his family great? doth not he make these necessities? And then he will come upon the people with this argument of necessity! ... It was, say some, the cunning of the Lord Protector (I take it to myself) it was the craft of such a man, and his plot that hath brought it about.

While he denied that he had 'yet known what it is to make necessities, whatsoever the judgements or thoughts of men are' his sensitivity to the charge of necessity was that it impugned the honour of God by assuming that men, rather than God, had the power to control events.

> Oh, what blasphemy is this! . . . To say that men bring forth these things, when God doth them, judge you if God will bear this. I wish that every sober heart, though he hath had temptations upon him of deserting the cause of God, yet may take heed how he provokes, and falls into the hands of the living God by such blasphemies as these.[12]

The final incident which seems a bad fit with the allegation of self-aggrandizement is Cromwell's comprehensive rejection of the crown offered to him in the spring of 1657. He may have demurred at the title of King and hereditary office as it was presented him to in an earlier version of the Instrument of Government but his rejection of kingship in 1657 was public, deliberate and definitive. Its key feature was respect for God's own decisiveness in blasting the title of King as well as 'blasting' the Stuart dynasty, and historians have recently come round to the view that this was a more important factor, in Cromwell's decision, than military opposition.[13]

There remains, however, a series of incidents, at best 'coincidences', which make it less easy to brush away the calculating politician, capable of subterfuge to attain his ends, from Cromwell's reputation. And, of course, the judgement with respect to his means will inevitably reopen questions about his objectives. Amongst the incidents falling into this category are several which have been focal in sustaining a less public-spirited reputation for him. First amongst them might be Cornet Joyce's seizure of the King on 4 June 1647. It seems unlikely that a relatively junior officer would have taken such a responsibility upon himself. Joyce had been at a meeting at Cromwell's house in Drury Lane, London on 31 May. The evidence is inconclusive but the deduction has frequently been made that Joyce was acting under Cromwell's instructions.[14] If that were the case, by what authority did Cromwell order the seizure of the King and with what intention? A second occasion which gave rise to accusations of perfidy and personal ambition came later in 1647 when Cromwell's simultaneous negotiations with the King in relation to The Heads of Proposals and his involvement in the famous debates at Putney over the Levellers' first Agreement of the People seemed to some to show a flexibility bordering on the hypocritical. In itself this may be readily dealt with. The accusations flung at Cromwell at this time can be categorized as expressions of frustration by those willing to embrace more radical courses than he was prepared to back at this stage. In particular, his role at Putney can be interpreted as that of trying to hold the army and as many other players as possible to the only formula on offer which held out the prospect of a parliamentary settlement which the King, the army, the godly and moderate constitutional reformers might be reasonably persuaded to accept, The Heads of Proposals. What immediately, however, alerts the suspicions of some are the circumstances of the King's escape from Hampton Court on 11 November 1647. Charles had been in the custody of Edward Whalley, Cromwell's cousin. Cromwell had written to Whalley warning him of rumours that some attempt might be made to seize or attack the King. Whalley had shown the letter to Charles and this probably precipitated his flight. Was this sequence premeditated? Was there complicity between Cromwell, Whalley and the King? The plot, if such it was, appears to thicken because, in his flight, Charles ended up in the Isle of Wight secured in Carisbrooke Castle under the custody of another kinsman of Cromwell's, Colonel Robert Hammond. It may be true, as Abbott affirmed long ago, that there is no evidence of Cromwell's complicity in Charles' escape but the series of 'coincidences' here have inevitably prompted speculation and have provided those who see Cromwell as a schemer with food for thought. A further incident, provocative of similar speculation, is Cromwell's long stay in the north of England, primarily at the siege of Pontrefract, while events unfolded in London in November/December 1648. In late November he was directly instructed by Fairfax to come south but it has been interpreted as no coincidence that it was the evening of 6 December, when the events of the day of Pride's Purge were virtually concluded, before he entered London.[15] From the Levellers' perspective this whole year and its outcome in the events of early 1649 was proof of Cromwell's self-serving treachery. He had, by their account, gulled them into burying their differences with the Grandees (as they called the senior officers of the New Model) in order to form a united front against the Royalist/Scots threat of the second civil war. The prospect had then been held out of their full involvement in finding an acceptable constitutional settlement and meetings with some of the Leveller leaders were held at Whitehall in November and December ostensibly for that purpose. By these means, it was alleged, Cromwell had kept the Levellers, and their radical allies in the army, quiescent while a military coup involving the purging of Parliament, the illegal trial and execution of the King and the dismemberment of the ancient constitution was carried through. In the event the Agreement of the People which emerged from the Whitehall discussions and was presented to the Rump on 20 January 1649 was ignored. The new regime, without a basis in consent, was tyrannical in the double sense of having usurped recognized authority and of ruling by will. As the spring of 1649 wore on, the Cromwellian junta was intent on crushing its opponents in the army and in the Leveller movement. The leaders of the Levellers were imprisoned and in Lilburne's case held in prison even after he had been acquitted by a London jury.[16] To the Levellers, then, the rule of the Rump, the trappings of the English Commonwealth, were no more than a mask concealing the brute facts of a military tyranny whose controller was Oliver Cromwell. Such a crude, conspiracy theory hardly does justice to the complex unfolding of events after 1648 nor to what, by this account, must look like the curious restraint of the military in setting up the machinery of the Commonwealth or in calling the Nominated Assembly or establishing the Protectorate.

It remains true, however, that from a relatively early stage self-aggrandizement, in particular the crown, were identified as Cromwell's underlying objectives. Did Cromwell aspire to the throne and, if so, for how long had it been his ambition? It was not unexpected that the fall of the Stuart dynasty should lead to speculation about its replacement. Europe was a continent of monarchies, not of republics, and for a territorially extensive state, like England, to be a republic was virtually unknown. That there should be speculation as to a new dynasty was natural. That, as time went on, such speculation should focus on Cromwell was understandable. The problem is that of distinguishing the rumour from the reality. In August 1649, in the first year of the Commonwealth, at least one newsbook was already prophesying Cromwell's ambition to be Lord Protector.[17] Two years later republicans were speculating on his monarchical ambitions in the wake of his triumph at Worcester.[18] On 10 December 1651 a meeting of MPs and senior officers at the Speaker's house discussed what was required to achieve a permanent settlement. The lawyers – Oliver St John, Bulstrode Whitelocke and William Lenthall, the Speaker himself – had argued that the nature of English law and governance was such that it was hard to imagine a permanent settlement 'without something of monarchy in it'. What is noteworthy is that Cromwell's position was that such a settlement might be 'very effectual' *provided that* 'it may be done with safety, and preservation of our Rights both as Englishmen and as Christians'. At this point, and if we can trust the sources on which this account is based, he had reservations about a monarchical solution. Furthermore, the discussion at this meeting was about whether Charles I's third son, the Duke of Gloucester, might be a potentially acceptable candidate. In other words, in so far as the renewal of monarchy remained an option, it was at this stage thought of in terms of hereditary legitimacy.[19] Almost a year later, in December 1652, Cromwell had a private discussion with Whitelocke. Their concern was the growing hostility between various factions both in Parliament and the army and between those two bodies. Cromwell was particularly concerned about the declining reputation of the Rump and the need for some constitutional 'Check' on their 'Exorbitancies'. It was in this context that he asked his famous question: 'What if a man should take upon him to be King?' Whitelocke's response was to suggest that the title would add nothing to Cromwell's existing powers, that any assumption of the title by him would alienate those of his allies who were committed to a 'Free State', and instead of the political choice for the majority being between monarchy and a Free State it would be between the two dynasties of Cromwell and Stuart. Oliver conceded the good sense of all of this and asked Whitelocke for alternative suggestions. Whitelocke's advice was to consider ways of doing a deal with the Stuarts with a view to their restoration.[20] If Whitelocke's account is to be trusted and, despite his habitually self-serving version of events, the consensus amongst historians is that it may be, then there was a moment in late 1652 when Cromwell considered the advisability of taking the throne. The evidence that underlying this was a settled ambition is, however, totally lacking and the assumption of such a disposition is hard to reconcile with his reaction on this occasion and later.

Nevertheless, the assumption of the Protectorate in December 1653 was, for many, a step too far in the direction of monarchy and away from a Free State. In January 1654, Captain John Williams was reported as having preached at Cannigull in Radnorshire that, for all they knew, they had a King already: 'in these dayes our sunn was gone down at noone day, and our light turned to darkness'.[21] Such anxieties were not kept from

Cromwell and they must have carried some weight with him. Adjutant-General William Allen, a Cromwellian and denounced as such by no less than John Lilburne, experienced genuine torment over Cromwell's assumption of the quasi-monarchical role of Lord Protector. From Dublin to a friend in London on April 1654 he wrote

> As to the person in chief place, I confess I love and honour him, for the honour God hath put uppon him, and I trust will yet continue; I mean that of uprightheartedness to the Lord, though this last change with his atendencyes hath more stumbled me than ever any did; and I have still many thoughts of heart concerning it. But time will tell us more of persons and things.[22]

Allen worried about the prospect that Cromwell was temporarily tainted by ambition in negotiating with the King in 1647; permanently by the assumption of the Protectorate in December 1653. Towards the end of 1654 he expressed these doubts directly to the Lord Protector. 'What my esteem hath been of you in some vertical forsaking days I believe you can remember; and I can truly say, if I have erred, it hath been I fear, in esteeming too highly of you.'[23] The evidence is that this kind of opinion, that of old, faithful comrades in arms weighed heavily with Cromwell.

In June 1655 the Swedish diplomat, Peter Julius Coyet, reported to his master, Charles X of Sweden, with a shrewd analysis of the balance of argument on Cromwell's possible assumption of the title of King. Custom and the nature of English law, the reconciliation of the English nobility and the reassurance of those who had benefited from property transfers, especially in Ireland, all favoured such a move. On the other hand, it would alienate many of the saints and the military. In terms of legitimacy the House of Cromwell could never compete with that of Stuart and it would be a move in defiance of the Act against Kingly power (the Act of 17 March 1649). A month later, Coyet wrote again, this time to report that opinion had moved against the desirability of the royal title. He stressed that a monarch's power would be even more circumscribed than that possessed by Cromwell already and that 'Protector' was beginning to be an established and accepted title.[24] In the spring of 1657, when his second parliament was offering him the crown, many godly congregations and old soldiers wrote to Cromwell begging him to reject it. William Bradford was one who had 'attended your greatest hazards'. 'I am of that number, my Lord, that still loves you, and greatly desire to doe so, I having gone along with you from Edge-hill to Dunbar.'[25] To the opinion of men such as this, as he insisted in his speech to the parliamentary committee sent to meet with him on 13 April 1657, Cromwell was sensitive.[26] Had ambition alone driven him, presumably he would have taken the throne when it was offered to him by a parliamentary majority but he did not. Providence and the loyalty of his most longstanding followers were against it. Even so there is no evidence that he ever coveted the title, that he ever thought of it as more than 'a feather in a Hatt'.[27]

To undermine personal ambition as the key to explaining Cromwell's political twists and turns is, however, merely to restate the problem. Was there any consistency at all in his politics over the 18 years from 1640 until his death or was it a pragmatic series of survivalist responses to changing situations? Looking back in his speech to both Houses of Parliament on 20 January 1658, he saw consistency in the twin causes of civil and religious liberty: 'our civil liberties as men, our spiritual liberty as Christians'. And he proudly reflected that what they had aimed at from the first they had now arrived at.[28] In this interpretation the good old cause which he personified might be seen as the cause of the political and religious networks to which he had belonged since the 1630s, the networks of St John, Hampden, Desborough, the Barringtons and 'the puritan Earl', Warwick. At once committed to liberty of conscience against oppressive episcopacy and to civil liberty against the centralizing reformism and oppressive taxation of the personal rule, these saintly patriots had been prepared to go to war to defeat the counsels of those who would direct government against civil and religious liberty. As we have seen, there was a congruence of kinship and religious and political networks in Cromwell's espousal of these causes and the military connections, through which he managed his contribution to the war effort, seemed, initially at least, to reinforce them. Cromwell's retrospective claim, in January 1658, was that his government, the Protectorate, finally secured the twin objectives of civil and religious liberty, the prize which he had consistently pursued throughout. The problem is the way in which the networks, which had underwritten his desire to achieve these aims, had been damaged or torn apart by the events, and Cromwell's stance in relation to them, of the intervening years. For example, the dispute over how the war should be fought and the kind of settlement which would be consistent with civil and religious liberty not only damaged Cromwell's relations with moderate conservatives like Manchester, Prynne and Baxter but with those at the other end of the spectrum like John Lilburne and the Levellers. The regicide, at least temporarily, alienated him from Oliver St John and cast a shadow over his relationship with Fairfax. His correspondence with Robert Hammond in late 1648 reveals how great the strain of this decisive event was on many of those close to him and indeed on himself. The expulsion of the Rump in April 1653 alarmed and alienated those, like Vane, who had been allies in the struggle for civil and religious liberty or, like Ludlow and Hutchinson had been comrades-in-arms in the military dimension of the same struggle. To Ludlow and the commonwealthsmen, the move to the Protectorate seemed not so much a diversion as a reversion, a return to all that they had fought against.[29] Thomas Harrison could endorse the expulsion of the Rump and the calling of the Nominated Assembly as evidence that Cromwell 'acted upon higher principles than civil liberty', that when civil and religious liberty were in conflict he would give priority to the latter. But, by December 1653, even he baulked at the adoption of the Instrument of Government and the establishment of the Protectorate.[30] In this way, successive layers of supporters and allies were alienated. Naturally, each of them saw themselves as consistent and Cromwell as swerving from or abandoning the principles which had bound them to him. By the mid-1650s, the Lord Protector was not only policing the radical forces which, in an earlier dispensation, he had helped to generate but the loyalty of his military network was stretched to the point where a number of colonels were petitioning against the power of the Protectorate.[31] When, in January 1658, Cromwell proclaimed his consistency and achievement in terms of civil and religious liberty, a cloud of witnesses could have been called to give evidence of his betrayal of the same principles.

Yet it would be a hard judgement which took disappointed and, in some cases, embittered, ex-allies as all the witnesses required to convict Cromwell of unprincipled inconsistency. Is there a defence case to be made against this evidence for the prosecution? Such a case might depend on re-reading the record with a more favourable bias towards Cromwell but, critically, it depends on looking to a core strategy, that of The Heads of Proposals for a key to his consistency. Drafted by a combination

of Lord Wharton, Viscount Saye and Sele, Henry Vane, Henry
Ireton and John Lambert, the Proposals were debated by the
Council of War of the New Model Army in July 1647. By this
stage a number of things were clear. Military victory had been
bought at a huge price. The financial and physical burden of war
had been great and was continuing to alienate those on whose
support any stable regime would depend. Parliament had shown
a potential for its own forms of tyranny, jeopardizing civil and
religious liberty. The army had recently shown a potential for
mutiny and indiscipline which could turn it from being a source
of strength to one of weakness. The saints, as Cromwell later
recalled, were indulging 'many unruly passions and troubles of
spirit, whereby they give disquiet to themselves and to others'.[32]
They had begun to demonstrate a potential for mutual acrimony,
verging on hatred. Divisions amongst the victors revealed allies
becoming enemies with a potential for multiplying war. In an earlier political crisis, that of late 1644, Cromwell had played a leading role in sustaining the causes of civil and religious liberty by
ensuring that Parliament had the means to win the war but not as
clients of the Scots. Providence had blessed the resolution of that
crisis with victory. But now, as the victors fell out amongst themselves, peace as well as civil and religious liberty were in jeopardy. It was to save all three that The Heads of Proposals were
hammered out.

The 'Presbyterian' majority in the House of Commons, led by
Denzil Holles, were in early 1647 developing a scheme to deal
with the financial and military burdens of the New Model Army.
It was to be reduced to a small security and garrison force, to be
commanded by Fairfax (after a vote with a majority of only 12)
and subject to subscription to the Covenant. The rest of its members were either to be disbanded or offered service in Ireland. As
a basis for settlement, the relatively harsh terms of the Newcastle
Propositions were put to the King. They provided for a
Presbyterian church settlement, parliamentary control of the
army and of the appointment of the King's ministers for 20 years
and a punitive deal over ex-Royalists. In March 1647, whatever
his personal feelings about this scheme, Cromwell was urging the
necessity for the army's obedience to their civilian, parliamentary
masters if any form of civil liberty were to be preserved. But anxiety over military grievances and the prospect of parliamentary
tyranny were proving unsettling in the army. In the second half of
March, a petition circulated amongst the soldiers and was dis-

cussed with the officers prior to its intended presentation to
Fairfax. Claiming to have fought for civil and religious liberties
and the privileges of Parliament, the petition called for the soldiers to be granted legal indemnification for acts of war, an audit
of military expenditures and the payment of arrears, provision
for soldiers' widows and maimed ex-soldiers, an end to free-
quarter (where soldiers were billeted on civilians in return for
promissory notes which were not always redeemed for cash) and
that volunteer troops should not be compelled to serve overseas.
When the petition, which was intended for Fairfax was reported
to the Commons on 27 March, they ordered him to suppress it.
But this was probably to ask the impossible and when the House
heard that it was still in circulation on 29 March, at the instigation of Holles, a 'Declaration of Dislike' was drafted and
endorsed by both Houses. In this it was declared that all those
who promoted the petition would be looked upon 'as enemies of
the state and disturbers of the public peace'.[33] From this point
onwards there was a growing estrangement between Parliament
and the officers and men of the New Model Army. The honour of
the army had been impugned and it seemed to be intolerable that
they could not present a petition to their own commander. The
ranks organized themselves through the election of representatives, called agents or agitators, and sought the cooperation of
their officers. This pressure eventually culminated in regular
meetings of the agitators and staff officers in the General Council
of the Army. Resentment at the high-handed attitude of the
Commons to military grievances and fear that behind it lay plans
for a Presbyterian coup, both of which were fanned by Leveller
pamphleteering, grew dangerously.

On 25 May the Commons decided that the army would be disbanded over the first two weeks of June with no concessions
made to the soldiers' grievances and no salve for their wounded
honour. Faced with the responsibility for implementing such a
disbandment, Fairfax called a meeting of his Council of War
which was attended by about 100 officers on 29 May. Several
regiments were close to mutiny and the demand for redress of
grievances before disbandment was growing. Two questions
were put to each officer present. Could the army be disbanded
without disturbance? To this 86 officers replied 'No'; three 'Yes'.
Should there be a general rendezvous of the army? Eighty-two
replied 'Yes'; five 'No'. Faced with this Fairfax and Cromwell
had to choose between compliance with Parliament and loss of

control of the army or moving with the army, if necessary in defiance of Parliament. A paper was drafted asking Parliament to reconsider its vote for disbandment without concessions and Fairfax wrote to William Lenthall, the Speaker of the Commons, 'I am forced to yield something out of order, to keep the army from disorder, or worse inconveniences'.[34]

The general rendezvous of six cavalry and seven infantry regiments at Newmarket on 4 and 5 June endorsed the Solemn Engagement by which it was agreed that the army would not obey the parliamentary order to disband until their grievances had been met and the civil liberties of the subject had been cleared. The General Council of the Army, consisting of the general staff officers plus two soldiers and two officers for each regiment, was to be responsible for dealings with Parliament. It was clear that those MPs with a record hostile to the New Model would be unacceptable parties to such dealings. This was confirmed in the Army's Declaration of 14 June in which it described itself as 'not a mere mercenary army' and, in defence of the people's just rights and liberties, called for a purge of Parliament, an end to the present Parliament, the setting up of a more 'equal representative' and the settling of the King's rights in so far as they were consistent with those of the subject. There was now a dangerous prospect of irreconcilable conflict between Parliament and its army. It was to address this that Cromwell joined those who were developing The Heads of Proposals. Their aim was to defuse a situation where the army and Parliament were estranged, the King was in the army's hands while Parliament was subject to mounting political pressure from Presbyterians in London and the army was slowly advancing on the capital.

Fundamental to The Heads of Proposals was the belief that any legitimate settlement should be arrived at on parliamentary authority and it was the intention of the framers of the document that its central features should be subject to parliamentary legislation.[35] The army was to be conciliated by provision for indemnity for acts of war and for the payment of arrears as well as by the clearing of their right to petition. The disposition of the armed forces and of the principal offices of state was to be vested in the Lords and Commons for 10 years. While the framework of the ancient constitution and the dignity of the monarchy was to be maintained, the desires of those who sought further constitutional change were to be met, in part at least, by biennial Parliaments elected by redistributed constituencies and by a strengthening of the government's accountability to Parliament. Local influence on the choice of juries, justices and sheriffs was also to be bolstered. Episcopacy and the Prayer Book, in a move which should have appealed to Charles I, were to be maintained, but, in deference to the godly, they were to have no coercive force and there would be liberty of conscience and practice for Protestants alongside this established church. Much more generous provision than in the Newcastle Propositions was made for ex-Royalists to reach a settlement with those who had achieved military victory over them. This was an impressive attempt to find a formula which would offer something to all the major players in the post-war political situation, except perhaps to those wedded to an exclusive, Presbyterian church settlement. The King and the ancient constitution would be restored, though on a modified basis. The Church of England would be part of that restored apparatus of settlement but it would come back without coercive powers and the godly would be free of the threat to liberty of conscience which both Landianism and Presbyterianism represented for many of them. Those who looked for constitutional protection for their civil liberties were offered regular parliaments, elected on a reformed basis and accountable, responsible government.

At the heart of the strategy of The Heads of Proposals was Cromwell's collaboration with Lord Wharton, Viscount Saye and Sele, Oliver St John and Henry Vane. This was a connection which had enjoyed some cohesion since 1640, if not before. Their appeal in 1647 was to address the immediate political crisis by reconciling competing interests into a coalition which gave each interest something of priority to them but gave none of them everything. For the longer term it gave to both saints and patriots, and crucially to the networks which Cromwell, St John, Wharton, Saye and Sele and Vane were central, guarantees of civil and religious liberty. The case for Cromwell's consistency on civil and religious liberty, if it is to be made at all, must be made around the principal features of The Heads of Proposals. The twists and turns of his search for a settlement, from late 1647 onwards, can be explained in terms of the tensions within the coalition of competing interests which he and his colleagues attempted to construct. The tragedy of many of these expedients was that, however driven by necessity (or, in Cromwell's terms, by Providence) they might have been, their effect was to deepen the irreconcileability of the elements upon which the settlement depended. What is remarkable is Cromwell's persistence after every setback, not only in attempting to stabilize the situation but to rebuild a strategy approximating as nearly as possible to that of The Heads of Proposals and delivering reconciliation along-side guarantees of civil and religious liberty. To the end of his life he may have had to work with 'solutions' which remained rough round the edges but the set of aspirations at their heart remained consistent and enduring.

In late autumn 1647 the New Model was camped on the out-skirts of London in a state of tension over the soldiers' griev-ances, the rights of the subject and possible threats to both from Westminster. The Levellers were deeply suspicious of the Grandees' negotiations with the King and determined to win the rest of the army over to more radical solutions. The critical fort-night was that from 28 October to 11 November. It began with the meetings of the General Council of the Army at Putney, with some civilians present, to discuss the nature of a settlement as proposals were being developed in rival documents. These famous debates at Putney are usually interpreted from a Leveller point of view, focusing on the issues raised in the Leveller's first Agreement of the People, which itself is usually viewed in a sym-pathetic light. But from Cromwell and Ireton's point of view, the debates are best seen as an attempt to keep the army to the com-mitment to The Heads of Proposals made by the Council of War at Reading on 17 and 18 July 1647. Had the debates gone the Levellers' way, it would have wrecked the prospect of a parlia-mentary settlement, would have alienated moderates and conser-vatives in the political nation, and would have required a force such as the army to dismantle the ancient constitution and *impose* a new one. However, on 4 November, The Heads of Proposals emerged from the debates virtually unscathed.[36] The major provisions of the Proposals had been introduced as Bills into Parliament by Wharton and Saye and Sele in October but, as November advanced, the policy they represented was wrecked by the intransigence of John Lilburne, and the Levellers, on the one side, and by Charles I, on the other.

Frustrated at Putney, the Levellers would not accept either defeat or compromise. They attempted to open a gulf between the commanders of the New Model, the Grandees, and their men. Lilburne and Wildman attacked Cromwell and Ireton as deceivers, in *Putney Projects* offering an account of recent events designed to show the two officers as prepared to sell out of the rights of soldiers and citizens alike. Sections of the army were close to mutiny and on 9 November it was agreed to assemble the troops at three rendezvous in order to restore order. But what made the Proposals as a strategy unworkable in 1647 was the duplicity and lack of realism of the King. Charles continued to believe himself to be the indispensable key to the situation and to underestimate the political difficulty which men like Cromwell faced in trying to hold together support for a set of proposals which were, in the circumstances, relatively generous to him. His escape on 11 November and his subsequent negotiations with the Scots made the deal impossible. By 26 November Cromwell had decided that he had to give priority to the unity of the army over the strategy of the Proposals. 'If we cannot bring the army to our sense, we must go to theirs'.[37] That imperative and the second civil war virtually destroyed any prospect of a revival of the Proposals with Charles I. Nevertheless, it took the failure of a further attempt by Cromwell and Saye and Sele to elicit a more reasonable response from the King at Carisbrooke (and so to avoid further bloodshed) for Cromwell to begin the process of readjusting his thinking.[38] It was still with reluctance that, in late 1648, he moved to what must have looked like the comprehensive demolition of the bases on which The Heads of Proposals might have been realized: the purging of Parliament, the execution of the King, the abolition of the House of Lords (which he opposed), and the declaration of a commonwealth.

The forms of government assumed in the proposals may have been destroyed but, despite his military preoccupations, Cromwell struggled to maintain as much of their spirit and potential as possible. He was energetic in seeking to reconcile moderates, to whom after all the Proposals were intended to appeal, back into Parliament and government. He was disillusioned by the Rump's failure to address the issue of the constitution but also by its punitive approach to ex-Royalists. Between October 1652 and April 1653 he seems to have convened as many as 10 or 12 meetings to discuss ways of moving towards a generally acceptable constitutional settlement.[39] Discussions of the possible revival of monarchy should be seen in the context of attempts to get back to something like the strategy of the Proposals. By the spring of 1653 it was impossible to hold the army and the Rump together in an alliance with shared goals. From this perspective, the Nominated Assembly was an attempt to get back in touch with the political nation; not a constitutional end point but a means towards a moderate and acceptable constitutional settlement, without running the risk that free elections might result in a parliament which could jeopardize both civil and religious liberty. The failure of that experiment, Cromwell's 'folly', led on to the Instrument of Government, drafted by Lambert who may also have played a part in shaping The Heads of Proposals. We will be considering the Instrument more closely in the next chapter when we examine Cromwell's reputation as a statebuilder. It is, however, worth noting that in its underlying principles the Instrument bears considerable similarity to the Proposals. Its great political liability was that it was an imposed solution, prescribed for the nation's good by Cromwell and, primarily, his military advisers. Cromwell was conscious of this and in his second speech to his first Parliament offered to embrace constitutional proposals from its members provided that four fundamentals were respected. They were: the joint rule of a single person and a Parliament; regular (i.e. not perpetual) parliaments; liberty of conscience alongside national religious provision; and joint, responsible, control of the militia. These were, of course, also fundamental to the Proposals and, if we put them alongside the existing constitutional provisions of the Instrument we can begin to see the Protectorate as an attempt to gain the benefits of the settlement envisaged in The Heads of Proposals by other means. Critical amongst those benefits were civil and religious liberty, at least in the terms in which Cromwell and many of his contemporaries would have understood them.

It is possible, then, to develop a case for some consistency in Cromwell's political career in the pursuit of civil and religious liberty within a governmental framework which would be acceptable to most of his compatriots. The failure of that strategy in 1647, compounded by the war of 1648 and its Providential outcome, pushed Cromwell and England into a series of crises where more immediate problems made that framework a less immediate priority. The reordering of priorities, or at least of the timetable for their achievement, had the effect of both alienating many of his former allies from him and of making him indispensable as the actor most likely to be able to manage the crises in such a way as to sustain some degree of stability. The fear of military instability and the concern for national security were potent forces pushing Cromwell from 1647 in the direction of temporary reorderings of priorities. But the devastation of the ancient constitution left him from 1653 with an overriding priority, that of statebuilding. It is to the issue of his politics with regard to this that we must now turn.

|8|

Statebuilder?

In an influential late Victorian assessment of the Lord Protector, S.R. Gardiner noted that Cromwell was admirably well-equipped for statesmanship.

> If large-mindedness, combined with an open eye for facts, together with a shrinking from violence till it seemed absolutely necessary to employ it, cannot fit a man to be a statesman, where can we hope to find statesmanship at all?

But, however positive and sympathetic Gardiner's assessment of the Lord Protector's capabilities might be, he felt obliged to conclude that the record was dismal. Nothing constructive endured. Oliver's success as a destructive force and his dependence on the military stood in the way. Having, however reluctantly, played a key role in the dismantling of the ancient constitution, he proved incapable of establishing a new state on a stable basis.

> it is impossible to resist the conclusion that he effected nothing in the way of building up where he had pulled down, and that there was no single act of the Protectorate that was not swept away at the Restoration without hope of revival[1]

A cruder version of the same verdict, more devastatingly put, was John Morley's observation that, 'Wherever force was useless, Cromwell failed'.[2]

This negative assessment of Cromwell the statebuilder has persisted, sometimes elevated to the status of a warning against allowing the military too free a role in post-conflict political reconstruction. At best, it is alleged, he destroyed one state system and failed to replace it with anything permanent. At worst, he destroyed one tyranny only to replace it with another. In one historiographical tradition he represents the failure of the Puritan Revolution, reliant on arms and fuelled by the narrow ideology of a godly minority; a failure mercifully redeemed by the Glorious Revolution of 1688–9, civilian in leadership, comprehensive in ideology and broadly in step with national sentiment. Of course, that assessment, particularly in its association with the Whig interpretation of English history, had its own self-serving aspects and has been subjected to searching criticism particularly in the last half–century. Nevertheless, there was at least one point in time when Cromwell himself appeared to endorse the view of his rule as a series of botched expedients, although he was anxious to deny responsibility for them. On 27 February 1657 he met with a delegation of about 100 army officers intent on persuading him against the Humble Petition and Advice and, in particular, against his assumption of the title of King. There are two manuscript reports of the meeting which differ in some respects but which are agreed in essentials.[3] In an angry speech, Cromwell berated his officers for leading him, often against his better judgement, through a series of ill thought out constitutional expedients. It was, he claimed, army pressure which had led him to dissolve the Rump. The Nominated Assembly had been the officers' idea and it was they who had nominated its members. When that body threatened liberty and property, it was got rid of. A group of army officers drafted the Instrument of Government, initially with the title of King in it. Cromwell had rejected the crown but, imperfect as it was, agreed to work with the Instrument. When Parliament sought to revise this constitution, a necessity with which Cromwell himself was not unsympathetic, the officers insisted that he dissolve it. A second Parliament had eventually been called, against Oliver's own judgement, and 120 members had had to be excluded in order to make it work. As Cromwell reminded them, the case of James Nayler was demonstrating that there could be no protection for liberty of conscience under a unicameral legislature and, therefore, constitutional reform was essential. Above all 'it is time to come to a settlement and lay aside arbitrary proceedings'. In one account of their confrontation presenting himself as 'their Drudge upon all occasions', there was an element of theatre in Cromwell's anger which was intended to shock his military colleagues out of their complacent opposition to any revision of the Instrument of Government. Nevertheless, here was Cromwell himself depicting 'his' rule post April 1653 (and, unknown to him, with only

18 months to run) as a series of botched expedients. Is this the view – abject failure – that we should settle for?

'Statebuilding' is commonly seen as one of the great challenges and problems facing early modern governments. To assess Cromwell's reputation in relation to it we need to clarify what we mean by the term and to establish the particular context of seventeenth-century England in which to judge him. The process of statebuilding refers to recurrent attempts to build fiscal and administrative systems which would enable the central government to have access to much greater resources than hitherto; to extend their fiscal and organizational 'reach'; to increase their creditworthiness and ability to sustain increased debt; to be able to muster and control much greater numbers of men, material and resources for longer periods of time, and to develop enlarged and more professional bureaucracies to organize all of this.[4] Two, interrelated, factors are frequently cited as causes of the early modern preoccupation with statebuilding. The first is war. The sixteenth and seventeenth centuries were witness to prolonged periods of both civil and international war of a scale and intensity which had barely been seen before. Whether the technology of warfare was also changing sufficiently rapidly to justify the terminology of a 'military revolution' has been the subject of controversy[5] but it is the case that the size of armies and navies and the complexity of their operations were increasing in the period. The second cause which stimulated governmental ambitions to control and administer complex problems was the growth of religious division, conflict and aspiration which we associate with the Reformation and Counter-Reformation. Not only did these developments fuel some of the rebellions, civil wars and international military conflicts which have already been mentioned, but territorial integrity acquired a new dimension, that of the confessional state, the desire to maintain uniformity of religion and an appropriate standard of godliness throughout society. These aspirations involved the development of states which could manage warfare on a new scale and which had the fiscal legitimacy and creditworthiness to command the requisite resources. The logistics of such operations were in turn dependent on new levels of bureaucratic efficiency and capability. To generate the base for such resources governments took a new interest in economic development, communications, education and even the technological applications of new scientific knowledge. Centralization was part of this drive towards the management of realms and their resources and this, in turn, involved developing agencies for the management and supervision of localities and regions on behalf of central government. Hindsight has tended to give the impression of greater tidiness and self-conscious purpose to this process of statebuilding than was ever likely to have been the case. Still, the demands of war and religious disturbances were relentless pressures towards greater claims by governing authorities and towards continuing preoccupation with the means of making those claims effective. What in the past has been rather crudely subsumed under the rubric of 'the rise of absolutism' may be seen as a series of attempts to free governments for the fiscal and military changes which would enable them to ensure order domestically and strength in international competition and conflict.

In England one dimension of the politics of the 1620s had been the desire of both the Court and Parliament to play a significant military role in the religious wars of Europe combined with Parliament's unwillingness to provide the resources to make such a role possible. The humiliations of English arms between 1624 and 1629 bore witness not only to mismanagement but also to the fact that the country lacked the fiscal resources, on a continuing basis, to fund the military and logistical apparatus required to make an international role for England sustainable. In this respect, England was no different to the many continental countries where governments aspiring to greater resources ran into resistance from assemblies representative of regional elites. In the 1630s Charles I tried to sidestep such resistance by dispensing with parliaments and exploiting non-parliamentary taxation, principally customs revenue and shipmoney, to render his government solvent and to build a navy. By 1637 that policy may have appeared to be bearing fruit but the willingness of his Scots subjects to fight a land war resisting his religious policies exposed the fact that the structure of government was too flimsy and lacking in the legitimacy of general support to bear the weight suddenly thrust upon it in 1639 and 1640. The demolition of the fiscal and institutional basis of independent monarchical rule in England in 1641 appeared to bring a halt to statebuilding aspirations. The suspicion that monarchical ambitions were not entirely dead and the fact that war in Ireland presented new demands and possibilities formed the backcloth to the breakdown to civil war. That war, its intensity and duration, had precisely the effect of reopening the problem of statebuilding, centralizing government, its fiscal rapacity and its threat to civil and religious liberties. The irony of the conflict was that, in order to fight a war for such liberties, Parliament itself had to engage with the fiscal, military and administrative challenges of state-building. By 1647 it was possible for its radical critics to identify a centralizing, tyrannical and religiously oppressive apparatus being built around Parliament's ostensibly representative legitimacy. The question brooding over the later 1640s was whether the consequence of the wars would be a breakthrough in terms of English statebuilding or whether such an outcome could be prevented by the restoration and stabilization of a relatively weak central government. By 1652, even after the removal of the old constitutional landmarks and further warfare in Ireland, Scotland and England, the removal of any serious, immediate, external threat meant that the choice between the two options remained open: the building of a 'modern' state around the New Model Army, the republican navy and a policy of imperial and commercial expansion, or a retreat to customary governance with greater safeguards for civil and religious liberty, a government more accountable to the local ruling classes and their resistance to statebuilding.[6] It is into this context that we must fit Cromwell's period as ruler and arbiter of England's political and constitutional destinies. Did he ever see himself as a statebuilder?

Peter Gaunt has warned us against identifying the Protectorate with the myth of an omnipresent, omnipotent Cromwell and there are good reasons for following his advice.[7] To what extent, even at the height of his authority, was Cromwell's power limited and constrained? In the first place, the constitutional arrangements under which the Protectorate operated were intended to prevent the evils of either an overmighty prince or an overmighty parliament[8] and, in practice, the most effective power in the day-to-day administration of government seems to have been exercised by the Council. In financial matters, the disposition of the militia, foreign policy and appointments to offices of state the Council exercised sustained control. Cromwell had no right of dismissal of his councillors and only a limited say in their appointment. Even decisions about when to call a Parliament and which members to exclude appear to have been taken by the Council. No aspect of government was beyond its reach but it would be wrong to see Cromwell as an entirely passive 'rubber-stamp'. 'Coordinate government', the sharing of power, an accountability on the part of the single person were all aspects of *responsible* government as it was understood by the political circles to which Cromwell had belonged since at least the early 1640s. Cromwell's own appetite for personal and continuing power, any ambition to control the levers of government, appears to have been severely limited. In 1653 he had refused to sit in either the Nominated Assembly or the Council. Under the Instrument, he was expected to work with the Council, as he did, but his absence from almost 60 per cent of its meetings is only partly explained by variable health. Moreover, his absences seem to have had little effect on the flow of business. The Council did not feel that its effectiveness was dependent on his presence and Cromwell was clearly of the same opinion.[9] Nevertheless, there were certain key decisions, which were obviously his, or in his hands: for example, the rejection of kingship or the decision to let the Major-Generals system collapse. Administration remained largely the Council's business. It is this sharing of power and responsibility which makes the shift, perceived by some historians, towards more authoritarian government in or about 1655 dangerous to identify simply with Cromwell's personal wishes.[10] The Protector's preoccupation was much more the political one of building networks of support and collaboration for the regime. The records of this activity are necessarily sparse since such meetings were unminuted. His weekly informal dinner with army officers in London no doubt exposed him to the pressures and lobbying which led to his verbal explosion at the meeting with them on 27 February 1657. But such pressure was an inevitable part of the close contact involved in building and maintaining effective political networks. It would be difficult to sustain the case that Cromwell was anything like the pawn, or 'drudge', of any particular group throughout the years of the Protectorate. At critical points he seems to have played his cards very close to his chest, and to have been almost solely reliant on his own conscience. John Thurloe, who worked closely with him as the only Secretary of State of the Protectorate, completely misread Cromwell's intention in early 1657 when he was sure that the Protector would accept the crown. Thurloe himself, almost inherited by Cromwell from Oliver St John whose servant he had been, is an example of Cromwell's networks in operation again. Within those networks were many groups with differing priorities and objectives. At this point in time, it is almost impossible to trace their influence in terms of specific policies and political strategies. An inner group, close to Cromwell in the first two years of the Protectorate, has been identified as Lords Broghill and Wharton, Sir Charles Wolsely, Bulstrode Whitelocke and Thorloe himself. By the end of 1655 they had been joined by Oliver St John, Henry Lawrence and Nathaniel Fiennes (second son of Viscount Say and Sele): all long-time connections of Cromwell's. But the specific influence of this group in shaping policy is more difficult to identify. When we look for answers to the question 'to what extent did Cromwell personally wield power in the Protectorate?' we are driven back to three considerations. The first is that he appears once more to be the team player; as far as we can tell, more than willing to accept the constitutional constraints upon his freedom of operation. The second is that his political role in building support for the regime involved him in close, familiar contact with a number of groups. Their direct influence on Protectoral policy is now difficult, if not impossible, to trace. Finally, there were a limited number of issues (kingship being the most obvious example) on which the decision was understandably his own. In the end what is striking with regard to these is the degree of his self-reliance.

Cromwell himself never used the language of 'statebuilding' and this may serve as a reminder that we should use what is an anachronistic terminology with due caution. Nevertheless, his own experiences in warfare and the logistics of war place him at the sharp end of some of the pressures pushing towards change in the reorganization of the state. The inadequacy of forces organized locally on a traditional basis, even of associations of such forces like the Eastern Association, and the move to the New Model Army can almost be read as paradigmatic of the evolution of a warfare requiring a corresponding adjustment by the state. In this scenario we might expect Cromwell to become a champion of the new military/fiscal state. He was certainly painfully aware of the consequences of failure to make the governmental adjustments to accommodate new military realities. Reluctance or inability to expand the state's fiscal base meant that the new army was repeatedly running into crises of underfunding, arrears of pay and reliance on free-quarter. These 'grievances' led in turn to military impatience and interference with the state, a response with which Cromwell was all too familiar and which, from some perspectives, he came to represent. So it would be possible to imagine Cromwell as the military man determined to reshape the governmental and administrative order of his country in order to meet the needs of war and, to some extent, the reputation of the Protectorate as a 'military dictatorship' was born out of this viewpoint. But Cromwell never showed the interest in fiscal policy, administrative structures, nor, critically, in the structure of local government through which national policy would need to be implemented. Even the Major-Generals experiment of 1655–7 cannot, as we will see later, be made to fit this bill. The state machinery of the Protectorate, both in structure and personnel, remained to a surprising degree what it had been even before the outbreak of the civil wars.[11] Both Cromwell's priorities and his underlying motivation after the experience of civil war are fundamental to explaining this lack of interest in statebuilding.

Like many soldiers who have been involved in the heat of battle and have witnessed its devastation, Cromwell came to fear the consequences of a return to civil war. God's will was peace. Men might defy Him but they would pay a terrible price. As late as January 1658 this was still a major preoccupation for Oliver. Addressing both Houses of Parliament at Whitehall he spoke of

> Dissension, division, destruction, in a poor nation under a civil war, having all the effects of a civil war upon it. Indeed if we return again to our folly, let every man consider if it be not like to be our destruction.[12]

Indeed it can be argued that from 1647 his priority, despite the fact that he was not personally free from armed conflict until 1651, was peacemaking.[13] In the aftermath of civil war, particularly after the second civil war, perhaps even more so after Worcester, there was a temptation for the victors to impose peace on their terms, to adopt an armed peace. Cromwell always favoured making, rather than imposing, peace; reconciliation rather than conquest rule. The path of the peacemaker inevitably involved moderation and conciliation. There were times when the pressures towards the renewal of conflict made such a role impossible but time and again in his speeches and his actions Cromwell returned to the task of reconciliation. He was always in favour of a moderate settlement with ex-Royalists. He sought to maintain the rule of known law through customary channels. He endeavoured to shift the post-war balance from soldiers to civilians, from swordsmen to gentlemen and lawyers. Of course, the record shows that this process was punctuated in political crisis by military interventions as in Pride's Purge and the expulsion of the Rump. But, on each occasion, Cromwell went back to a search for ways of bringing some representative legitimacy back to the process of government, back to the path of reconciliation and moderation. There was a balance to be struck between this process and the security of the regime and of the nation but what is also significant is Cromwell's persistence in winding down the size of the military establishment. From about 60,000 at the end of 1652 the numbers of military personnel fell to about 53,000 in 1654, and to about 45,000 in 1657. Even that political and public relations disaster, the Major-Generals experiment, is now seen as 'part of a plan to reduce the overall size and structure of the military'.[14] But the shift from military to civilian rule could not of itself produce the transition from a climate of aggression, suspicion and hostility to one of fairness, tolerance and sympathetic understanding on which genuine peace and reconciliation must rest. Cromwell had no faith that the 'dross and dung' of formal institutional or constitutional structures could achieve that. Instead, and we shall see more of this later in this chapter, he sought to win over old and new adversaries by establishing common ground, by 'no compulsion, but that of light and reason' and by insisting on and offering 'impartial justice'.[15] Reconciliation, as he told the first Protectoral Parliament on 4 September 1654, necessitated 'a reciprocation' if 'scatterings, division and confusion' were not to be perpetuated.[16] In all of these ways Cromwell saw himself not as a statebuilder but, as he himself said, as a constable; an arbitrator between disputants and a keeper of the peace.

Perhaps the closest we can get to the bedrock of Cromwell's thinking in this regard is by looking at the views he expressed at the Putney debates on 1 November 1647. On that day he had to chair a meeting, in the aftermath of a divisive debate over *The case of the Armie* and the first *Agreement of the People*, with the knowledge that there was heated resistance in the army and outside to any continuance of a determinative voice for the monarch and the Lords in parliamentary legislation. Cromwell's desire to defend the army's commitment to The Heads of Proposals with its moderate and measured attempt to reconcile antagonists around a modified version of the *status quo* was confronted by a challenge to accepted concepts of the political nation, the state, civil and religious liberty. In these circumstances he was obliged to articulate a view of what was politically possible and desirable in the crisis of late 1647. In doing so, he came as close as he was ever to do to spelling out the philosophical basis of his politics.

He began by responding to a claim by Captain Francis Allen that the godly recognized that the task before them was to take away the negative voice of the King and the House of Lords.[17] Cromwell's initial response was to agree that the King had transgressed but, in a New Testament spirit, to acknowledge that there was none amongst them free of transgression. What, he insisted, was really at issue was whether a group such as that gathered at Putney could possess an authority to reconstruct the state in England. The members of the army were under a Parliament which had first called them into existence. If they went against Parliament, how could they construct a new authority. 'If they be no Parliament, they are nothing and we are nothing likewise. If they be a Parliament, we are to offer it [ie. the Proposals to which the army was committed] to it.' So his first argument was about authority and the fact that the army had a subordinate or delegated authority only. But Cromwell immediately followed this with an argument about priorities which was couched in religious terms. The constitutional forms, to which the Levellers and their allies gave such importance, were, to use St Paul's words, but 'dross and dung in comparison of Christ'. To fight over temporal forms, over things which, in the end, were of little consequence, would reduce 'the State . . . to desolation'. They should therefore support Parliament in its attempts to settle the Kingdom and they had a moral obligation and a Christian duty to do so. Personally, Cromwell admitted, he would like to see constituency reform and provision for regular parliamentary elections but provision for settlement also extended to the view that Parliament should offer the King those things which would reasonably secure his compliance and that of his followers. There was, then, no civil warrant for attempting to impose a radical revision of the constitution on Parliament or on the country independently of Parliament. Equally, there was no religious warrant for pursuing constitutional reforms derived from human reason to the point of renewed civil war and consequent desolation.

But, of course, as someone who had repeatedly invoked the living God and His providential interventions against the conclusions of fleshly reason and carnal wisdom, Cromwell might be thought vulnerable to the argument that God's will was precisely a radical remodelling of the English state. Lieutenant-Colonel Goffe urged exactly such a consideration when he reported that 'It seems to me clear that a voice from heaven has told us that we have sinned against the Lord by tampering with his enemie.'

Replying, Cromwell offered two preliminary considerations: we must be careful how we judge what it is that God is telling us and that the engagements we are all committed to must play some part in the pursuit of justice and righteousness. But he conceded that it was possible that God's will might indeed be for a radical overthrow of the existing constitution. Picking up terms used by Edward Sexby, he agreed that, if God had written off the ancient constitution, then they should not attempt to reform it: 'to heal Babylon when God had determined [to destroy her]' was to 'fight against God'. But, in his view, three powerful arguments, all of which related to the nature of God and His will, stood in the way. The first of these was that God was not a God of contradictions and yet those debating at Putney were in a confused and contradictory state. How were they to escape this? The first step was to acknowledge those things that they were agreed about, the consensus that they shared, and here Cromwell's summary was masterly. They were agreed, he claimed, in the objectives of accomplishing the work of God, 'to deliver this nation from oppression and slavery' and 'to establish our hopes of justice and righteousness'. They were all worried about the future roles of the King and the House of Lords. They differed over whether their shared objectives could be achieved in collaboration with, or only without, King and Lords. Some, including Cromwell, believed that the monarchy and the second chamber could not be nullified without injustice and an associated hazard to security. Others believed that there could be no security without the removal of the negative voice of King and Lords and that security must take priority even if there were some hazard to justice. At this point of apparent impasse, Cromwell drew on his second and third arguments. The hallmarks of God's will were 'meekness and gentleness and mercy and patience and forbearance and love'. Given the doubts about, or obscurity of, God's will in these circumstances those counsels which led away from justice to 'the ways of force' had to be seen as leading away from this spirit. But, thirdly and finally, if it was God's will to destroy the King and the Lords, He would do it without scandal or sin. They should wait upon God knowing that 'what God would have us do, He does not desire we should step out of the way for it'.

Rather than seeing Cromwell at Putney as using any argument to hand which would block his opponents, we should recognize how much he conceded. God *might* sanction the destruction of the ancient constitution, the overthrow of Babylon (as indeed He was to do in later 1648). But one had to have sure grounds for knowing that to be His intention. In the meantime, one should follow the values of reconciliation – 'forbearance and love' – and work with constituted authorities for such a reconciliation and for the justice and righteousness in which the honouring of engagements would play a part.

For the constituted authorities to have any chance of successfully implementing their policies, however, they needed to build an operational consensus, a network of key actors who were agreed in working together for common ends. Cromwell may have had no theory of 'statebuilding' in the sense of seeing a necessity to develop an English version of the military/fiscal state. He may not even have possessed a language appropriate for such an exercise, but he attached great importance to the building and maintenance of operational consensus. Indeed, he may have seen the operation of government and its stabilization as more a matter of building consensual networks rather than institutional structures and constitutional contrivances. The government of early modern England was reliant on a small number of paid officials and a host of unpaid officers from parish constables to Lords Lieutenant of counties to ambassadors representing the country abroad. Without the conscientious commitment of these individuals and groups very little, beyond the customary, could be achieved, as Charles I found when he tried through their agency to raise an army to confront his rebellious Scots subjects in 1639 and 1640. He simply had not established an operational consensus for the policies which his government had come to represent to the vast majority of those who governed England in the 1630s. In 1647 it became equally clear that a badly paid army, anxious about the terms of a post-war settlement and affronted that its honour had been attacked in Parliament, would no longer unquestioningly obey the orders of its political masters. The control of its senior officers was also in doubt. The Putney debates were, in large part, for Cromwell a struggle to establish, or reestablish, an operational consensus with his military colleagues and subordinates. The establishment and maintenance of networks of like-minded individuals and groups was a key theme in Cromwell's politics. Whether in peace or war his instinct was to build consensual relationships as a means of operating effectively. But we should also note that he was never satisfied with consensus for its own sake, never prepared to settle for the lowest, common, consensual denominator. The networks to which he belonged, or which he led, had to be committed to some purpose – the defence of civil and religious liberty, winning the war, godly reformation on an irenic, Protestant basis. Even 'healing and settling' was insufficient to him as a final goal. It was simply consensus writ large. Even towards the end of his career, as John Morrill puts it, 'He was unable to settle for what he had already achieved, a world made safe for the gentry and the propertied, a prudent measure of religious pluralism, an effective English imperialism, especially within Britain.'[18] So, operational consensus was a key to his politics and his understanding of governance and leadership but it was never an end in itself.

The crisis which precipitated the English civil war was brought about by the erosion of consensual support for the government by Charles I and its policies and by Charles' inability to establish the basis for a new parliamentary consensus on the back of the reforms of 1641. The parliamentary side in that civil war was a coalition which had repeatedly to struggle for some degree of internal consensus in order to maintain its operational effectiveness. In that context Cromwell was a dynamic, increasingly powerful, but never straightforward builder of networks and player for consensus. In recruiting his own troops he looked for like-minded men, those who had the root of the matter in them. His formal requirements, in terms of social background or religious conformity, were minimal. What mattered were a shared understanding of the cause and enthusiasm for it. In command, he was a team player, consulting others before important decisions and acting in agreement with them.[19] Through the 1640s he engaged in a dogged struggle to maintain as general as possible a consensus between the army and Parliament as well as within the army. He was, however, willing to disrupt consensus where its objectives, as he saw it, were imperilled. The most obvious case of this in the first civil war was his attack on Manchester, provoked when the cause of civil and religious liberty seemed to be in jeopardy as a result of Manchester's willingness to make peace, or avoid outright victory, at almost any price. He was also a participant in three events which ruptured his own consensual networks: passively in Pride's Purge, actively in the regicide which followed it and explosively in the expulsion of the Rump in April 1653. Networks and consensus were rent asunder. In all three cases, Cromwell could claim that a greater danger, the revanchist victory of the cause against which they had fought, appeared in prospect. Even so, as David Underdown demonstrated some time ago, after the regicide it was Cromwell who was most active and assiduous in attempting to re-establish the pre-Purge coalition.[20] Consensus as the basis for the achievement of agreed objectives remained a political bedrock as long as those objectives were a common aspiration and priority. By 1649 his political tactics in military campaigning were informed by the aim of sowing disunity amongst his enemies while preserving and, where possible, extending the unity of those backing the cause for which he fought. Both the Irish and the Scots campaigns of 1649–51 bear witness to this. Where policy could not command consent and the objective was not an overwhelming priority, caution ensued. For example, Cromwell looked favourably on the campaign for the readmission of the Jews to England in the mid-1650s. But, before acting, he looked for consensus on the issue. He called a conference at Whitehall in 1655 to seek such agreement. When the outcome proved ambiguous he proceeded cautiously and informally.[21] His moments of apparent indecision, as in respect to the offer of the crown in 1657, are almost always associated with dilemmas over the maintenance of consensus. Healing and settling meant, in religious terms, attempting to draw into the consensual framework as many moderate Protestant groups as possible. So much so that John Rogers was complaining in the mid-1650s that liberty extended too far, even to 'Commonprayer men and such like'.[22] Making, rather than imposing, peace was the path of the consensualist and Cromwell, as we shall see, committed himself to that path from the moment that the expulsion of the Rump placed effective power in his hands. There is then a key transition in Cromwell's political development from the ruthlessness of the 'holy warrior' to the moderation and desire for reconciliation of the consensual politician. It was not a black into white transition. Men of different persuasions had to be harnessed to work together in order to win the war. The demands of peacetime consensus were even greater and might involve networks extending even to onetime enemies.

What we are interested in here are not so much Cromwell's objectives – win the war, break tyrannical rule or make peace – so much as the means by which he sought to achieve those ends. What sort of consensus-builder or peacemaker was he? Two issues are critical in his history from this point of view: the limits of consensus and how to operate in accordance with conscience within those limits.

Of course, in looking at Cromwell's behaviour as a consensual politician, objectives are important and must come back into the picture. There could be no sustained working together, no networking with those who did not prize civil and religious liberty (as Cromwell understood them); no compromise, as in Ireland, with the Roman Catholic mass. Religion in forms which promoted immorality or idolatry was beyond the pale as was military indiscipline. The maintenance of order against those who would have engendered disorder became another brake on the consensual arrangements he was prepared to reach. The restriction of participation in parliamentary elections to those with a permanent, fixed interest or some substance as property owners, and the social hierarchy that went with this became a principle beyond which he would not go in envisaging constitutional change. Similarly, the rule of law, obedience to the established authorities, provided they did not jeopardize civil and religious liberties, were part of the framework in which he tried to maintain his consensual politics. The politics of what he liked to refer to vaguely as the 'honest' cause, the politics of 'honest, godly people', was essentially to be contained within the limits, the boundaries of the principles which we have just enumerated.

Operating according to conscience within those limits was sometimes a problem and his correspondence with Robert Hammond in late 1648 is perhaps the most graphic example we have of Cromwell trying to work through such a problem of conscience. The letters to Hammond of 6 November and 25 November 1648 were written at the height of a political crisis when the moderate settlement proposed in The Heads of Proposals seemed to have been rendered unrealizable by the intransigent idealism of the Levellers and the elusiveness of the King. The options beginning to stare them in the face were a retreat to the old constitutional landmarks with no safeguards for the good old cause, civil and religious liberty, or the destruction of the ancient constitution to embark on an administration of uncertain authority. These men had taken the oath of The Solemn League and Covenant 'to preserve the rights and privileges of the Parliaments, and to preserve and defend the King's Majesty's person and authority in the preservation and defence of the true religion and liberties of the kingdoms, that the world may bear witness with our consciences of our loyalty, and that we have no thoughts or intentions to diminish His Majesty's just power and greatness'.[23] This and other engagements bound them in conscience to uphold King and Parliament as well as true religion and liberties. What was to be done when, after two civil wars, the majority in Parliament seemed prepared to do an unconditional deal for the restoration of a King who could not be trusted with regard to true religion and civil liberties? This was a crisis of conscience as well as a political crisis. It was as an adviser on conscience, a casuist, that Cromwell wrote to Hammond in November 1648 and it is worth looking again at that correspondence in this context. As the tensions in the two letters reveal, the conscience under counsel was Cromwell's own as well as his cousin's.

The first letter goes straight to the issue of conscience: 'look to thy heart, thou art where temptations multiply'.[24] 'How easy it is to find arguments for what we would have' but it was 'most dangerous to go against the will of God' to achieve peace. Sir Henry Vane had argued that the choice was between restoring the King with an intolerant, Presbyterian church or, better, with a moderate episcopacy. Cromwell doubted the wisdom of that choice. It might be easier for the King 'to tyrannise' with a system which he knew and liked rather than with one which was alien to him. But Cromwell did not believe that these were the only alternatives. It was necessary to go back to the issue of conscience:

> we have walked in this thing (whatsoever surmises are to the contrary) in plainness and godly simplicity, according to our weak measure, and we trust our daily business is to approve our consciences Godward, and not to shift and shirk, which were exceeding baseness in us to do, having had such favour from the Lord, and such manifestations of His presence.

The choices apparently confronting them were 'an evil business' but he was content in the knowledge 'that innocency and integrity loses nothing by a patient waiting upon the Lord'. As regards the Scots, the Presbyterians, 'God hath justified us in their sight.' Victory in the second civil war was a sign of God's approval so far. 'Robin, be honest still. God keep thee in the midst of snares. Thou hast naturally a valiant spirit. Listen to God and he shall increase it upon thee, and make thee valiant for truth.'

As custodian of the King, Hammond was both in a key position and under great pressure to commit himself. Cromwell urged patience, the avoidance of simplistic solutions and attention to conscience. In his second letter, written just over two

weeks later, Cromwell was exploring a way forward, the possible
purging of Parliament, and its implications for the consciences of
both of them.[25] He began with a description of his own spiritual
condition. 'I am such a one as than didst formerly know, having
a body of sin and death, but I thank God, through Jesus Christ
our Lord there is no condemnation, though much infirmity, and I
wait for redemption.' As regards worldly events, God's 'presence
hath been amongst us, and by the light of his countenance we
have prevailed'. Of God's direct dealings with them Hammond
himself had, Cromwell suggested, recent experience. He had
sought refuge in the quiet calm of the Isle of Wight, but God had
steered Charles I in his direction and so had not allowed him to
escape the eye of the storm: 'seek to know the mind of God',
Cromwell urged him, 'in all that chain of Providence, whereby
God brought thee thither, and that person to thee'. In searching
out God's will in all of this Cromwell ominously put forward his
own view of it. 'I dare be positive to say that it is not that the
wicked should be exalted.'

Hammond was disturbed that God required obedience to the
authorities set over them;[26] in England's case, to Parliament.
Cromwell agreed that 'Authorities and powers are the ordinance
of God'. But, in a standard argument, he claimed that *the specific
form* which authority took in each realm was of human institution, not a matter of divine will. Accordingly, human authorities
could not do anything and claim divine sanction: 'all agree, there
are cases in which it is lawful to resist'. So the crucial question
was whether the present circumstances presented such a case in
relation to the authority of Parliament.

In addressing that case, Cromwell began with three considerations impinging on the issue of whether the authority of
Parliament might be defied. One was where the safety of the people, by which he probably meant social order and the avoidance
of further civil war, made it necessary. A second was where

> the whole fruit of the war [was] like to be frustrated, and all
> most like to turn to what it was, and worse . . . contrary to
> engagements, declarations, implicit covenants with those
> who ventured their lives upon those covenants and engage-
> ments.

The third consideration was whether the New Model Army was
'a lawful power, called by God' which might justifiably oppose
Parliament, when it acted to frustrate the purposes for which it

had called that army into being. But, however significant these
three considerations might be (and their value should be tested
and assessed), 'truly these kinds of reasonings may be but fleshly'.
Ultimately, the saints must turn away from carnal reasoning to
look more deeply into the reading of God's will. 'My dear friend,
let us look into providences; surely they mean somewhat. They
hang so together; have been so constant, so clear and unclouded.'
Here was the surer guide to conscience in these difficult circumstances. What, Cromwell asked, did Hammond think of
Providence disposing so many of the godly, in the army and outside of it, to the belief that the army must cut through the
Gordian knot of the present crisis? When so many of God's people were persuaded that this was His will, to act decisively would
not be tempting God even when there were competing claims of
obligation and morality. In these circumstances, 'the more the
difficulties, the more the faith'. There could be no expectation of
good from Charles I, 'this man against whom the Lord hath witnessed; and whom thou knowest'. In the end, therefore, to sit
passively by while Parliament restored him to power and authority was unacceptable.

Here we see Cromwell wrestling to resolve the central dilemma
of the crisis of 1648–9. A wartime alliance, a consensus, had been
built around shared commitments to defend civil and religious
liberty *but also* to preserve King and Parliament. Men were conscientiously committed to all of these elements but it now
appeared impossible to maintain them all. So consensus operated
and was built within the limits of shared objectives but under the
pressures of crisis those limits would have to be breached and
consensus might consequently be disrupted. Consciences which
had been operating within the limits set by consensus, and the
oaths which formalized that consensus, had then to seek for guidance. Fleshly reasoning, the arts of casuistry, might take the conscientious some way towards the resolution of their difficulties
but the key indicator of divine approval when consensual limits
were breached or had broken down was Providence.

This way of thinking was not only central to Cromwell in managing his way through political crisis but also informed his view
of statebuilding. We can see this well illustrated in his attempt to
reconstruct a governmental hold on the political nation after a
second revolution (that of the overthrow of the Rump in April
1653) by the symbolic act which inaugurated the first full year of
Protectorate, the national day of Solemn Fasting and

Humiliation called for 24 March 1654. Timed for the last day of
the calendar year and in preparation for the new, the day can be
seen as a way of calling for a new consensus, binding a divided
nation together under the Protectorate. The declaration calling
for the observation of the Fast Day pointed to God's undeniable
appearance in the deliverance of the nation from the 'bondage
and thraldome, both Spiritual and Civil' into 'a just Liberty'.[27]
How was the nation to be worthy of such a deliverance? Over a
dozen questions were offered for consideration during the day of
fasting. Their implication was that 'worthiness' involved grati-
tude, 'Brotherly Love and a Healing Spirit', mutual tolerance and
respect, with priority given to the things of the spirit over the
ambitions of the flesh. The exercise of Solemn Fasting and
Humiliation was designed therefore to give the whole population
a day in which to ponder how to reconcile themselves one with
another in a spirit of reciprocity and under the current magistracy. Just as exercises of this kind were perceived as instrumental in building a godly army, so the hope was that they could be
effective in building a godly nation. Reprogramming a divided
society's networks and ethos was an essential part of what
Cromwell might be thought to have considered the essence of
'statebuilding'. In retrospect and in the light of its failure, that
aspiration may look naïve. Cromwell himself was reduced to
wringing his hands over, for example, the unwillingness of many
sectarians to embrace consensus with him. This should not blind
us to the importance, for him, of the spiritual and behavioural
drive towards rebuilding society and the state.

    Where it is effective and effectively maintained, consensus is
inevitably constraining. In a conservative society it put a substantial brake on the potential for revolution. But, as we have
seen, there could be circumstances and situations in which
Cromwell was prepared to break the limits within which consensus operated and to risk the existence of the consensual community itself. Were there elements within his make up and within the
situations in which he found himself, revolutionary impulses,
potentials and opportunities, which could have led him to break
entirely free from those restraints and to have overridden his
desire for consensus? Perhaps it is Ireland which came closest to
having this potential. There was considerable talk of a conquered
Ireland as a *tabula rasa* or, changing the metaphor, as clay available for remoulding. The schemes for large-scale transplantation
and resettlement were premised on just such chilling notions. In

family letters written even on the eve of his departure for Ireland in August 1649, Cromwell was invoking the 'mercy' of God which had delivered that country into English hands.[28] Did Cromwell ever subscribe completely to this vision? And, if it had been given free rein, could an Irish revolution have presaged a British revolution?[29] Whatever the dream, the reality was that the English in Ireland were drawn back to the limits of the possible. It was beyond their material and administrative resources to carry out their plans completely, horrifying though the attempt to do so and its consequences were. From Henry Cromwell's effective assumption of responsibility in Ireland in 1654, pragmatism and the recognition that the country could only be governed with, and not against, the Irish returned.

As in Ireland so elsewhere, we, like Cromwell and his associates, are brought back to the socio-political possibilities and realities of early modern society. Without the consent or consensual support of the broad governing classes of that society, the achievements of magistrates or godly ministers, even of Major-Generals, remained severely limited. The consent of those governing classes was, by and large, in favour of normality and in the medium-term it was some version of normality in the operation of the Cromwellian state which triumphed – at a price. As Derek Hirst has pointed out, the alliance of ministers, magistrates and godly households which, like Cromwell himself, aspired to a godly reformation of society were, in the 1650s, not rejoicing in their success but struggling with a sense of failure. They had neither the institutional framework nor the numbers to carry whole communities with them. In the case of religious reformation, they were too divided amongst themselves. In terms of the reformation of manners, godly reformation had failed, as Hirst concludes, to put down adequate roots amongst the constables and jurymen of the parishes and counties.[30] However consistently he adhered to the desire for a godly nation, in the end Cromwell lacked the coercive machinery (for which he possibly had no desire) and the widespread community support which was required. The history of the Major-Generals experiment of 1655–7 epitomizes the problem. In the late summer of 1655 Cromwell appointed 'a number of his closest military colleagues' to head up 10 (later 11) regions into which England was divided. The Major-Generals were given responsibility for putting regional security on to a cheaper basis, for disarming malignants and for assessing and collecting a 'decimation' tax on known

Royalists and delinquents. Almost as a logical extension of this
they were charged with the moral reformation of their regions.
As Cromwell himself said 'I think reformation, if it be honest and
thorough and just, it will be your best security'. When it was first
established the scheme aroused high hopes and there was a wave
of enthusiastic responses from the localities to central government. But they were the welcome of local minorities, of 'small
but dedicated cadres of 'well-affected' local Puritans'. The question remained as to whether those minorities could command the
regional community and its institutions of self-government.
Within just over a year the evidence was clear that they could
not. There were just not enough of them to make up the necessary rosters of JPs, juries and constables. Those who would col-
laborate were, as often as not, more interested in the
opportunities for settling old scores. When in July 1656 the decision was taken to call a new Parliament the elections were frequently seen locally 'as a referendum on the rule of the generals
and their godly allies'. The result was an overwhelming disappointment to the godly. Everywhere their adversaries swept the
board.[31]

The ability to win the consent and support of local communities and the broad range of people who participated in their governance was, if the hand of coercion was to be stayed, critical. As
Charles I had found, so Cromwell too discovered, their opposition, even their sullen indifference, was no basis for effective state
action, let alone statebuilding. When the perspective moved from
England to Britain or on to an even wider, imperial horizon the
problem was simply multiplied. The conquest of Ireland and
Scotland may have created a 'British moment' but to sustain it
there needed to be a grass roots culture of Britishness. Such affec-
tations as there were amongst the Protectoral rulers have been
described as shallow and chauvinistic and, as the costs to the
English of maintaining control of Scotland and Ireland became
apparent, disillusion set in.[32] However much the admirers of
Roman imperialism might urge Cromwell to become the emperor
of a new Rome in the west, the reality was more sobering. To create an effective imperial administration in the British Isles alone
would have required the building of a state able to command
vastly more of society's resources, with the military and bureaucratic systems and the political culture to match. But as political
thinkers as diverse as Hobbes, Harrington and Milton saw, this
could only finally be paid for in the coin of what Cromwell and

his contemporaries called civil liberty.[33] So the equation turned round. To build a state, a new regime, which defended existing civil and religious liberty, the basis of rule would have to be in the consent and cooperation of the governors of the counties and boroughs. Their innate conservatism immediately limited the possibilities. Aspirations to greater things might flicker but survival depended upon a realistic adjustment to the possible. Cromwell's instinctive reaching out to build consensual networks kept him in touch with these realities and much of the drift of his policy in the 1650s was in terms of adjustment to them. But it is important to recognize how much of his approach to building and stabilizing a regime was through developing, managing and maintaining consensual networks. In that respect he was more akin to the leader of a great Congressional party than to the President of the United States or to the Chairman of a British political party rather than the Prime Minister. But consensual networking, as a basis for government, could be ideologically and culturally sterilizing, reaching out for the reassurance of old forms, symbols and rituals.[34]

Obviously, Cromwell's freest hand, with regard to the reshaping of the central constitutional and administrative apparatus of government in England, came in the period from the expulsion of the Rump in April 1653 down to the end of his Protectorate in September 1658. The best guide to his thinking (or absence of it) on issues of statebuilding in this period are his speeches to the Nominated Assembly and the Protectoral Parliaments. In the earlier seventeenth century, Parliament had been a focus of resistance to Stuart statebuilding. It remained *the* institution which had to be reassured or won over if Cromwell intended to maintain an operational consensus with the political nation. *The Declaration of the Lord General and his Council of Officers*, which followed swiftly on the expulsion of the Rump, announced that authority would be delegated to 'known persons, men fearing God, and of approved integrity'; in other words, to men of the godly network. By this means, it was hoped, the people might 'forget monarchy, and understanding their true interest in the election of successive Parliaments, may have the government settled upon a true basis'.[35] The implication was that the Nominated Assembly, an unelected body, was to take part in the work of settling government upon a true basis. When, however, Cromwell first spoke to the Assembly on 4 July 1653, he presented them with an Instrument 'drawn up by the consent and advice of the

principal officers of the army'. His speech was then devoted to an
explanation of God's dealings in bringing them to this point and
a justification for the expulsion of the Rump. It was, he told
them, the desire of himself and his fellow officers to divest themselves of civil authority. Beyond that all he could advise the
Assembly was that they were 'called by God to rule with Him,
and for Him', to protect the godly and to promote the Gospel: 'it
is better that we should pray to you than to advise you'.[36]
'Statebuilding' would be an entirely inappropriate description for
the commission given by Cromwell to this gathering. Indeed,
even guidance on what might form a true basis for the settlement
of the nation was lacking. A distrust of forms, which at best were
secondary to God's workings in the world, His providence, is on
display in this forum just as antiformalism marked Cromwell's
religious thinking. He hoped that it was 'written in their hearts to
approve yourselves to God'. Scriptural texts were deployed to
reinforce the message of submission to Him. They were truly
'called by God to rule with Him, and for Him'.[37] For Cromwell
in such a disposition the appropriate responses were to enlist the
support of as many of the godly persuasion as possible, networking and consensus, spiritual preparation, prayer, fasting and
hearing the word of God. The machinery of state was not a priority.

By the time of his next address to a national representative
assembly, however, things had changed. The weakness of the
Nominated Assembly had been exposed and in December 1653
the Protectorate had been inaugurated. In the process the desirability of formal constitutional machinery had been confronted
in the adoption of the Instrument of Government. A Protector
was to govern in coordination with a Council both of whom
were accountable to regularly elected, unicameral parliaments.
Constitutional provision for a standing army of 30,000 troops
meant the necessity for an adequate tax base and an appropriate
state machine to manage and control its enterprises. With a large
and professional army and navy it would seem essential that the
Protectorate confront the problem of the military/fiscal state. The
first means available for addressing the problems of statebuilding
were Protectoral ordinances (which would have to be confirmed
by a future Parliament) and parliamentary legislation. Between
January and September 1654 Cromwell endorsed over 180 ordinances prepared by his Council, some of them on policy matters.[38] But his opening speech to the Parliament assembled in

September 1654 was essentially about a crisis of religious enthusiasm.[39] The interests of the three great nations of England, Scotland and Ireland were 'the interest of all the Christian people in the world' but to rehearse all the wonderful providences of God demonstrating this would take too long. Israel was out of Egypt but why was it languishing in the wilderness? Something had gone wrong. Every man was against every other. 'Christ and the Spirit of God' had been 'made the cloak of all villainy and spurious apprehensions'. Civil and religious liberty, 'two as glorious things to be contended for as any God hath given us', were abused. 'Carnal divisions and contentions among Christians' were not signs of Christ's kingdom coming. What must be done? Bills were in preparation for law reform. The administration of the law had been put into the hands 'of just men, men of the most known integrity and ability'. The court of Chancery had been reformed. Some headway (the ordinances establishing the Triers and Ejectors) had been made to put 'a stop to that heady way . . . of every man making himself a Minister and a preacher'. Parliament, as must have been blindingly obvious to all present, had been called. Foreign policy needed to be sorted out. Some temporary abatement of taxation had been made.[40] The plantation of Ireland should be carried forward. And that was essentially it. They must progress out of the wilderness and not repine there forever.

> I do therefore persuade you to a sweet, gracious, and holy understanding of one another, and of your business, concerning which you have had so good counsel this day as it rejoiced my heart to hear it,[41] so I hope the Lord will imprint it upon your spirits: wherein you shall have my prayers.

As a speech on 'statebuilding', the challenges of matching governmental resources to the necessities of its naval and military establishment, this barely made sense but, of course, Cromwell's perspective, objectives and approach were otherwise. His vision was of the nation coming through a series of spiritual tests and crises in which the primary objective had to be to understand and work with the will of a living God. The means which made most sense to him in addressing this objective were those which had built a godly coalition, committed to civil and religious liberty and, above all, to instrumentality in the hands of the Lord, and which enthused that coalition with service under that God. Behind the formal façade of state occasions and the business of conciliar government, much of Cromwell's time was spent in informal discussions, seeking to win over opponents, onetime allies who had become disillusioned or saints who were running to extreme causes. The records only give us a glimpse of a small proportion of these contacts but even what we do see is impressive in its range and persistence. With Edmund Ludlow and other 'commonwealthsmen', who thought of the expulsion of the Rump as the great betrayal, he sought reconciliation at meetings in mid-December 1655 and again in late July and early August 1656. He met with members of various sects in October 1653 to plead for mutual forbearance and tolerance. With Quakers, in their most disruptive phase, he took counsel, meeting with Anthony Pearson on 16 July 1654, and with George Fox in late February 1655, in October 1656, twice in the week of 23 March 1657 and again shortly before his death. He wrote encouraging the Presbyterian ministers of the north-east along the path of tolerance in December 1656. In early 1656 he was in informal discussions with Anglicans about a potential rapprochement. In April 1656, in a conciliatory gesture and possibly out of a genuine respect, he contributed to the funeral expenses of Archbishop Ussher. Even extremists, like Christopher Feake who was for 'rending and dividing yet more',[42] could not entirely escape the Cromwellian embrace of conciliation. Cromwell had met with Feake and other Anabaptists on 29 November 1653. He held conferences with Feake and his followers on 21 and 23 December 1654. Personal interviews with Fifth Monarchists were held in late July and August 1656. In Cromwell's mind the net of potential consensus spread wide and he was assiduous in the endeavour to catch as many as possible within it. We should have this continuing background activity in mind as perhaps what the Lord Protector considered as important to the success of his rule as the elaboration of administrative structures and the modification of constitutional machinery. He carried conciliation so far as to worry both his opponents and his supporters. His opponents who feared that he might be too successful in stabilizing the Protectoral regime, and his supporters who feared that his approach gave too much credence to dangerous individuals and groups. On 26 December 1655 Henry Cromwell wrote to John Thurloe expressing reservations about his father's conciliation of opponents.

It is good to use tenderness towarde them. I have done it, and shall doe it; but shall withall be carefull to keep them from power, whoe, if they hade it in their power, would express little tenderness to those that would not submitt to their way.[43]

If there was a balance to be struck between time spent attempting to conciliate inveterate opponents and preparing to deal with them more harshly, the Cromwell of the 1650s could be accused of erring in the former direction. It was part of a consciousness that it was more important to win men over than to perfect systems of government. Nevertheless, very quickly in the course of his first Protectoral Parliament, the need to make the Instrument of Government, the machinery of state, acceptable and workable was forced on that consciousness. Within the first week of Parliament's sitting, the implacable opponents of the Protectorate had dominated proceedings in wide-ranging attacks on the Instrument of Government and its, shakily based, claims to legitimate authority. However much of a priority, the machinery was in danger and Cromwell was forced to address its importance. In a second speech to the members on 12 September 1654, his approach was fundamentally different. There was still án appeal to the mutual understanding, 'a reciprocation', of consensus, but it was also necessary to discuss the nature of the present constitutional provision and its justification. There were, he insisted, four non-negotiable fundamentals: rule by a single person and a Parliament, to guarantee order; parliaments which were not perpetual, to protect civil liberty; liberty of conscience, the guarantee of religious liberty; and a militia placed equally under the authority of Protector and Parliament. For the rest, members would be called upon to sign a recognition of his authority but would be free to discuss revision of the constitution, exclusive of the four fundamentals.[44] But the issue of the military/fiscal state the question – of state provision for the army and navy and of the kind of state necessary to sustain such provision – hovered in the wings. When Cromwell dissolved his first Parliament, at the earliest possible opportunity, on 22 January 1655, it was provision for the military which was the critical failure. Of course, Cromwell complained about lack of communication and a level of parliamentary inaction which had allowed division in the country to fester but the critical failure was to provide for the army whose pay was, he alleged, now 30 weeks in arrears and who were dependent once again on free-quarter.[45]

When he next met a Parliament, on 17 September 1656, Cromwell was still appealing for unity, or at least consensus.[46] But an urgency had been leant to the appeal by the publication in the spring of the year of Sir Henry Vane's *The Healing Question* with its claim that Cromwellian government represented an abandonment of the good old causes of civil and religious liberty. The weakness of the reliance of the system of Major-Generals on godly minorities in the regions had been exposed and repudiated in the parliamentary elections. The notoriously unpopular decimation tax appears to have failed to cover even the costs of the Major-Generals' operations. War with Spain and other military costs were obliging the government to look for parliamentary support. In this context, Cromwell's speech was revealing of the dilemmas he faced and his intended approach to them.

On the one hand, he deployed a traditional appeal for unity. The nation was threatened from without and the enemy was an inveterate one, Spain. Ever since the Reformation, Spain had been the sworn enemy, the agent of Rome, and one assiduously campaigning and intriguing against all Protestant nations but especially against God's 'most peculiar interest', the English. It was the appeal to unity of an enemy-at-the-gates speech and one wonders if Cromwell might have recalled Charles I's striking lack of success with a similar appeal at the opening of the Short Parliament in 1640. The other side of the speech was preoccupied with the growth of an anti-Protectoral consensus. The Levellers (now, he suggested, renamed 'Common Wealth's men') were strangely joined by some men of great estates and fortunes. This consortium now had links with the Cavaliers and thereby with the papists. In another direction they were allied with the Fifth Monarchists. It was an admission that, in his mind at least, Cromwell saw a menacing coalition whose consensual bond was their detestation of the Protectorate. Many of its members were his one-time allies now prepared to bury the hatchet with their old foes. Was Cromwell losing the consensual struggle?

> There is a generation of men in this nation that cry up nothing but righteousness and justice and liberty; and these are diversified in several sects and sorts of men. And though they may be contemptible, in respect they are many and so not like to make a solid vow to do you mischief, yet they are apt to agree *in aliquo tertio*, they are known, yea well enough, to shake hands together, I should be loath to say

with Cavaliers, but with all the scum and dirt of this nation, to put you to trouble.

The remedies, he proposed for the nation's problems abroad and at home, were security and reformation. The pursuit of war with Spain and the maintenance of armed vigilance at home ran alongside the protection of religious liberty, the reformation of manners and the reform of the law to ensure reasonable penalties and consistency of judgement. But where were the proposals that would address the problems of military/fiscal statebuilding? Not only were they conspicuous by their absence from this speech but within the year Cromwell was turning his back on them. His reduction, in June 1657, of the assessment to £35,000 a month was designed to conciliate the traditional governing classes but, without corresponding reductions in the armed forces, it precipitated the financial crisis which in part accounts for the collapse of the Protectorate after his death.[47]

In Cromwell's mind the problems facing him and his Parliament in the autumn of 1656 were to be addressed not by new institutions and processes of state but, just as it had been in the first civil war, by a coalition of men of spirit. 'Doubting, hesitating me,' he told his MPs, 'they are not fit for your work ... Give me leave to tell you, those that are called to this work, it will not depend upon formalities, nor notions, nor speeches.' As before, it was the work of

> men of honest hearts, engaged to God, strengthened by providence, enlightened in his words to know his word; to which he hath set his seal, sealed with the blood of his Son in the blood of his servants. It is such a spirit as will carry on this work.

In his public utterance at least, Cromwell's approach was still antiformalist. The challenges facing them had to be met by likeminded men of spirit. But, given that defections of former allies into hostility had weakened Cromwell's old consensual coalitions where were such combinations now to be found? Parliament was not long in suggesting an answer: a more conservatively inclined and more civilian coalition built around the proposals hammered out in the Humble Petition and Advice. Moreover, the Petition offered the great merit of a legitimacy arising from the initiative of elected representatives rather than, as in the case of the Instrument, a solution imposed on those representatives by the army. In other words, it was a solution and a coalition which sought Cromwell out rather than one which he painstakingly had to build or repair. It is not surprising that Cromwell would want to take it very seriously or that the army officers should be alarmed at the prospect of the consensual basis of his power being moved on to a more civilian and inevitably more conservative basis.

The problem of government for Cromwell was then not one of the development of new agencies, bureaucratic instruments and fiscal potential. It was rather one of finding effective networks of support built around an operational consensus to which he could subscribe. Constitutional adjustment to facilitate the building of such a consensus was something which he remained open to even if it alarmed or alienated others of his allies: the commonwealthmen in April 1653, the sectarian saints in December 1653, and the military supporters of the Instrument in the spring of 1657. Constitutional matters could engage his attention when they impinged on the project of building the great, stable and committed coalition which would deliver not only stability but the enduring goals of civil and religious liberty.[48] But his thoughts and energies never seem to have engaged with what modern historians call the process of statebuilding and its instruments: fiscality, bureaucracy, regulation, uniformity and supervision. To assess his record from the point of view of statebuilding, in this sense, may therefore be both inappropriate, to fail him for something he never intended to achieve, and anachronistic.

Given, instead, that his objective was to build a firm government, protective of civil and religious liberty, adequately networked amongst those who could share his objectives and work together to deliver effective, just and godly government at all levels of society, how well did he do? Here the perspectives of contemporary observers and the struggles of anti-Cromwellians to form a coalition against him are significant. Those who had the greatest interest in his failure, the Royalists in exile, provide a useful guide to the measure of his success. The fear that he could win over moderate Anglicans went back to the early 1650s.[49] After Worcester, in late 1651, there was great fear of the erosion, to the point of collapse, of remaining Royalists sympathies.[50] In the mid-1650s, anxieties about the damage to their cause, were Cromwell were to assume the throne, haunted the exiles.[51] On the other hand, the publication in 1657 of that notorious call for the assassination of the Lord Protector, *Killing Noe Murder*, witty and scathing though it might be, was also a tacit admission that disgruntled republicans were not going to be able to undermine Cromwell's support by more conventional means. Of course, these impressions are no more than that. To know, with any certainty, how effectively Cromwell was beginning to build a governing consensus with which he could work both in Parliament and in the localities we need much more research on local administration and politics in the mid-1650s.

One of the great themes of the history of modern Europe has been the creation of a 'modern' state, whether in kingdoms or republics, with the capacity to deliver to the 'nation' in terms of military, political, economic, welfare and cultural capability. Only in the last 20 or 30 years have we witnessed the waning of that capability (or perhaps its inability to keep pace with aspirations) and a growing resort to regional or supra-national institutions. It is often assumed that the seventeenth century was an era of state formation, that it saw the beginnings of a three-century long dominance of the 'nation' state. Cromwell has featured ambiguously in this process. On the one hand, he is perceived as having given 'Britain' a meaning and the international characteristics of a strong 'nation' state: under him Britain was feared abroad. On the other hand, the machinery he used was either inherited (the central bureaucracy and judiciary), flawed (the Nominated Assembly or the Major-Generals) or extremely temporary. But we need to ask two questions. First, how could a new state be built in the circumstances of the 1650s? Initiatives like the Major-Generals turned out to be dependent on unpopular and unrepresentative local minorities. The traditional governors of the regions wanted stability, continuity and the reassurance of the familiar after a decade of unprecedented civil conflict and heavy taxation. They were likely to be most resistant to collaborating in the permanent expansion of the tax base if a new state was to be built. Nevertheless, if he was to govern with security and stability and was to have some hope of realizing his aspirations towards civil and religious liberty, Cromwell had to have a basis for effective government. He sought it by the most traditional of means, by trying to develop networks of support built around consensually agreed objectives. Necessarily, this involved compromises and, if he was to escape reliance on violent minorities, some moves in the direction of conservative sentiments.

The *sine qua non* for healing and settling was therefore a government which could claim the substantial allegiance of those who participated in the governance of England. The price would be customary means and the preservation of social hierarchy. The two key attempts at the post-war settlement of England, The Heads of Proposals and the Humble Petition and Advice, for this reason have essential features in common. Both offered liberty of conscience with an unoppressive, national church settlement. Both proposed a responsible monarchy (or single person) accountable to a Council and Parliament, a constitution of checks and balances. Both relied on the representation of the traditional governors of the counties and towns across the land, and both envisaged the ratification of the settlement by legislation pursued through parliaments representing them.

The kind of state which 'statebuilding' envisages was not what Cromwell sought. Within the framework of government to hand, and this became progressively more traditional, he worked to build a coalition of governance, a network with which he could work and which would sustain the work of healing, settling and, where possible, of reformation. Whether he would have been tempted to other causes, had the civil war coalition, of which he became a leader, held together with greater cohesion, it is now impossible to say. The point is that it fractured, disintegrating over definitions of civil and religious liberty as it was to do again in 1659–60. It proved impossible to govern through them as an alliance and it was impossible to govern through any one element in that spent coalition without coercion. Cromwell, still trying to maintain old links, was forced to look elsewhere and the obvious place, in the end, was amongst those who had always run the parishes, boroughs, hundreds and shires and whose priorities, one suspects, were order rather than ideology and ambitious state enterprises.

|9|

Conclusion

Oliver Cromwell and the English Revolution

Behind Cromwell's reputation for paradox, with which we started this enquiry, lies the apparent paradox of the English Revolution of the mid-seventeenth century. And it is a double paradox. First, how did the conservative defenders of civil and religious liberty, most of whom firmly believed that both were already enshrined in the English constitution and an Erastian church established by statute, come to destroy the very ancient constitution they had set out to defend? Second, how was it that the revolutionary acts of regicide, the abolition of aristocratic privilege and the House of Lords, the demolition of the Church of England and the declaration of a republic were the prelude, not to revolutionary change in England, but to the search for a consensual, conservative, hesitantly reforming settlement?

If we put those two questions together, the paradox begins to unravel. Having unleashed the dogs of war to liberate their King from the baleful influence of evil advisers, essentially conservative men and women found themselves struggling with the capacity of civil war to engender unintended consequences, to generate unexpected demands and to complicate circumstances to the point of confounding existing ideological resources. The journey from conservative resistance, the defence of civil and religious liberty from the menace of innovatory and tyrannical men, to 'revolution', with its own implicit threats to liberty, and thence to a search for consensual healing and settling, was a sequential story of frustration by unfolding circumstances. As that narrative unfolds, Cromwell becomes an actor of increasing importance. But how his role is depicted, the basis of his reputation, depends to a large extent on what form that narrative is given.

The simplicities of the Great Rebellion or of the Puritan Revolution, two of the great meta-narratives of these events, will no longer satisfy us. The story of Cromwell as the arch-rebel, assumed, like all rebels, to be disloyal and treacherous is transparent propaganda. But, equally, the Revolution as nonconformist liberation, with Cromwell as the archetypal Puritan, pays too little heed to the complexities of the relationships within the coalition which triumphed in the English Civil Wars. Both Christopher Hill and Professor Barg provide us with brilliant summations of the paradox of a revolution which devours its children and turns against its own trajectory. They see the parliamentary side in the civil war as essentially a coalition; an alliance between, on the one hand, the propertied, landowning classes, intent on preserving their property (and the civil and religious liberties which protected it) from the threat of an authoritarian monarchy, and, on the other hand, the masses, over whom they normally exercised governance in the countries and boroughs. The rhetoric of their campaign and the collapse of controls over press and pulpit allowed radical groups from the masses to articulate more revolutionary definitions of the nature of the struggle. These tensions within the parliamentary alliance were reflected in the Parliament/Army stand-off of 1647, in the rise of the Levellers and in proliferating sectarianism. In 1648–9 the Gordian knot was cut. On the one hand, the King and the more conservative members of the parliamentary coalition were removed from the scene. On the other hand, those who threatened to radically redefine the purposes of that coalition, the Levellers, were suppressed and military discipline was reasserted. The 1650s then became a drift back to a world safe for the substantial landed classes and the respectable bourgeoisie. Barg and Hill, therefore, resolve the paradoxes of the Revolution in terms of its social underpinning, an alliance between social groups, or classes, which were shown in victory to have divergent interpretations of the Revolution's stated objectives. In this formulation Cromwell becomes the saviour of the 'respectable revolution', rescuing it from the spectre of a more plebeian and 'genuine' revolutionary threat.[1] This has been an influential interpretation of the paradox seen to be inherent in the context of Cromwell's life and place in English history. The problem with it is that few historians would now accept this social description of the conflict as accurate or justified by the findings of the critical mass of research over the last half-century. A further difficulty is that, while there clearly were strains and tensions within the parliamentary alliance of the 1640s, they are complex and very rarely reducible to group affiliations. Indeed they are sometimes epitomized in the strains and tensions internal to an individual conscience as illustrated, for example, in Cromwell's correspondence with Robert Hammond in November 1648. Associating social groups, however flexible their economic determination might be, with particular views of the Revolution and its desirable outcomes has, in the end, been more productive of questions than answers.

Cromwell made allusions to his belief in the value of social hierarchy – 'a nobleman, a gentleman, a yeoman'[2] – but it would be misleading to describe him as anything like the consistent advocate of the interests of a socially determined group. He was well aware of the paradoxical development of the struggle on which he had so enthusiastically embarked in 1641, of its strange twistings and turnings. He would have explained those paradoxes in terms of providences of a just, merciful and occasionally angry God whose more immediate purposes sinful human beings could only dimly perceive, and whose promptings they fumbled blindly after. This is a view of history, as the footsteps of the living God, to which we can no longer universally subscribe. It has seemed, then, to a growing number of historians that we are left with explanation in terms of the complexity and limitations of human interaction with other individuals, groups and social forces and that such an explanation can only be arrived at through the imaginative understanding of a carefully researched and artfully constructed narrative. This set of events, the interaction of individual lives within it, may only be understandable as a story. Otherwise, these interactions and relationships, are robbed of their richness and complexity by the conventional categories of analysis and obscured by the invocation of paradox and greatness.[3]

In such a narrative, it could reasonably be argued, Cromwell would almost certainly appear as an increasingly decisive influence on the unfolding of events. It is hard, for example, to imagine Parliament winning the first civil war as decisively as it did, or in the way that it did, without Cromwell's contributions at Marston Moor, in the struggle with Manchester over war management, and at Naseby and Langport. Equally, in the period 1647–9 he was a key figure in preventing the escalation of military disorder even if this was ultimately at the price of purging

the Commons, executing the King and abolishing the Lords.
Cromwell may have shared some of Fairfax' distaste for these
'solutions' but he differed from him in a willingness to grasp the
unpalatable nettle when the alternative appeared to be a further
erosion of order in the direction of anarchy. The creation of a
'British Moment' through the conquest of Ireland and Scotland
owed much to Cromwell's campaigning skills, vigour and ruthlessness. The fact that the Protectorate could reconcile the tone of
godliness and the aspiration to godly reformation with an
antiformalist openness to varieties of Protestant practice and
expression owes almost everything to the temper of Cromwell's
own godliness. The institutionally and constitutionally unsettled
nature of the years 1653–8 is intertwined with Cromwell's own
political shifts. If we see this phase as exemplified by Cromwell's
expulsion of the Rump in April 1653, it can look like little more
than a series of ad hoc responses to a sequence of crises.
Cromwell begins, in this case, to appear as a pragmatist preoccupied with political survival, his own short-termism contributing
to the continuing instability. On the other hand, it is possible to
see him as a creative political actor, remaining, despite some of
his colleagues, committed to finding a consensual basis for the
renewal of stability and the rebuilding of the state, agnostic
about constitutional forms but returning repeatedly to the principles underlying The Heads of Proposals. But, however we shape
the narrative of the English Revolution, Cromwell remains a
decisive, if not a dominant, figure in the story. This is why, from
whatever perspective he is viewed, his 'greatness' has so often
appeared undeniable. But the precise nature of his reputation, the
character of that 'greatness', will ultimately depend upon the narrative shape we give to the English Revolution.

Can we allow him a final determinative word in informing the
way in which we see his role in that climacteric of English history,
the Revolution? In one of his few, but most often quoted, pieces
of self-reflection, Cromwell appears to concede a great deal to
those who portray him as little more than a pragmatist, hanging
on to the comet of revolution with little of consistent principle
intact at the end of the ride. 'I can tell you, Sirs, what I would not
have; tho' I cannot what I would.' What happens if we take this
'negativity' principle seriously and apply it to his part in the story
of the English Revolution? How does the issue of consistency and
principle look, if we explore it in terms of what Cromwell *did not
want* at each stage of his political career?

In the first 18 months of the Long Parliament his efforts were predominantly directed *against* episcopal religious oppression and imposed religious formality. His attention to John Lilburne's case, involvement with the Root and Branch issue, scepticism about the future of the Prayer Book, all bear witness to this. His detachment from the destruction of Strafford might suggest that civil liberty was less of a priority but his interest in statutory provision for regular parliaments is evidence that it was, nevertheless, a concern. What the Cromwell of 1640–1 did not want was the recurrence of threats to religious and civil liberty or the rule of ministers he associated with such threats. By 1642 his immediate priority had shifted to *not* being defeated in a civil war. He quickly came to identify two subordinate things that he would rather not have. A lukewarm approach to the war, not only exposed his side to the possibility of defeat, but, prolonging the conflict, it imposed greater burdens which dishonoured Parliament's soldiers and exposed the cause to the charge that it too was destructive of civil liberty. The second thing which he came to oppose was the threat to religious liberty, springing now from within his own side and its alliances: from the Scots and from some interpretations of a Presbyterian church settlement. His concern for tender consciences in 1644 and anxiety at military footdragging after Marston Moor came together in a desire to be rid of the old military order and rid of dependence on the Scots. All of this found expression in the Self-Denying Ordinance and the formation of the New Model Army. The avoidance of military defeat was replaced, in the aftermath of victory, by the desire to avoid political defeat after such a costly triumph. Negotiations which restored the King, however punitively his followers were treated, alongside a religiously oppressive church would represent just such a defeat.

The crucial context of these years was the Solemn League and Covenant, the great binding oath intended to be taken by all 'noblemen, barons, knights, gentlemen, citizens, burgesses, ministers of the gospel, and commons of all sorts in the kingdoms of England, Scotland and Ireland, by the providence of God living under one King, and being of one reformed religion'.[4] Sworn by the House of Commons on 25 September 1643, it remained a reference point for individuals as diverse as Gerrard Winstanley, who subscribed to it on 8 October 1643, and Cromwell himself who took the oath on 5 February 1644. In a society where the management of conscience and conscientious obligations was seen as not only vital to social order and coherence, but a matter between those who swore and a living, watchful and jealous God, the importance of such an oath cannot be overestimated. The Covenant bound all who took it against popery and malignants, for the reformation of the Church and, in humility, under a God easily provoked. But the key commitment, in terms of the post-war negotiations of 1646, 1647 and 1648 was clause III.

> We shall with the same sincerity, reality and constancy, in our several vocations, endeavour with our estates and lives mutually to preserve the rights and privileges of Parliaments, and the liberties of the Kingdoms, and to preserve and defend the King's Majesty's person and authority, in the preservation and defence of the true religion and liberties of the Kingdoms, that the world may bear witness with our consciences of our loyalty, and that we have no thoughts or intentions to diminish His Majesty's just power and greatness.

It is this conscientious and specific commitment, the desire *not* to break a solemn engagement which dominated Cromwell's political conduct through the post-war crisis. A settlement which protected civil and religious liberty had also to preserve Parliament, the King's person and his just power and greatness. The Heads of Proposals was the formulation which Cromwell backed to square this circle and honour this engagement. Its failure opened up the chasm of a tragic dilemma. If Parliament itself threatened religious liberty or was to provoke military disorder, what was to be done? In 1647 this meant, for Cromwell, being prepared to bring pressure to bear on a Presbyterian-dominated Parliament and a willingness to debate the future settlement of the Kingdom with the General Council of the Army. The year of 1648 and the second civil war made the dilemma even more sombre. If preserving the person of a particular King and the power and greatness of the crown meant continuing instability, defiance of the judgements of Providence and risking the radicalization and loss of control of the army, Cromwell chose to break the engagement of the Covenant to follow what Providence and necessity seemed to require. But it bore all the tragic hallmarks of a choice between two evils. Parliament was preserved by a fictional whisker. Cromwell did not want it to end there but the greater imperative was to forestall a solution which would put power back into the hands of the enemies of civil and religious liberty. The campaigns of 1649–51, in Ireland, Scotland and England, were, in no small measure, designed to prevent such an outcome. But by 1652–53 what could *not* be borne was the self-perpetuation of a non-reforming, corrupt establishment which appeared to risk, in its approach to constitutional settlement, the overthrow of all that had been fought for from 1642. Having overthrown the Rump, Cromwell did *not* want a naked military regime: hence the Nominated Assembly. Towards the end of 1653 he had decided, with others, that he did *not* want an unsettling, 'parliamentary' radicalism and that to prevent it he should accept the Assembly's surrender of authority. With the Instrument of Government and the inauguration of the Protectorate, Cromwell reverted to a number of constants on his list of undesirables. He did *not* want military rule, nor the threat to civil liberty which the rule of a single person, unconstrained by a Council and a Parliament might bring. Through the system of Triers and Ejectors, he avoided threats to religious liberty while preventing religious disorder. He did not want inflexibility in the face of parliamentary concerns about the constitution but, at the same time, he wished to avoid the financial destabilization of the regime and the alienation of the military. These were, perhaps, the most difficult issues to reconcile in the first phase of the Protectorate. The failure of his first Parliament saw his attention turned in 1655 to the prevention of internal and external threats to security and to an attempt to avoid the further loss of providential favour by a programme for the moral reformation of the nation. These concerns coalesced in the Major-Generals' experiment. That programme's reliance on unpopular local minorities left him wanting *not* to alienate further those who normally governed the localities. In the Humble Petition and Advice he was offered, and attracted by, the opportunity to avoid a non-parliamentary settlement, an unbalanced constitution (potentially menacing to both religious and civil liberty) but he could only accept it on terms which would not alienate the army and his providential God.

If, then, we track what Cromwell *would not have*, certain key and continuing themes clearly emerge. The preservation of religious and civil liberty within a customary framework was the starting point, as it was for so many who supported the legislative programme of 1641. To rid the King of advisers, who could not be trusted to respect those liberties nor the statutory constraints which had been erected to neutralize the crown's capacity to act against them, a civil war had to be fought vigorously and decisively. Not only that campaign but the long political struggle for settlement which followed were informed by principles enshrined in the Solemn League and Covenant and The Heads of Proposals: godly reformation with liberty of conscience; a parliamentary settlement; constitutional protection for civil and religious liberties; a responsible, accountable monarchy. In the end, Charles I's manipulative responses to these offers and the growing threat that they would unleash a counter-response in the direction of military insubordination and more radical solutions, meant that it was impossible to sustain this formulation. Cromwell's tragedy was that, in the cause of preserving some sort of order, he was pushed into destroying the monarchy and violating the rights of Parliament. His conscience coped with his betrayal of the oath of the Covenant by throwing reliance on Providence and his willingness to follow a living God, the God of Abraham.

What is remarkable is that he recognized, at the same time, that governance of the nation at large was dependent on regaining the cooperation, compliance and collaboration of a much broader coalition than the narrow military backing which had given him the coercive force to cut the Gordian knot of 1648–9 and to expel the Rump in April 1653. The attempt to maintain a civilian basis for government in the Nominated Assembly and under the Instrument reflects this. So too does the desire to respond positively to the civilian, parliamentary initiative of constitutional reform represented by the Humble Petition and Advice. The *leit motif* of Cromwell's political career after 1653 remained essentially true to the principles of the Solemn League and Covenant and The Heads of Proposals: guarantees for civil and religious liberties; regular and representative parliaments; a single person responsible to and constrained by a Council and a Parliament; and a church settlement which sustained godliness without jeopardizing religious liberty. His Achilles heel was the need to provide for an expensive naval and military establishment if the security of England and control of Ireland and Scotland were to be maintained. The consequences of this were high taxation and extensive borrowing which alienated the very governing classes he wished to win over. At the prospect of a rapprochement with them in 1657, he cut the monthly assessment to drastically low levels. His death, the following year, left no one with the status and authority to reduce the military establishment by a corresponding proportion. The inevitable result was a collapse of government credit, virtual bankruptcy and the end of the Protectorate. The numbers, that he revealingly confessed not to understand,[5] finally caught up with him. A vigorous warrior in the cause of God and His chosen people, Cromwell's political instincts were to seek moderate solutions of the civil problems of rule. A monarch who abused trust to the point of legitimating the identification of monarchy with Babylon, helped to engender a revolutionary situation in which moderate men could only struggle to make an ordered and stable society out of the wreckage. This was Cromwell's tragedy. His greatness is that he did so much more than cling on to the debris. By 1657 he had gone a long way towards finding a stable civilian basis for the regime, a basis not altogether removed from the principles he and others had fought for in the 1640s. But time was running out and the settlement was never to be consolidated. It was a settlement far less radical than those who have aspired to an English Revolution, then and since, would have wished. Nor could it ever possess the hereditary legitimacy of those sympathetic to the fate of the 'martyr' King or sticklers for the untarnished rule of law. But it was admirable none the less.

Notes

Chapter 1 Enigma or hero?

1. John Buchan, *Cromwell* (London, 1970; first published 1934) pp. 19–20.
2. Christopher Hill, 'Oliver Cromwell' in *idem, Collected Essays*, (Brighton, 1986) III, pp. 68–94.
3. John F.H. New, 'Cromwell and the Paradoxes of Puritanism', *Journal of British Studies*, 5:1 (1965) pp. 53–9; *idem* (ed.), *Oliver Cromwell: Pretender, Puritan, Statesman, Paradox?* (New York, 1972).
4. Antonia Fraser, *Cromwell: Our Chief of Men* (London, 1973) ch. 24 especially p. 700. Fraser's biography is still in print.
5. Serialized in *The Times*, 22 November 1999, p. 41.
6. C.H. Firth, *Oliver Cromwell and the Rule of the Puritans in England* (London, 1928; first published 1901) pp. 53, 478.
7. Buchan, *Cromwell*, p. 479. See also The Preface.
8. Sir Ernest Barker, *Oliver Cromwell and the English People* (Cambridge, 1937) pp. 14, 28.
9. The Cromwell Day Addresses are published in the annual issues of the Association's journal *Cromwelliana*.
10. John West, *Oliver Cromwell and the Battle of Gainsborough* (Boston, Lincolnshire, 1992). Cf. Peter Young's Cromwell Day Address for 1975.
11. The nearest I have come is an anonymous review essay in the *Church Quarterly Review* 58 (1904) pp. 395–421. The author asks why the language of idealism should be applied to a merely opportunist politician.
12. Roger Howell Jr, *Cromwell* (London, 1977). Introduction.

Chapter 2 Why Cromwell's reputation matters: the record

1. For an interesting discussion of a key example see Peter Gaunt's discussion of the documentary problems relating to the first

Protectorate Parliament in 'Law-Making in the First Protectorate Parliament', in Colin Jones, Malyn Newitt and Stephen Roberts (eds), *Politics and People in Revolutionary England* (Oxford, 1986) pp. 163–86.

2. Roger Howell, Jr, *Cromwell* (London, 1977) ch. 1.
3. Nicholas Rogers and Christopher Parish, *Cromwell and Sidney Sussex* (Cambridge, 1999) p. 1.
4. See C.H. Firth (ed.), *The Memoirs of Edmund Ludlow, Lieutenant-General of the Horse in the Army of the Commonwealth of England 1625–1672* (2 vols, Oxford, 1894). The problem of Toland's editorial influence on the text and the possibility of the reconstruction of a pre-Toland text is brilliantly handled in A.B. Worden (ed.), *Edmund Ludlow: A Voyce from the Watch Tower: Part Five 1660–1662*, Camden, Fourth Series, 21, Royal Historical Society (London, 1978).
5. On Carlyle see D.J. Trela, *'Cromwell' in Context: The Conception, Writing and Reception of Carlyle's Second History* (Edinburgh, 1986). On Abbott, John Morrill, 'Textualizing and Contextualizing Cromwell', *The Historical Journal*, 33:3 (1990) pp. 129–39.
6. See, amongst many others, Frederic Harrison, *Oliver Cromwell* (London, 1890) p. 11. Harrison relies on the evidence of the inscription hung over the effigy which lay in state after Oliver's death. For a convenient text of the inscription see Roy Sherwood, *Oliver Cromwell: King in All but Name 1653–1658* (Stroud, Gloucestershire, 1997) p. 148.
7. See the suggestion made by John Morrill, 'The Making of Oliver Cromwell', in Morrill (ed.), *Oliver Cromwell and the English Revolution* (London, 1990) p. 24. This essay is now the indispensable piece on Cromwell's early life.
8. *Ibid.*, pp. 34–6.
9. *Ibid.*, p. 37.
10. *Ibid.*, pp. 44–5.
11. The sums offered by Cromwell appear to have been considerable and it would be interesting to know where they came from if he was contributing in his own right or if he was acting as an agent for others. For various estimates of his contributions see Howell, *Cromwell*, p. 38; Peter Gaunt, *Oliver Cromwell* (Oxford, 1996) p. 34; Barry Coward, *Oliver Cromwell* (London, 1992) p. 17.
12. See the depositions assembled in John Bruce and David Masson (eds), *The Quarrel Between The Earl of Manchester and Oliver Cromwell*, Camden Society, New Series XII (London, 1875).
13. See G.E. Aylmer, 'Was Oliver Cromwell a Member of the Army in 1646–47 or Not?', *History*, 56:187 (1971) pp. 183–8.
14. The Council met regularly, on 6 and 17 July at Reading, on 18 August at Kingston and on 9 September at Putney, for example. It did not replace the Council of War and was not responsible, as has sometimes been suggested, for running the army. The essential account of these events is Austin Woolrych, *Soldiers and Statesmen: The General Council of the Army and its Debates, 1647–1648* (Oxford, 1987).

15. The definitive accounts are David Underdown, *Pride's Purge* (Oxford, 1971); Blair Worden, *The Rump Parliament* (Cambridge, 1974).

16. A good account of the campaigns and their impact on Scotland is to be found in John D. Grainger, *Cromwell Against the Scots: The Last Anglo-Scottish War 1650–1652* (East Lothian, Scotland, 1997).

17. C.H. Simpkinson, *Thomas Harrison: Regicide and Major-General* (London, 1905) p. 184.

18. For a recent, highly suppositious but entertaining attempt to argue the case that Cromwell was killed by poisoning and that it was not his corpse but a substitute which was exhibited and defiled at Tyburn see H.F. McMains, *The Death of Oliver Cromwell* (Lexington, Kentucky, 1999/2000).

Chapter 3   The cat's paw of history: Cromwell's reputation through time

1. For pioneering work on the popular reputation of Cromwell see the 'Nineteenth-century Cromwell' project sponsored by the journal *Past and Present*. T.W. Mason, 'Nineteenth century Cromwell' in J.S. Bromley and E.H. Kossmann (eds), *Britain and the Netherlands: vol. V: Some Political Mythologies* (The Hague, 1975) pp. 141–63; Alan Smith, 'The Image of Cromwell in Folklore and Tradition', *Folklore* (The Folk-Lore Society) 79 (1968) pp. 17–38.

2. This reached its definitive summation in *A True and Faithful Narrative of Oliver Cromwell's Compact with the Devil* (1720).

3. Hartlib mss., Sheffield University Library, 7/118/1A Polier to Hartlib, 8 October 1655; Alan Macfarlane (ed.), *The Diary of Ralph Josselin* (Oxford, 1976) p. 225 – entry for 27 December 1650.

4. For Cromwell's providentialism see Blair Worden, 'Providence and Politics in Cromwell's England', *Past and Present*, 109 (1985) pp. 55–99; J.C. Davis, 'Cromwell's Religion' in John Morrill (ed.), *Oliver Cromwell and the English Revolution* (London, 1990) pp. 181–208.

5. Hartlib mss., 54/27A – 30B, Peter Cornelius to Oliver Cromwell, 4 June 1657; *ibid.*, 9/17/41A – 42B, Figulus to Hartlib, 25 October 1658.

6. [William Prynne]. *The Machiavellian Cromwellist and Hypocritical New Statist* (1648).

7. Mercurius Melancholicus, *Craftie Cromwell: Or, Oliver ordering our New State. A Tragi-Comedie* (1648).

8. *The British Bell-man* (1648).

9. Lilburne, *An Impeachment* (1649) p. 8.

10. See, for example, Aaron Guerdon, *A Most learned, Conscientious and Devout Exercise* (1649); *A Curse Against Parliament Ale* (1649); Philo Regis, *The Right Picture of King Olivre from Top to Toe* (1649).

11. See, for example, *Remarkable Observations on God's Mercies towards England* (1651); T.M. jun., Esq., *Veni; Vidi; Vici: The Triumphs of the Most Excellent and Illustrious Oliver Cromwell* (1652).
12. John Spittlehouse, *A Warning Piece Discharged* (1653).
13. In 1656 Edmund Ludlow upbraided Thomas Harrison for supporting Cromwell in 1653 and 1654. Harrison's reply was that he did so because Cromwell was prepared to back men 'who acted upon higher principles than those of civil liberty'. C.H. Firth (ed.), *The Memoirs of Edmund Ludlow* (2 vols, Oxford, 1894) II, p. 7.
14. John Spittlehouse, *An Answer to One Part of the Lord Protector's Speech* (1654). For similar charges of backsliding or apostacy – potential or realized – see *Sighs for Righteousness: Or the Reformation This day calls for* (1654); George Rofe, *The Righteousness of God to Man* (1656).
15. Colonel Edw. Lane, *An Image of our Reforming Times: Or Jehu in his proper Colours* (1654).
16. George Fox, *To Thee Oliver Cromwell* (1655).
17. Christopher Feake, *A Beam of Light Shining in the Midst of much Darkness and Confusion* (1659) especially p. 56.
18. *Britania Trumphalis: A Brief History of the Warres and other State Affairs of Great Britain* (1654) p. 168.
19. Samuel Richardson, *An Apology for the Present Government and Governour* (1654). See also John Moore, *Protection Proclaimed (through the loving kindness of God in the Present Government)* (1655).
20. *Killing is Murder* (1657) p. 49.
21. For example, John Saunders, *An Iron Rod* (1655?); *idem, An Iron Rod Put into the Lord Protectors Hand* (1655).
22. [William Sedgewick], *Animadversions upon A Letter and a Paper* (1656). Sedgewick preached several Fast Sermons to Parliament during the civil war and was appointed town preacher of Ely in 1644. He probably knew Cromwell personally.
23. Samuel Morland, *The History of the Evangelical Churches of the Valleys of Piemont* (1658).
24. *The Commonwealth Mercury*, September 2–9, 1658; *Upon the much Lamented Departure of the High and Mighty Prince, Oliver, Lord Protector of England, Scotland and Ireland* (1658?); George Lawrence, *PEPLUM OLIVARII* (1658); *The True Manner of the most Magnificent Conveyance of his Highnesse Effigies* (1658); Tho. Davies, *The Tenth Worthy* (1658).
25. Thomason catalogue: E1787 (1).
26. Robert Pitilloh, *The Hammer of Persecution* (1659).
27. William Winstanley, *The Loyall Martyrology* (1665).
28. Roger Howell, Jr, '"That Imp of Satan": The Restoration Image of Cromwell', in R.C. Richardson (ed.), *Images of Oliver Cromwell: Essays for and by Roger Howell, Jr* (Manchester, 1993) pp. 33–47.
29. John Hacket, *Serinia Reserata* (1693) pp. 223–4.
30. *Arbitrary Government Display'd: In the Tyrannic Usurpation of the Rump Parliament and Oliver Cromwell* (1683) pp. 51, 89, 92, 93.

31. Firth (ed.) *Memoirs of Edmund Ludlow*, I, pp. 282, 344; II, pp. 9–10. For Toland's editorship see A.B. Worden (ed.) *Edmund Ludlow: A Voyce from the Watch Tower: Part Five 1660–1662*, Camden, Fourth Series, 21, Royal Historical Society (London, 1978) Introduction. Ludlow was not alone in this view of Cromwell. Cf. Henry Neville, *Plato Redivivus* (1681); Edward Philips, *Life of John Milton* (1694) p. 52; John Toland, *Life of John Milton* (1698) p. 145. From a non-republican standpoint Thomas Hobbs' *Behemoth*, first officially published in 1682, portrayed Cromwell as run by ambition to gain the throne.

32. The phrase is from another Royalist's verdict recorded on the day of Cromwell's death in 1658. Andrew Browning (ed.) *Memoirs of Sir John Reresby*, Royal Historical Society (London 1991, 2nd edn) pp. 22–3.

33. W. Dunn Macray (ed.), *The History of the Rebellion and Civil Wars in England by Edward, Earl of Clarendon* (6 vols, 1888: 1958) IV, pp. 304–8; V, p. 281; VI, pp. 91–2.

34. Robert Latham and William Matthews (eds), *The Diary of Samuel Pepys* (11 vols, 1970–1983) I, p. 309.

35. Essentially true, for example, of Laurence Echard, *The History of England* (1718); John Oldmixon, *The History of England* (1730); Gilbert Burnet, *History of My Own Time* (1724).

36. [John Banks], *A Short Critical Review of the Political Life of Oliver Cromwell* (1739).

37. *Biographica Britannica: or, The Lives of the Most Eminent Persons Who have flourished in Great Britain and Ireland* (1750) III, pp. 1537–79.

38. Catherine Macaulay, *The History of England* (1768) V, pp. 19, 58, 97, 102–7; VI, pp. 112, 200.

39. *Ibid.*, IV, pp. 169, 313: V, pp. 100, 219.

40. Quoted in Roger Howell, Jr, 'Images of Oliver Cromwell', in Richardson (ed.), *Images*, pp. 27–8.

41. Peter Karsten, *Patriot-Heroes in England and America: Political Symbolism and Changing Values over Three Centuries* (Madison, Wisconsin, 1978) ch. 3.

42. Peter J. Kitson, '"Sages and Patriots that being dead do yet speak to us": Readings of the English Revolution in the late Eighteenth Century', in James Holstun (ed.), *Pamphlet Wars: Prose in the English Revolution* (London, 1992) pp. 205–30.

43. 'The Life of Cromwell', *The Quarterly Review*, 25:50 (July, 1821) pp. 205–347.

44. Kenneth R. Johnston and Joseph Nicholes, 'Transitory Actions, Men Betrayed: The French Revolution and the English Revolution in Romantic Drama', *The Wordsworth Circle*, 23:2 (1992) pp. 76–96.

45. William Godwin, *History of the Commonwealth of England* (4 vols, 1824–1828) II, pp. 199–204, 409; III, p. 533; IV, pp. 13, 587–8. A darker version of the same theme was presented earlier by John Millar in *An Historical View of the English Government* (4 vols, 1812). Cromwell's virtues were vigour and decision; his failing,

ambition which led him into experiments unsupported by the political nation.

46. D.J. Trela, *A History of Carlyle's 'Oliver Cromwell's Letters and Speeches'* (New York, 1992) pp. 165–7.

47. Mark Noble, *Memoirs of the Protectoral House of Cromwell* (2 vols, London, 1787) I, p. iii.

48. I am grateful to Professor Blair Worden for allowing me to see the text of his 1999 Ralegh Lecture on Carlyle and Cromwell prior to publication and his 'The Victorians and Oliver Cromwell', in Stefan Collini *et al.* (eds), *British Intellectual History 1750–1950* (Cambridge, 2000) pp. 112–35.

49. See Trela, *Carlyle's Cromwell*, ch. 7. Trela's is now the standard study of Carlyle's *magnum opus*.

50. For the Squire letters see Trela, *Carlyle's Cromwell*, pp. 85–92; Walter Rye, *Two Cromwellian Myths* (Norwich, 1925).

51. Trela, *Carlyle's Cromwell*, p. 107.

52. Roger Howell, Jr, '"Who needs another Cromwell": The Nineteenth Century Image of Oliver Cromwell', in Richardson (ed.), *Images*, p. 103; Trela, *Carlyle's Cromwell*, p. 169.

53. Karsten, *Patriot-Heroes*, pp. 75, 143.

54. J.P.D. Dunbabin, 'Oliver Cromwell's Popular Image in Nineteenth-Century England', in J.S. Bromley and E.H. Kossman (eds), *Britain and the Netherlands; volume V: Some Political Mythologies* (The Hague, 1975) p. 155.

55. Roy Strong, *And when did you last see your father? The Victorian Painter and British History* (London, 1978) p. 141.

56. *Ibid.*, pp. 146–9.

57. Dunbabin, 'Cromwell's Popular Image', p. 143.

58. Karsten, *Patriot-Heroes*, pp. 6–7.

59. Smith, 'Cromwell in Folklore', pp. 17–39.

60. The work of Toby Barnard is seminal here. See Barnard, 'Irish Images of Cromwell', in Richardson (ed.), *Images*, pp. 180–206.

61. John P. Prendergast, *The Cromwellian Settlement of Ireland* (London, 1865; reprinted 1996) pp. iii, xxxix, 149.

62. For Froude see Barnard, 'Irish Images', p. 194. His was one of the earliest expressions of Cromwell as the strong, iron-fisted hero that was to become an important strain in his reputation down to the 1940s.

63. *Ibid.*, pp. 180, 195.

64. I am grateful to Blair Worden for providing me with a typescript of his essay 'A Statue for Oliver Cromwell'. One of the leading opponents of the statue, Lady Helen Clifford-Nellor accused Cromwell of 'despotism' and 'insolent Caesarism'. Karsten, *Patriot-Heroes*, p. 159.

65. Examples of this are: C.H. Firth, 'Cromwell and the Insurrection of 1655', *English Historical Review*, 3 (1888) pp. 323–50; Frederic Harrison, *Oliver Cromwell* (London, 1890); D.W. Rannie, 'Cromwell's Major Generals', *English Historical Review*, 10 (1895) pp. 471–506; S.R. Gardiner, *Cromwell's Place in History* (London, 1897).

66. J.R. Seeley, *The Expansion of England* (1883) and the excellent discussion in Timothy Lang, *The Victorians and the Stuart Heritage: Interpretations of a Discordant Past* (Cambridge, 1995) ch. 5.
67. S.R. Gardiner, *Cromwell's Place*, pp. 28, 31, 84–5, 113–16. See also Lang, *The Victorians and the Stuart Heritage*, pp. 199–213.
68. Howell, 'Who Needs Another Cromwell', pp. 96–7.
69. Karsten, *Patriot-Heroes*, p. 75.
70. Dunbabin, 'Cromwell and the Inter-war European Dictators', in Richardson (ed.), *Images*, pp. 108–23, especially p. 110.
71. Sir George MacMunn, *Leadership through the Ages* (London, 1935).
72. Twenty years later Ashley was to repudiate even these qualified views. Maurice Ashley, *The Greatness of Oliver Cromwell* (London, 1957).
73. W.C. Abbott (ed.), *The Writings and Speeches of Oliver Cromwell* (4 vols, Oxford, 1988: reissue of Oxford, 1937–47) III, pp. xi, 134.
74. Sir Ernest Barker, *Oliver Cromwell and the English People* (Cambridge, 1937).
75. Richardson, 'Cromwell and the Dictators', pp. 113–14, 116–17; H.N. Brailsford, *The Levellers and the English Revolution* (London, 1961). Brailsford began writing this in the 1940s. For the definitive demolition of the Cromwellian dictorship see Austin Woolrych, 'The Cromwellian Protectorate: A Military Dictatorship?', *History*, 75:244 (1990) pp. 207–31.
76. Hilaire Belloc, *Cromwell* (London, 1934) pp. 87, 272–3, 298, 374.
77. H.R. Trevor-Roper, 'Oliver Cromwell and his Parliament', in *idem*, *Religion, the Reformation and Social Change* (London, 1967) pp. 345–91. This essay was first published in 1954. Roger Howell, Jr, 'Cromwell and his Parliaments: the Trevor-Roper Thesis Revisited', in Richardson (ed.), *Images*, pp. 124–35. This essay was first published in 1987–8.
78. A good but rather more lenient discussion may be found in Roger Howell, Jr, 'Cromwell's Personality: the Problems and Promises of a Psycho Historical Approach', in Richardson (ed.), *Images*, pp. 136–57. First published in 1978.
79. Beginning with the work of Geoffrey Nuttall (especially his *The Holy Spirit in Puritan Faith and Experience* (Oxford, 1946)) this reappraisal culminates in the work of Blair Worden: 'Providence and politics'; 'Toleration and the Cromwellian Protectorate' in W.J. Shiels (ed.), *Persecution and Toleration: Studies in Church History 21* (Oxford, 1984) pp. 199–233; 'Oliver Cromwell and the Sin of Achan', in Derek Beales and Geoffrey Best (eds), *History, Society and the Churches* (Cambridge, 1985) pp. 125–45. See also Davis, 'Cromwell's Religion'.
80. Barry Coward, *Oliver Cromwell* (London, 1992) especially pp. 3–4; Peter Gaunt, *Oliver Cromwell* (Oxford, 1996); *idem*, 'Cromwell's Purge: Exclusions and the First Protectorate Parliament', *Parliamentary History*, 6:1 (1987) pp. 1–22; *idem*, 'Drafting the Instrument of Government 1653–1654', *Parliamentary History*, 8 (1989) pp. 28–42; *idem*, '"The Single Persons Confidants and

Dependents"? Oliver Cromwell and his Protectoral Councillors', *The Historical Journal*, 32:3 (1989).

81. As well as the numerous county studies the following appraisals are important: Derek Hirst, 'The failure of Godly Rule in the English Republic', *Past and Present*, 132 (1991) pp. 33–66; *idem*, 'The English Republic and the Meaning of Britain', *Journal of Modern History*, 66:3 (1994) pp. 451–86; Anthony Fletcher, 'Oliver Cromwell and the godly Nation', in Morrill (ed.), *Cromwell and the English Revolution*, pp. 209–33; *idem*, 'Oliver Cromwell and the Localities: the Problem of Consent', in Colin Jones, Malyn Newitt and Stephen Roberts (eds), *Politics and People in Revolutionary England: Essays in Honour of Ivan Roots* (Oxford, 1986) pp. 187–204.

82. See Tom Reilly, *Cromwell: An Honourable Enemy: The Untold Story of the Cromwellian Invasion of Ireland* (Dingle, County Derry, 1999). Compare Jason McElligott, *Cromwell: Our Chief of Enemies* (Dundalk, 1994).

83. Interesting in this respect are Sean Kelsey, *Inventing a Republic: The Political Culture of the English Commonwealth 1649–1653* (Manchester, 1997); Roy Sherwood, *Oliver Cromwell: King in All But Name 1653–1658* (Stroud, 1997); Laura Lunger Knoppers, *Constructing Cromwell: Ceremony, Portrait and Print 1645–1661* (Cambridge, 2000).

84. Dunbabin, 'Cromwell's Popular Image', p. 158.

85. Smith, 'Cromwell in Folklore', p. 17.

86. Norman Davies, *The Isles: A History* (London, 1999); William Rees-Mogg, 'Cromwell, Where are You? ... We Need Another Man of Destiny', *The Times*, 25 January 1999. 'A brave bad man' was the title given to an exhibition (and the associated web page) mounted by Cambridge University Library to mark the Cromwell quarter-centenary in 1999.

87. D.H. Pennington, 'Cromwell and the Historians', in Ivan Roots, *Cromwell: A Profile* (London, 1973) pp. 221–30. A decade ago, acknowledging the recycling of judgements on Cromwell, John Morrill called for historians to go back much more systematically to the original documents and to see them afresh. We are fortunate to have a brilliant historian, Blair Worden, engaged on precisely that process for what promises to be the most important biographical study since those of Gardiner and Firth. The rest of this study consists of a series of attempts to show where we might expect fresh thinking about Cromwell to have most impact. John Morrill, 'Textualizing and Contextualizing Cromwell', *The Historical Journal*, 33:3 (1990) p. 639.

Chapter 4 The self-made man risen from obscurity

1. Quoted in Roger Howell, Jr, *Cromwell* (London, 1977) p. 47. Manchester's identification of socially subversive attitudes with Cromwell is, of course, quite explicit in 1644. See John Bruce and

David Masson (eds), *The Quarrel Between The Earl of Manchester and Oliver Cromwell*, Camden Society, New Series, XII (London, 1875) pp. lxxi, 59–70.
2. Blair Worden, 'The Victorians and Oliver Cromwell', in Stefan Collini *et al.* (eds), *British Intellectual History 1750–1950* (Cambridge, 2000) pp. 112–35.
3. Roy Strong, *And when did you last see your father? The Victorian Painter and British History* (London, 1978) pp. 145, 150.
4. For Hume's attitudes, in many ways a classic formulation of the darker view of Cromwell's rise from obscurity see David Hume, *The History of England from the Invasion of Julius Caesar to the Revolution in 1688* (6 vols, London, 1778; reprint 1983) V, pp. 452–3, 468–70.
5. Antonia Fraser, *Cromwell: Our Chief of Men* (London, 1973) p. 705.
6. Peter Gaunt, *Oliver Cromwell* (Oxford, 1996) p. 23. Much the same assessment was made in Howell, *Cromwell*, p. x.
7. Michael A.G. Haykin, *To Honour God: the Spirituality of Oliver Cromwell*, Classics of Reformed Spirituality (Dundas, Ontario, 1999) p. 20.
8. John Morrill, 'Introduction' in Morrill (ed.) *Oliver Cromwell and the English Revolution* (London, 1990) pp. 3, 14, 19. The rest of the argument here is reconstructed from his seminal essay, 'The Making of Oliver Cromwell', in the same volume pp. 19–48.
9. *Ibid.*, pp. 19–21.
10. On social mobility see Keith Wrightson, *English Society 1580–1680* (London, 1982) pp. 26–30; J.A. Sharpe, *Early Modern England: A Social History 1550–1760* (London, 1987) pp. 19, 220–1.
11. Morrill, 'The Making', p. 22.
12. In 1640 his income was modest by comparison with other MPs elected to the Long Parliament. Mary Frear Keeler, *The Long Parliament 1640–1641: A Biographical Study of Its Members* (Philadelphia, 1954) p. 26.
13. For Cromwell's election for Cambridge see Morrill, 'The Making', pp. 44–5. Morrill explores the possibility of Rich patronage. Holland was chancellor of the university. But, as Morrill concedes, the evidence is tantalizingly elusive.
14. For the declining gentry thesis of the origins of the Civil War and for Cromwell as exemplifying that group see H.R. Trevor-Roper, *The gentry, 1540–1640*, Economic History Review supplement no. 1 (Cambridge, 1953).
15. M.A. Barg, *The English Revolution of the 17th Century Through Portraits of Its Leading Figures*, translated by Cynthia Carlile (Moscow, 1990).
16. *Ibid.*, p. 194. See also pp. 6, 118, 130–6, 146–9, 153–64, 176–7, 184–5. The essential elements of the same argument were present in Christopher Hill's brilliant Historical Association pamphlet of 1958; reprinted in Hill, *Collected Essays*, vol. 3 (Brighton, 1986) pp. 68–94. It is much muted in Hill, *God's Englishman: Oliver Cromwell and the English Revolution* (London, 1970).

17. G.E. Aylmer, 'Gentlemen Levellers?', *Past and Present*, 40 (1970) pp. 120–5; John Gurney, 'Gerrard Winstanley and the Digger Movement in Walton and Cobham', *The Historical Journal*, 37:4 (1994) pp. 775–802.
18. John Morrill, *The Nature of the English Revolution* (London, 1993), part one.
19. Michael Walzer, *The Revolution of the Saints* (London, 1966); Nicholas Tyacke, *Anti-Calvinists: the Rise of English Arminianism c.1590–1640* (Oxford, 1987).
20. Christopher Hill, *Society and Puritanism in Pre-Revolutionary England* (London, 1966) ch. 1; Patrick Collinson, *The Elizabethan Puritan Movement* (London, 1967); *idem*, *The Religion of Protestants* (Oxford, 1982); *idem*, *The Birthpangs of Protestant England* (London, 1988).
21. C.H. George, 'Puritanism as History and Historiography', *Past and Present*, 41 (1968) pp. 77–104.
22. William Lamont, *Puritanism and Historical Controversy* (London, 1996).
23. R.S. Paul, *The Lord Protector: Religion and Politics in the Life of Oliver Cromwell* (London, 1955).
24. Sarah Gibbard Cook, 'The Congregational Independents and the Cromwellian Constitutions', *Church History*, 46:3 (1977) pp. 335–57.
25. For Cromwell's antiformalism see J.C. Davis, 'Cromwell's Religion', in Morrill (ed.) *Cromwell and the English Revolution*, pp. 181–208.
26. The theme of David Underdown's magisterial study *Pride's Purge* (Oxford, 1971).
27. W.C. Abbott (ed.), *Writings and Speeches of Oliver Cromwell* (4 vols, Oxford, 1988) IV, p. 452.
28. Mark Noble, *Memoirs of the Protectoral House of Cromwell* (2 vols, London, 1787) I, p. 99. Noble thought that the Hampdens were also involved.
29. *Ibid.*, p. 132; Pauline Gregg, *Oliver Cromwell* (London, 1988) p. 36; Morrill, 'The Making', pp. 42–4.
30. Morrill, 'The Making', pp. 44–5; see also Gregg, *Cromwell*, p. 50.
31. Keeler, *The Long Parliament*, p. 16.
32. One of the latter was John Williams, Bishop of Lincoln and from 1641 Archbishop of York, to whom Cromwell wrote in September 1647 typically reminding him of their kinship connection: 'I shall study to serve him for kindred's sake; among whom let not be forgotten, My Lord, Your cousin and servant, Oliver Cromwell'. Abbott (ed.), *Writings and Speeches*, I, p. 501. Keeler, *Long Parliament*, pp. 29–30; D. Brunton and D.H. Pennington, *Members of the Long Parliament* (London, 1954) pp. 31, 35, 113, 123. By 1647 the number of Cromwell's close kin in the House of Commons had risen to 23. Stanley J. Weyman, 'Oliver Cromwell's Kinfolk', *English Historical Review*, 6 (1891) pp. 56–7.
33. Weyman, 'Cromwell's Kinfolk', p. 48.
34. The best discussion of Cromwell's conversion and early religious background is now Morrill, 'The Making', especially pp. 34–6.

35. For example, six of his cousins had been imprisoned for resisting the forced loan of 1627. Howell, *Cromwell*, p. 5.
36. Abbott, *Writings and Speeches*, I, pp. 96–7.
37. *Ibid.*, I, pp. 258–9.
38. *Ibid.*, I, pp. 264–5. This letter is part of a mobilization of his cousinage against the charge that he was recruiting an army of sectaries.
39. *Ibid.*, I, pp. 287–8.
40. J.R. Jones, *Marlborough* (Cambridge, 1993) p. 10.
41. Abbott, *Writings and Speeches*, III, p. 452.
42. Jon Disbrowe (Desborough) to Cromwell, 30 September 1650 in John Nickolls (ed.), *Original Letters and Papers of State Addressed to Oliver Cromwell* (London, 1743) p. 26.

Chapter 5   Swordsman

1. John Adair, *Roundhead General: A Military Biography of Sir William Waller* (London, 1969) pp. 22, 24–5. As Adair points out, Waller's pre-civil war military experience has continued to be exaggerated.
2. Clive Holmes, *The Eastern Association in the Civil War* (Cambridge, 1974) p. 54; John Buchan, *Cromwell* (London, 1934; reprint 1970) p. 128.
3. Cf. Austin Woolrych, 'Cromwell as a Soldier', in John Morrill (ed.), *Oliver Cromwell and the English Revolution* (London, 1990) pp. 95–6.
4. See, for example, W.C. Abbott (ed.), *The Writings and Speeches of Oliver Cromwell* (4 vols, Oxford, 1988) I, pp. 262, 204, 278. My emphasis.
5. Adair, *Roundhead General*, pp. 179–80.
6. Maurice Ashley, *Cromwell's Generals* (London, 1954) pp. 21–2.
7. Holmes, *Eastern Association*, pp. 113, 177.
8. *Ibid.*, pp. 200–1.
9. *Ibid.*, pp. 202–5.
10. Woolrych, 'Cromwell as a Soldier', p. 96.
11. Holmes, *Eastern Association*, pp. 206–7.
12. John Bruce and David Masson (eds), *The Quarrel Between The Earl of Manchester and Oliver Cromwell*, Camden Society, New Series, XII (London, 1875) pp. lxvii–lxx, 78–95, 96–99.
13. *Ibid.*, pp. lxxxi, 59–70.
14. Abbott (ed.), *Writings and Speeches*, I, pp. 314–15.
15. A good account of these deliberations and their outcome is given in Mark A. Kishlansky, *The Rise of the New Model Army* (Cambridge, 1979) ch. 2.
16. Ian Gentles, *The New Model Army in England, Ireland and Scotland 1645–1653* (Oxford, 1992) p. 25.
17. Kishlansky, *Rise of the New Model*, p. 62.
18. William Waller made much the same points as Cromwell but in more muted terms.
19. For example see Austin Woolrych, 'Cromwell as Soldier', p. 104.

When he was Lord Protector, Cromwell kept an open table at a weekly dinner for any army officer who happened to be in London. It was the team player maintaining his military networks.

20. For example by John Buchan, *Cromwell*, pp. 96, 158, 400; Sir Charles Firth, *Oliver Cromwell and the Rule of the Puritans in England* (Oxford, 1966) pp. 29–30. Cromwell's confession, in August 1655, to the Swedish ambassador that Gustavus Adolphus had been his hero is little more than a Protestant conventionality. See Michael Roberts (ed.), *Swedish Diplomats at Cromwell's Court*, Camden, Fourth Series, 36, Royal Historical Society (London, 1998) p. 133.

21. See, for example. *The Swedish Intelligencer* (1632); cf. Henry Bynneman, *All the famous Battels that have been fought in our age throughout the world* (1578?); *idem, The second part of the book of Battailes, fought in our age* (1587) which cover battles of the French wars of religion and the revolt of the Netherlands and were much studied by those interested in the European Protestant cause.

22. Barry Coward, *Oliver Cromwell* (London, 1991) p. 27.

23. Firth, *Oliver Cromwell*, p. 88.

24. Buchan, *Cromwell*, pp. 158–66.

25. Bruce and Masson (eds), *The Quarrel Between Manchester and Cromwell*, p. lxxxviii.

26. The argument here is indebted to the discussion of his campaigns in 1643 by Clive Holmes, *Eastern Association*, pp. 70–5.

27. Quoted in Roger Howell, Jr, *Cromwell* (London, 1977) p. 70.

28. Keith Lindley and David Scott (eds), *The Journal of Thomas Juxon, 1644–1647*, Camden, Fifth Series, 13 (Cambridge, 1999) p. 80.

29. Abbott (ed.), *Writings and Speeches*, I, p. 365.

30. Cf. Gentles, *New Model Army*, p. 354. See also James Scott Wheeler, *Cromwell in Ireland* (Dublin, 1999).

31. Ably described in John D. Grainger, *Cromwell Against the Scots: The Last Anglo-Scottish War 1650–1652* (East Lothian, Scotland, 1997).

32. Gentles, *New Model Army*, p. 388.

33. Barry Coward, *Oliver Cromwell* (London, 1991) pp. 73–4.

34. Abbott (ed.), *Writings and Speeches*, II, p. 142. Cromwell to William Lenthall, 14 October 1649.

35. See, for example, Derek Hirst, *England in Conflict, 1603–1660: Kingdom, Community, Commonwealth* (London, 1999) pp. 262–3.

36. Abbott (ed.), *Writings and Speeches*, II, p. 127. Cromwell to Lenthall, 17 September 1649. He was, of course, writing this after Drogheda but before Wexford.

37. See Jason McElligott, *Cromwell: Our Chief of Enemies* (Dundalk, 1994) especially p. 36. In the 1940s, Irish schoolchildren were taught that Cromwell in Ireland was responsible for 'one of the most horrible massacres in history'. *Ibid.*, p. 32.

38. Tom Reilly, *Cromwell: An Honourable Enemy: The Untold Story of the Cromwellian Invasion of Ireland* (Dingle, County Derry, 1999) pp. 3, 7.

39. *Ibid.*, pp. 51, 56.

40. *Ibid.*, pp. 74–81 and ch. 3.
41. *Ibid.*, ch. 5. See also Woolrych, 'Cromwell as a Soldier', p. 111.
42. S.R. Gardiner, *History of the Great Civil War 1642–1649* (New York, 1965) II, pp. 362–5; Gaunt, *Oliver Cromwell*, pp. 64–5; Howell, *Cromwell*, pp. 78–9. Gardiner has 100 killed, 300 taken prisoner.
43. Abbtt (ed.), *Writings and Speeches*, I, p. 387; Cromwell to Lenthall, 14 October 1645.
44. Hirst, *England in Conflict*, p. 263.
45. Hickman to Cromwell, 16 November 1650 in John Nickolls (ed.), *Originall Letters and Papers of State Addressed to Oliver Cromwell* (London, 1743) pp. 29, 31. Hickman believed, like James Harrington, that, if the republic was to prosper, decapitating the King was not enough. The foundations of society, the distribution of land, must also be changed.
46. Abbott (ed.), *Writings and Speeches*, II, p. 142.
47. *Ibid.*, II, pp. 127, 142, 186. My emphasis.
48. David Stevenson. 'Cromwell, Scotland and Ireland', in Morrill (ed.), *Cromwell and the English Revolution*, pp. 171–80. In a sensibly balanced assessment of Cromwell in Ireland, James Scott Wheeler has pointed out that the harsh policy looking for a speedy end to the conflict, has to be balanced against the tendency of atrocities to lead to irreconcilable conflict. Even in military terms, massacres, like Drogheda and Wexford, could be seen as counterproductive. Wheeler, *Cromwell in Ireland*, p. 162.

Chapter 6 Man of God

1. W.C. Abbott (ed.), *Writings and Speeches of Oliver Cromwell* (4 vols, Oxford, 1988) IV, p. 11.
2. S.R. Gardiner (ed.), *Constitutional Documents of the Puritan Revolution 1625–1660* (Oxford, 1906) p. 321.
3. Abbott (ed.), *Writings and Speeches*, I, p. 512. Cromwell was one of the tellers in favour of the motion, an indication that he was one of the movers of it.
4. For a discussion of the biblicism of this letter see Robert S. Paul, *The Lord Protector: Religion and Politics in the Life of Oliver Cromwell* (London, 1955) Appendix II, pp. 399–400; John Morrill, 'King-killing No Murder: Cromwell in 1648', *Cromwelliana 1998*, p. 15.
5. Abbott (ed.), *Writings and Speeches*, III, pp. 434–5, 436–7, 442. Michael Walzer, *Exodus and Revolution* (New York, 1985) pp. 3–4.
6. Abbott (ed.), *Writings and Speeches*, III, pp. 579–93; IV, pp. 260–79; D.J. Trela, *A History of Carlyle's Oliver Cromwell's Letters and Speeches* (New York, 1992) p. 131.
7. Abbott (ed.), *Writings and Speeches*, III, p. 65; Morrill, 'King-killing No Murder', pp. 15–16.
8. Abbott (ed.), *Writings and Speeches*, IV, p. 473.
9. 'God did tempt Abraham'. Genesis xxii:I.
10. Patrick Collinson, *The Birthpangs of Protestant England: Religious and Cultural Change in the Sixteenth and Seventeenth Centuries* (London, 1988) p. 154.

11. Cornelius Burgess, *The First Sermon Preached to the Honourable House of Commons now Assembled in Parliament at their Publique Fast, November 17, 1640* (1641) p. 34.

12. Stephen Marshall, *A Sermon Preached before the Honourable House of Commons ... At their Publique Fast, November 17, 1640* (1641) pp. 25, 24, 26.

13. Stephen Marshall, *A Peace Offering to God* (1641).

14. Edmund Calamy, *England's Looking-Glass* (1642) pp. 3, 6.

15. Jeremiah Burroughs, *Sion's Joy* (1641) A2.

16. Cornelius Burgess, *Another Sermon* (1641) p. 1.

17. John Arrowsmith, *The Covenanting Avenging Sword Brandished* (1643).

18. Simon Ash, *The Best Refuge for the Most Oppressed* (1642) p. 25; Edward Corbett, *God's Providence* (1643).

19. Jeremiah Whittacker, *Eironopolis: Christ the Settlement of Unsettled Times* (1648) pp. 27, 21, 68.

20. Peter Sterry, *The Clouds in which Christ Comes* (1648) pp. 38, 47–8.

21. Abbott (ed.) *Writings and Speeches*, II, p. 127.

22. John Nickolls (ed.), *Original Letters* (1743) pp. 24–6.

23. Derek Wilson, *The King and the Gentleman* (London, 1999) p. 346.

24. People of New England to the Lord General Cromwell, 31 December 1650, Nickolls (ed.), *Original Letters*, pp. 44–5.

25. Erberry to Cromwell, 19 July 1652, *ibid.*, p. 88.

26. Cromwell to Generals Blake and Montagu, 28 April 1656, Abbott (ed.), *Writings and Speeches*, IV, pp. 148–9.

27. Cromwell to Lieutenant-Colonel Wilks, January 1655, *ibid.*, III, p. 572.

28. *Ibid.*, III, p. 53. My emphasis.

29. *Ibid.*, III, pp. 53–4.

30. *Ibid.*, III, p. 285.

31. *Ibid.*, IV, p. 473.

32. *Ibid.*, IV, p. 277. Speech opening Parliament, 17 September 1656.

33. *Ibid.*, II, p. 37. Speech to the General Council of the Army at Whitehall, 23 March 1649.

34. *Ibid.*, I, pp. 341, 377.

35. Nickolls (ed.), *Original Letters* (1743) p. 19.

36. Alan MacFarlane (ed.), *The Diary of Ralph Josselin 1616–1683* (Oxford, 1976) entry for 31 December 1650.

37. Norwich to Nicholas, June 1655, in George F. Warner (ed.), *The Nicholas Papers: Correspondence of Sir Edward Nicholas, Secretary of State*, Camden Society: New Series, 50 (1892) p. 318.

38. Sir Charles Firth, *Oliver Cromwell and the Rule of the Puritans in England* (Oxford, 1966) p. 131.

39. Blair Worden, 'Providence and Politics in Cromwellian England', *Past and Present*, 109 (1985) pp. 55–99.

40. Abbott (ed.), *Writings and Speeches*, I, p. 644. For Vane's reply see *ibid.*, n. 99.

41. Cromwell to Lord Wharton, 2 September 1648, *ibid.*, I p. 646.

42. Cromwell to William Lenthall, 11 July 1648, *ibid.*, I, p. 621.

43. Cromwell to Robert Hammond, 6 November 1648, *ibid.*, I, pp. 676–7.
44. Cromwell to Hammond, 25 November 1648, *ibid.*, 1, pp. 696–9.
45. Nickolls (ed.), *Original Letters*, pp. 72–4.
46. Abbott (ed.), *Writings and Speeches*, III, pp. 225–8.
47. For a searching treatment of this episode see Blair Worden, 'Oliver Cromwell and the Sin of Achan', in Derek Beales and Geoffrey Best (eds), *History, Society and the Churches* (Cambridge, 1985) pp. 125–45. Achan brought down the wrath of God upon the Israelites, after their successful capture of Jericho, by taking plunder, 'the accursed thing'.
48. William Hickman to Cromwell, 16 November 1650, Nickolls (ed.), *Original Letters*, pp. 30–1.
49. Cromwell to Lenthall, 20 August 1650, Abbott (ed.), *Writings and Speeches*, I, p. 638.
50. *Ibid.*, II, p. 340.
51. For a discussion of these themes see J.C. Davis, 'Against Formality: One Aspect of the English Revolution', *Transactions of the Royal Historical Society*, sixth series, III (1993) pp. 265–88.
52. John Owen, *Complete Collection of Sermons* (1721) pp. 73, 221–2, 562–5.
53. Sterry, *Clouds in which Christ Comes*, pp. 47–8.
54. For a wider discussion of the Cromwellian church see Davis, 'Cromwell's Religion' and Anthony Fletcher, 'Oliver Cromwell and the Godly Nation', in Morrill (ed.), *Cromwell and the English Revolution*, pp. 209–33; Claire Cross, 'The Church in England 1646–1660', in G.E. Aylmer (ed.), *The Interregnum: the Quest for Settlement 1646–1660* (London, 1972) pp. 99–120.
55. From *A Proclamation Prohibiting the Disturbance of Ministers*, 15 February 1645, Abbott (ed.), *Writings and Speeches*, III, p. 626. On the theme of liberty of conscience see Davis, 'Cromwell's Religion'; Blair Worden, 'Toleration and the Cromwellian Protectorate', in W.J. Sheils (ed.), *Persecution and Toleration: Studies in Church History 21* (Oxford, 1984) pp. 199–233.
56. Cromwell to George Willingham, February 1641, Abbott (ed.), *Writings and Speeches*, I, p. 125.
57. *Ibid.*, I, p. 294.
58. *Ibid.*, I, p. 360 and n. 130.
59. *Ibid.*, I, pp. 377–8 and n. 172.
60. *Ibid.*, I, p. 534.
61. *Ibid.*, III, p. 89.
62. *Ibid.*, III, pp. 461, 89, 92, 225–7, 436, 459, 615, 756; IV, pp. 221, 267, 278. For examples of Cromwell's attempts to conciliate the sects see *ibid.*, III, pp. 116, 119, 125–6, 373.
63. *Ibid.*, III, pp. 459, 586.
64. Davis, 'Cromwell's Religion', pp. 196–9.
65. Derek Hirst, 'The Failure of Godly Rule in the English Republic', *Past and Present*, 132 (1991) pp. 33–66.
66. Fletcher, 'Oliver Cromwell and the Godly Nation'. For continuity in local government administration see Stephen Roberts, 'Local

Government Reform in England and Wales during the Interregnum: A Survey', in Ivan Roots (ed.), *Into Another Mould: Aspects of the Interregnum* (Exeter, 1981) pp. 24–41.
67. Abbott (ed.), *Writings and Speeches*, II, p. 104.
68. *Ibid.*, III, p. 64.
69. *Ibid.*, II, p. 215.

Chapter 7 The politician

1. W.C. Abbott (ed.), *Writings and Speeches of Oliver Cromwell* (4 vols, Oxford, 1988) I, p. 128. For the Protestation see S.R. Gardiner, *The Constitutional Documents of the Puritan Revolution* (Oxford, 1906) pp. 155–6.
2. Cromwell to Mr Storie, 11 January 1635, in Abbott (ed.), *Writings and Speeches*, I, p. 80.
3. *Ibid.*, I, p. 519.
4. John Adamson, 'Oliver Cromwell and the Long Parliament', in John Morrill (ed.), *Oliver Cromwell and the English Revolution* (London, 1990) pp. 49–92.
5. Cromwell to Mr. Willingham, February 1641, Abbott (ed.), *Writings and Speeches*, I, p. 125.
6. Cromwell appears to have rejected the title of King and a hereditary protectorship as first envisaged in the Instrument.
7. George F. Warner (ed.), *The Nicholas Papers: Correspondence of Sir Edward Nicholas, Secretary of State* (2 vols, London, 1886/1892) I, p. ix.
8. John Buchan, *Cromwell* (London, 1934/1970) p. 403.
9. Cf. *ibid.*, p. 425. 'Now, as after Worcester, he could have made himself King.'
10. Johann Sommerville, 'Oliver Cromwell and English political thought', in Morrill (ed.), *Cromwell and the English Revolution*, p. 255.
11. Nicholas to Edward Hyde, 8 December 1653, Warner (ed.), *Nicholas Papers*, II, p. 32.
12. Abbott (ed.), *Writings and Speeches*, III, pp. 591–2.
13. John Morrill, 'King Oliver?' in *Cromwelliana 1981–1982*, pp. 22–4. Morrill's argument is, in part, that members of the army might not have liked the prospect of Cromwell assuming the royal title but they would have come to terms with it.
14. As it was by S.R. Gardiner, *History of the Great Civil War 1642–1649* (4 vols, New York, 1965) II, pp. 266–7.
15. Cf. Peter Gaunt, *Oliver Cromwell* (Oxford, 1996) p. 102 for the speculation that this was not coincidental. The timing of his arrival in London is not entirely clear and there is some inconclusive evidence that he was there from at least 2 December.
16. See, for example, [Richard Overton], *The Hunting of the Foxes ... or the Grandie-Decievers Unmasked* (1649) in Don M. Wolfe (ed.), *Leveller Manifestoes of the Puritan Revolution* (London, 1944/1967) pp. 358–85.

17. Abbott (ed.), *Writings and Speeches*, II, p. 182.
18. *Ibid.*, II, p. 472.
19. *Ibid.*, II, pp. 506–7.
20. *Ibid.*, II, pp. 587–92; Ruth Spalding (ed.), *The Diary of Bulstrode Whitelocke 1605–1675*, Records of Social and Economic History, New Series, 13 (Oxford, 1990) pp. 281–2.
21. Thomas Birch (ed.), *A Collection of the State Papers of John Thurloe, Esq.*, (7 vols, London, 1742) II, p. 46.
22. *Ibid.*, II, pp. 214–15. For his identity as an agitator in 1647 and former member of Cromwell's own troop see C.H. Firth (ed.), *The Clarke Papers* (2 vols, London, 1992) I, pp. 430–3.
23. P.H. Hardacre, 'William Allen, Cromwellian Agitator and "Fanatic"', *The Baptist Quarterly*, New Series, 19 (1961–2) p. 301.
24. Michael Roberts (ed.), *Swedish Diplomats at Cromwell's Court 1655–1656*, Camden, Fourth Series, 36 (London, 1998) pp. 75–7, 98–9, 122.
25. John Nickolls (ed.), *Original Letters and Papers* (London, 1743) pp. 141, 139–40.
26. Abbott (ed.), *Writings and Speeches*, IV, p. 472.
27. Speech to army officers, 27 February 1657. B. L. Add. Mss. 6125 fo. 285. On Cromwell's personal uninterest in the crown and regality see Laura Lunger Knoppers, *Constructing Cromwell: Ceremony, Portrait and Print 1645–1661* (Cambridge, 2000) pp. 56, 70, 118.
28. Abbott (ed.), *Writings and Speeches*, IV, p. 705.
29. C.H. Firth (ed.), *The Memoirs of Edmund Ludlow* (2 vols, Oxford, 1894) 1, p. 435.
30. *Ibid.*, II, pp. 7–8.
31. Derek Hirst, 'The Lord Protector 1653–1658', in Morrill (ed.), *Oliver Cromwell and the English Revolution*, p. 124; Barbara Taft, 'The Humble Petition of Several Colonels of the Army*: Causes, Character, and Results of Military Opposition to Cromwell's Protectorate', *Huntington Library Quarterly*, 42 (1978–9) pp. 15–41.
32. Cromwell speech to Parliament, 22 January 1655 in Abbott (ed.), *Writings and Speeches*, III, p. 590.
33. Austin Woolrych, *Soldiers and Statesmen: The General Council of the Army and its Debates 1647–1648* (Oxford, 1987) pp. 35–8.
34. *Ibid.*, pp. 98–103.
35. For the text see Gardiner (ed.), *Constitutional Documents*, pp. 316–26.
36. Woolrych, *Soldiers and Statesmen*, p. 259. This is now the indispensable account of the debates.
37. Roger Howell, Jr, *Cromwell* (London, 1977) p. 105.
38. Adamson. 'Cromwell and the Long Parliament', p. 76.
39. *Ibid.*, p. 82.

Chapter 8   Statebuilder?

1. Samuel Rawson Gardiner, *Cromwell's Place in History: Founded on Six Lectures Delivered in the University of Oxford* (London, 1897) pp. 103–4.

2. John Morley, *Oliver Cromwell* (London, 1904) p. 6.

3. British Library: Landsdowne. Mss. 821 fo. 314 and Add. Mss. 6125 fo. 285.

4. For recent discussions of statebuilding in England see John Brewer, *Sinews of Power: War, Money and the English State, 1688–1783* (New York, 1989); M.J. Braddick, *The Nerves of State: Taxation and National Finances 1558–1714* (Manchester, 1996); James Scott Wheeler, *The Making of a World Power: War and the Military Revolution in Seventeenth-Century England* (Stroud, Gloucestershire, 1999). Brewer would place the formation of the military/fiscal state in England after 1688. Wheeler argues that in terms of a professional army and navy, 'modern' forms of taxation, state credit and administration, the process was an evolutionary one commencing in the later sixteenth century. In Wheeler's account the Cromwellian period is a significant step in this evolution.

5. A debate ably summarized in Wheeler, *Making of a World Power*, ch. 1.

6. A third alternative, the radical redefinition of the political nation, had been decisively and forcibly rejected by 1652; ironically perhaps by decisions and actions taken in 1649.

7. Peter Gaunt, *Oliver Cromwell* (Oxford, 1996) p. 6.

8. Derek Hirst, *England in Conflict, 1603–1660: Kingdom, Community, Commonwealth* (London, 1999) p. 285.

9. See Peter Gaunt, '"The Single Person's Confidants and Dependants"? Oliver Cromwell and the Protectoral Councillors', *The Historical Journal*, 32:3 (1989) pp. 537–60; *idem*, 'Cromwell's Purge? Exclusions and the First Protectorate Parliament', *Parliamentary History*, 6:1 (1987) pp. 1–22; *idem, Cromwell*, pp. 162–3.

10. Cf. Ronald Hutton, *The British Republic* (London, 2000) pp. 67–9. Barry Coward, *Oliver Cromwell* (London, 1992) pp. 126–7.

11. G.E. Aylmer. *The State's Servants: The Civil Service of the English Republic 1649–1660* (London, 1973). For a recent restatement of the argument that we err in placing too much emphasis on institutional/constitutional statebuilding in this period see Jonathan Scott, *England's Troubles: Seventeenth-century English Political Instability in European Context* (Cambridge, 2000).

12. W.C. Abbott (ed.), *The Writings and Speeches of Oliver Cromwell* (4 vols, Oxford, 1988) IV, p. 720.

13. J.C. Davis, 'Oliver Cromwell: Peacemaker', *Cromwelliana: The Journal of the Cromwell Association* (1998) pp. 2–7.

14. Mark Kishlansky, *A Monarchy Transformed: Britain 1603–1714* (London, 1996) p. 210.

15. Abbott (ed.), *Writings and Speeches*, I, pp. 377, 690.

16. *Ibid.*, III, pp. 452, 401.

17. The text examined here is to be found at *ibid.*, I, pp. 539–64.

18. John Morrill, 'Cromwell and his Contemporaries', in Morrill (ed.), *Oliver Cromwell and the English Revolution* (London, 1990) p. 281.

19. Perhaps the most famous instance was his consultation with

Lambert, Fleetwood and Whalley immediately before the battle of Dunbar. But see also the comments on Cromwell's collaborative approach to military command in James Scott Wheeler, *Cromwell in Ireland* (Dublin, 1999) p. 161. Peter Gaunt has also emphasized this quality in Cromwell's dealings with the Protectoral Council. Peter Gaunt, '"The Single Person's Confidants and Dependents"?' pp. 537–60.

20. David Underdown, *Pride's Purge* (Oxford, 1971). See also Abbott (ed.), *Writings and Speeches*, II, pp. 6–7.
21. David Katz, *Philo-Semitism and the Readmission of the Jews to England 1603–1655* (Oxford, 1982) pp. 195, 203–24.
22. R.S. Paul, *The Lord Protector: Religion and Politics in the Life of Oliver Cromwell* (London, 1955) p. 329, n. 2.
23. S.R. Gardiner (ed.), *The Constitutional Documents of the Puritan Revolution 1625–1660* (Oxford, 1906) p. 269.
24. The text of the letter of 6 November 1648 is at Abbott (ed.), *Writings and Speeches*, I, pp. 676–8.
25. The text of the letter of 25 November 1648 may be found at *ibid.*, I, pp. 696–9.
26. The classic text was Romans 13.
27. The text of the declaration is at Abbott (ed.), *Writings and Speeches*, III, pp. 225–8.
28. *Ibid.*, II, pp. 102–4.
29. For some indication of the possibility see the officers' petition of 12 July 1649, in *ibid.*, II, p. 93.
30. Derek Hirst, 'The Failure of Godly Rule in the English Republic', *Past and Present*, 132 (1991) pp. 33–6. See also *idem*, 'The Failure of National Reformation in the 1650s', in Gordon J. Schochet (ed.), *Religion, Resistance and Civil War*, The Folger Institute for the History of British Political Thought: Proceedings, vol. 3 (Washington, 1990) pp. 51–62.
31. This paragraph owes much to Christopher Durston, '"Settling the Hearts and Quieting the Minds of All Good People": The Major-Generals and the Puritan Minorities of Interregnum England', *History*, 85:278 (2000) pp. 247–67. (The quotations are from pp. 249 and 265.) See also *idem*, 'The Fall of Cromwell's Major-Generals', *English Historical Review*, 113 (1998) pp. 18–37; Anthony Fletcher, 'Oliver Cromwell and the Localities: Problems of Consent', in Schochet (ed.), *Religion, Resistance and Civil War*, pp. 13–19; *idem*, 'Oliver Cromwell and the Godly Nation', in Morrill (ed.), *Oliver Cromwell and the English Revolution*, pp. 209–33.
32. Derek Hirst, 'The English Republic and the Meaning of Britain', *The Journal of Modern History*, 66:3 (1994) pp. 451–86. Hirst estimates that 42,000 out of 53,000 English troops were serving outside of England and Wales in 1654, predominantly in Scotland and Ireland. Scotland's garrison was at a net cost of £130,000 per annum with a similar amount required for Ireland.
33. See David R. Armitage, 'The British Empire and the Civic Tradition 1656–1742', PhD thesis, Cambridge University, 1992.
34. Cf. Sean Kelsey, *Inventing a Republic: The Political Culture of the*

English Commonwealth 1649–1653 (Manchester, 1997); Roy Sherwood, *Oliver Cromwell: King in All But Name 1653–1658* (Stroud, Gloucestershire, 1997).
35. 22 April 1653, Abbott (ed.), *Writings and Speeches*, III, pp. 6–7.
36. For the text of the speech see *ibid.*, III, pp. 52–66. The Instrument (*ibid.*, p. 67) gave authority to the Assembly to sit until 3 November 1654, to nominate their successors and 'to take care for a succession in Government'.
37. *Ibid.*, III, p. 61.
38. See Gaunt, *Cromwell*, pp. 176–7.
39. The text of the speech of 4 September 1654 is at Abbott (ed.), *Writings and Speeches*, III, pp. 434–41.
40. The monthly assessment was reduced from £120,000 to £90,000 and in December 1654 to £60,000. Wheeler, *Making of a World Power*, p. 193.
41. Cromwell is here referring to the sermon which had been preached to members earlier in the day by Thomas Goodwin.
42. In a sermon preached at All Hallows on 5 January 1657, Feake argued that greater division was the only way of keeping away from anti-Christ and out of Babylon. See Thomas Birch (ed.), *A Collection of the State Papers of John Thurloe* (7 vols, London, 1742) V, p. 758.
43. *Ibid.*, IV, p. 348.
44. The text of the speech is at Abbott (ed.), *Writings and Speeches*, IV, pp. 451–62.
45. Text of the speech at *ibid.*, III, pp. 579–93.
46. The text of the speech is at *ibid.*, IV, pp. 260–79.
47. Wheeler, *Making of a World Power*, p. 193.
48. However much the basis of his consensual support may have moved, his commitment to civil and religious liberty remained intact. See the oath he took at his second installation and his speech to Parliament on 22 January 1658. Abbott (ed.), *Writings and Speeches*, IV, pp. 565, 705.
49. See Sir Edward Nicholas to Sir Richard Browne, from Utrecht, 5 July 1650, in George F. Warner (ed.), *The Nicholas Papers: Correspondence of Sir Edward Nicholas, Secretary of State*, 2 vols, Camden Society, New Series, 40, 50 (London, 1886, 1892) II, p. 187.
50. *Ibid.*, I, p. 268. See also pp. 283–4, 310.
51. *Ibid.*, II, pp. 32, 42, 64.

Chapter 9 Conclusion: Oliver Cromwell and the English Revolution

1. Christopher Hill's voluminous writings contain various versions of this theme; from *The English Revolution: 1640* (London, 1955) to *God's Englishman: Oliver Cromwell and the English Revolution* (London, 1970) to *The World Turned Upside Down: Radical Ideas*

During the English Revolution (Harmondsworth, 1975). M.A. Barg, *The English Revolution of the 17th Century Through Portraits of Its Leading Figures* translated by Cynthia Carlile (Moscow, 1990).

2. See also his observation in a speech to Parliament on 17 September 1656: 'we would keep up the nobility and gentry'. W.C. Abbott (ed.), *The Writings and Speeches of Oliver Cromwell* (4 vols, Oxford, 1988), IV, p. 273.

3. Two prime examples of the illumination to be gained by such narrative are Austin Woolrych, *Soldiers and Statesmen: The General Council of the Army and its Debates, 1647–1648* (Oxford, 1987); and Anthony Fletcher, *The Outbreak of the English Civil War* (London, 1971).

4. The text of the Solemn League and Covenant is in S.R. Gardiner, *The Constitutional Documents of the Puritan Revolution 1635–1660* (Oxford, 1906) pp. 267–71. See also Cromwell's reported comment of 20 October 1647 that it was the intention of the army from the beginning 'to serve the King and establish the power of the monarchy'. Abbott (ed.), *Writings and Speeches*, I, p. 512.

5. See his speech to a parliamentary committee 21 April 1657. 'Somewhat that is indeed exceedingly past my understanding, for I have as little skill in Arithmetic as I have in the Law.' *Ibid.*, IV, p. 496.

Further reading

The most accessible and still indispensable introduction to Cromwell's own words remains W.C. Abbott (ed.), *The Writings and Speeches of Oliver Cromwell* (4 volumes, Cambridge, Massachusetts, 1937–1947) which was reprinted by Oxford University Press in 1988. The limitations of Abbott's edition are comprehensively set forth in John Morrill, 'Textualizing and contextualizing Cromwell', *The Historical Journal*, 33:3 (1990) pp. 629–39. The very useful Ivan Roots (ed.), *Speeches of Oliver Cromwell* (London, 1989) fell inexplicably out of print in the year after Cromwell's quartercentenary.

The best currently available biographies are Barry Coward, *Oliver Cromwell* (London, 1991) and, with the same title, Peter Gaunt (Oxford, 1996). Both are trenchant, well informed and strongly argued. Also impressive is Roger Howell, *Cromwell* (London, 1977) and worth reading, amongst the popular biographies, are Anthonia Fraser, *Cromwell: Our Chief of Men* (London, 1973) (also published as *Cromwell: The Lord Protector* (New York, 1973)) and John Buchan, *Cromwell* (London, 1934). Now dated but worth reading as the work of a great and influential historian is Christopher Hill's *God's Englishman: Oliver Cromwell and the English Revolution* (London, 1970). The best introduction to recent scholarship on aspects of Cromwell's life, career and contemporary reputation is the collection of essays by various authorities edited by John Morrill under the title *Oliver Cromwell and the English Revolution* (London, 1990).

In what remains a difficult period to keep abreast of, there are now some excellent general accounts which relate the flow of events to recent historical analysis and interpretation, much of it, inevitably, controversial. For the period as a whole, Barry

Coward's *The Stuart Age: England 1603–1714* (2nd edition, London, 1999) is exemplary. Mark Kishlansky's *A Monarchy Transformed: Britain 1603–1714* offers an exhilarating narrative. For a magisterial and enormously stimulating reinterpretation of the period as a whole and within a European context see Jonathan Scott, *England's Troubles: Seventeenth-Century English Political Instability in European Context* (Cambridge, 2000). A lucid and reliable guide to the fascinating complexities of the 1640s and 1650s is Derek Hirst in his *England in Conflict 1603–1660: Kingdom, Community, Commonwealth* (London, 1999).

For his contemporary reputation the obvious starting point is John Morrill, 'Cromwell and his contemporaries' in Morrill (ed.), *Cromwell and the English Revolution*, pp. 259–81. Laura Lunger Knoppers provides a stimulating reading of contemporary visual, ritual and textual representations of Cromwell in *Constructing Cromwell: Ceremony, Portrait and Print 1645–1661* (Cambridge, 2000). She also provides valuable bibliographical guidance. Essays on Cromwell's reputation over a long span of time are to be found in R.C. Richardson (ed.), *Images of Oliver Cromwell: Essays for and by Roger Howell, Jr* (Manchester, 1993). The development of Cromwell's reputation in North America and Britain is given interesting, comparative coverage in Peter Karsten, *Patriot-Heroes in England and America: Political Symbolism and Changing Values over Three Centuries* (Madison, Winconsin, 1978). D.J. Trela provides a broad perspective for the mid-nineteenth-century reinstatement of Cromwell in *A History of Carlyle's 'Oliver Cromwell's Letters and Speeches'* (New York, 1992). One of the outstanding works of recent historiographical literature, containing a seminal chapter on Cromwell, is Timothy Lang's *The Victorians and the Stuart Heritage: Interpretations of a Discordant Past* (Cambridge, 1995).

On Cromwell's early life see the indispensable John Morrill, 'The Making of Oliver Cromwell', in Morrill (ed.), *Cromwell and the English Revolution*. For the military background the strong collection of essays and the bibliographical suggestions in John Kenyon and Jane Ohlmeyer (eds), *The Civil Wars: A Military History of England, Scotland and Ireland* (New York, 1998) are now the starting points. Charles Carlton in *Going to the Wars: The Experience of the British Civil Wars* (London, 1994) brings home the reality of civil war in an attempt to weigh the human and social costs. Clive Holmes, *The Eastern Association in the English Civil War* (London, 1974) remains the established authority on the theatre of Cromwell's early military activity. An account of the origins of the New Model and a corrective to much mythology about its early character is to be found in Mark Kishlansky, *The Rise of the New Model Army* (Cambridge, 1979). The definitive account of that army is now Ian Gentles, *The New Model Army in England, Ireland and Scotland 1645–1653* (Oxford, 1992).

On Cromwell in Ireland see the relevant chapters in T.W. Moody, F.X. Martin and F.J. Byrne (eds), *A New History of Ireland*, vol. III *Early Modern Ireland, 1534–1691* (New York, 1976) and Toby Barnard, *Cromwellian Ireland: English Government and Reform in Ireland, 1649–1660* (New York, 1975). A revisionist account of Cromwell's military conduct in Ireland is given by Tom Reilly, *Cromwell: An Honourable Enemy: The Untold Story of the Cromwellian Invasion of Ireland* (Dingle, County Derry, 1999). The story of the Scots campaigns is ably told in John D. Grainger, *Cromwell Against the Scots: The Last Anglo-Scottish War 1650–1652* (East Lothian, Scotland, 1997). F.D. Dow, *Cromwellian Scotland, 1651–1660* (Edinburgh, 1979) remains useful.

On Cromwell's religion the work of Blair Worden is indispensable: 'Toleration and the Cromwellian Protectorate', in W.J. Shiels (ed.), *Persecution and Toleration: Studies in Church History*, 21 (Oxford, 1984) pp. 199–233; 'Providence and politics in Cromwellian England', *Past and Present*, 109 (1985) pp. 55–99; 'Oliver Cromwell and the sin of Achan', in Derek Beales and Geoffrey Best (eds), *History, Society and the Churches* (Cambridge, 1985) pp. 125–45. See also J.C. Davis, 'Cromwell's religion' in Morrill (ed.), *Cromwell and the English Revolution*, pp. 181–208.

Cromwell's political life still requires authoritative and comprehensive treatment. A start is made in John Adamson, 'Oliver Cromwell in the Long Parliament' in Morrill (ed.), *Cromwell and the English Revolution*, pp. 49–82. A fuller examination must await Blair Worden's much anticipated biography. In the meantime valuable background is provided in Austin Woolrych, *Soldiers and Statesmen: The General Council of the Army and Its Debates* (Oxford, 1987); Robert Ashton, *Counter-Revolution: The Second Civil War and its Origins* (New Haven, 1994); David Underdown, *Pride's Purge* (Oxford, 1971); Blair Worden, *The*

Rump Parliament (Cambridge, 1974) and Austin Woolrych, *Commonwealth to Protectorate* (Oxford, 1982). For the Protectorate, valuable work has been done by Peter Gaunt, Derek Hirst, Anthony Fletcher and Christopher Durston. See: Gaunt, ' "The Single Person's Confidents and Dependents"? Oliver Cromwell and his Protectoral Councillors', *The Historical Journal*, 32:3 (1989) pp. 537–60; *idem*, 'Cromwell's Purge? Exclusions and the First Protectorate Parliament', *Parliamentary History*, 6:1 (1987) pp. 1–22; Hirst, 'The failure of Godly Rule in the English Republic', *Past and Present*, 132 (1991) pp. 33–6; *idem*, 'The failure of National Reformation in the 1650s' in Gordon J. Schochet (ed.), *Religion, Resistance and Civil War* (Washington, 1990) pp. 51–62; *idem*, 'The English Republic and the Meaning of Britain', *The Journal of Modern History*, 66:3 (1994) pp. 451–86; Fletcher, 'Oliver Cromwell and the Godly Nation', in Morrill (ed.), *Cromwell and the English Revolution*, pp. 209–33; *idem*, 'Oliver Cromwell and the Localities: problems of consent', in Schochet (ed.), *Religion, Resistance and Civil War*, pp. 13–19; Durston, ' "Settling the Hearts and Quieting the Minds of the Good People": The Major-Generals and the Puritan Minorities of Interregnum England', *History*, 85:278 (2000) pp. 247–67; *idem*, 'The Fall of Cromwell's Major-Generals', *English Historical Review*, 113 (1998) pp. 18–37. Protectoral foreign policy is treated by Steven Pincus, *Protestantism and Patriotism: Ideologies and the Making of English Foreign Policy 1650–1668* (Cambridge, 1996) and by Timothy Venning, *Cromwellian Foreign Policy* (New York, 1995). The Protectorate lacks a good, modern, synthetic history embracing Council, Parliament, the localities and the sinews of state as well as the Lord Protector's vexed relationship with the judiciary.

Chronology 1599–1658

1599
25 April   Oliver Cromwell born in Huntingdon.
29 April   Baptized: St John the Baptist, Huntingdon.

1616
23 April   Registered at Sidney Sussex College, Cambridge as a fellow commoner.

1617
24 June   Death of Cromwell's father; Cromwell left Cambridge.

1620
22 August   Cromwell marries Elizabeth Bourchier.

1621   Birth of son Robert.

1623   Birth of son Oliver.

1624   Birth of daughter Bridget.

1626   Birth of son Richard.

1627   The Earl of Manchester purchases Hinchingbrooke.

1628   Birth of son Henry.
Cromwell elected MP for Huntingdon.

1629   Birth of daughter Elizabeth.

1630

7 May   Sale of Huntingdon property leading to move
                    to St Ives.

1632

January   Birth and death of son James.

1636   Death of Sir Thomas Steward: Cromwell the
                    main beneficiary.

1637   Birth of daughter Mary.

1638

6 December   Birth of daughter Frances.

1639   Death of son Robert.

1640

25 March   Elected MP for Cambridge for the Short
                    Parliament.
27 October   Elected MP for Cambridge to the Long
                    Parliament.

1641

Early May   Zealous for the Protestation.
21 May   Root and Branch Bill introduced.
September   Cromwell speaks critically of the Prayer
                    Book.
October   Irish rebellion and alleged 'massacres' of
                    Protestants.
27 November   The Grand Remonstrance.

1642

26 March   Cromwell signs subscription list for loan on
                    Irish lands (£500).
April–July   Invests £2050 on Irish lands.
29 August   Musters a troop of cavalry at Huntingdon.
23 October   At the battle of Edgehill.

1643

February   Cromwell a Colonel in the Eastern
                    Association.

11 May	Involved in the recovery of Grantham, Lincolnshire.
13 May	Involved in the victory at Belton, Lincolnshire.
July	Cromwell made Governor of the Isle of Ely.
20 July	Involved in the successful relief on Gainsborough, Lincolnshire.
10 October	Battle of Winceby.

1644

January	Instrumental in stopping provocative preaching at Ely Cathedral.
Late January	Appointed Lieutenant-General.
5 February	Signs the Solemn League and Covenant.
7 February	Appointed to Committee of Both Kingdoms.
2 July	Battle of Marston Moor.
13 September	Speech on tender consciences.
27 October	Second battle of Newbury.
9 November	Royalists relieve Donnington Castle.
23 November	Parliament instructs the Committee of Both Kingdoms to consider the reorganization of the army.
25 November	Cromwell attacks Manchester's war management; Zouch Tate Committee set up to consider.
28 November	Manchester replies in the Lords.
2 December	Manchester's case presented in writing.
9 December	Tate's committee reports; Cromwell's conciliatory and constructive speech.
19 December	Self-Denying Ordinance sent from Commons to Lords.

1645

9 January	Committee of Both Kingdoms reports on the reorganization of the army.
13 January	Lords reject the Self-Denying Ordinance.
18 January	Military reorganization agreed in the Commons.
21 January	Fairfax appointed General; Skippon Major-General of the foot; Lieutenant-General of the Horse left vacant.
27 January	Third reading of the New Model Army ordinance in the Commons.

3 April	Final version of the Self-Denying Ordinance.
14 June	Battle of Naseby, Northamptonshire.
10 July	Battle of Langport, Somerset.
23 July	Royalist surrender of Bridgewater, Somerset.
10 September	Fall of Bristol.
14 October	Storming of Basing House, Hampshire.

1646

13 January	Elizabeth marries John Claypole, Holy Trinity, Ely.
March	Ordinance establishing Presbyterianism in England approved by the House of Lords.
April	Cromwell denounces Ireton for not revealing the King's attempt to negotiate directly with the army.
15 June	Bridget marries Henry Ireton.
24 June	Royalists surrender Oxford.
9 October	Abolition of episcopacy approved by the Lords (12 present).

1647

20 March	Cromwell assures the Commons that the army would obey.
27 March	Fairfax ordered to suppress soldiers' petition.
29 March	'Declaration of Dislike' promoters of the soldiers' petition declared 'enemies of the state' by the Commons.
16 May	Cromwell at Saffron Walden urging army compliance with Parliament.
21 May	Cromwell reporting to the House of Commons on army moderation and grievances.
25 May	The Commons vote that the army disband in the first two weeks of June.
29 May	Council of War: 100 officers report that the army could not be disbanded without disorder.
1 June	Newmarket rendezvous.
1 June	Joyce secures Oxford artillery.
4 June	Joyce secures the King.
5 June	*Solemn Engagement* of the Army: General Council of the Army established.

8 June	King at Newmarket.
10 June	Grandees prepared to comply with Presbyterianism.
15 June	Army's Representation.
17/18 July	Council of War debates The Heads of Proposals at Reading.
20 July	Eleven MPs ask leave to go into exile.
26 July	'Presbyterian' mob invades House of Commons: Speaker, 57 MPs and nine peers seek protection of the army.
28 July	King's dismissal of The Heads of Proposals.
2 August	The Heads of Proposals published.
6 August	Army enters London.
14 August	Agitators call for purge of Parliament.
18 August	General Council issues Remonstrance.
20 August	Parliament complies.
7 September	Charles advises Parliament that he favours The Heads of Proposals.
October/ November	Putney debates.
18 October	Case of the Armie presented to Fairfax.
8 November	Agitators sent back to regiments.
9 November	Agreement on three rendezvous.
11 November	King escapes from Hampton Court.
15 November	King arrives at Carisbrooke.
15 November	Ware rendezvous.
17 November	St Albans rendezvous.
18 November	Kingston rendezvous.
19 November	Cromwell's Norman Yoke speech.
23 December	Council of Officers votes for the prosecution of the King.

1648

3 January	Cromwell supports the Vote of No Addresses.
27 March	Accession day demonstrations in London in favour of the King.
28 April	Commons vote for no alteration in the fundamental government of the kingdom.
May–November	Cromwell commanding the New Model cavalry.
May–June	Cromwell in active command in South Wales.
11 July	Pembroke surrenders to Cromwell.

17 August	Cromwell's victorious command at the battle of Preston.
24 August	Parliament repeals the Vote of No Addresses.
4–7 October	Cromwell in Edinburgh as the 'guest' of the Earl of Argyll and the Covenanters.
6–29 November	Cromwell oversees the siege of Pontefract Castle, Yorkshire.
15 November	Leveller/Independent discussion at the Nag's Head.
16 November	Council of Officers offer terms to King.
17 November	King sets them aside.
18 November	Council of Officers endorses Ireton's Remonstrance.
20 November	Army Remonstrance before the Commons.
1 December	Fairfax has Charles moved to Hurst Castle.
6 December	Pride's Purge; probable date of Cromwell's return to London.
19 December	Charles moved to Windsor.
21 December	Council resolved on King's death.
23 December	Committee of Rump to consider trial process.

1649

1 January	Trial of the King approved by the Commons.
3 January	Vote of No Addresses.
4 January	'People ... the original of all just power'.
6 January	Ordinance for trial of Charles Stuart approved.
20 January	Officers' Agreement presented to Commons.
30 January	Execution of the King.
February	Cromwell a member of the Council of State.
15 March	Named as Commander-in-Chief for the Irish expedition.
13/14 May	Cromwell suppresses mutiny at Burford.
2 August	Jones' victory at Rathmines.
15 August	Cromwell lands in Ireland.
10–11 September	Storming of Drogheda.
11 October	Storming of Wexford.
2 December	Cromwell forced by sickness to abandon siege of Waterford.

1650

3 February	Fethard, County Tipperary surrenders.
24 February	Caher, County Tipperary surrenders.

18 March	Thomastown, County Limerick surrenders.
27 March	Kilkenny surrenders.
19 April	Lord's Day Observance Act.
10 May	Adultery Act.
18 May	Clonmel, County Tipperary surrenders.
26–28 May	Cromwell travels back to England from Ireland.
June	Appointed Captain-General and leaves for Scotland.
28 June	Act against swearing.
3 September	Cromwell's victory in the battle of Dunbar.
7 September	Cromwell enters Edinburgh which is to be his base for the rest of the Scottish campaign.

1651

Spring and summer	Campaigning in the Scottish lowlands.
20 July	Lambert's victory at Inverkeithing, Fife.
2 August	Surrender of Perth to Cromwell.
3 September	Cromwell's victory at Worcester.
12 September	Cromwell back in London from where he rarely moves far for the rest of his life.
18 November	Date for dissolution of the Rump set for 3 November 1654.
10 December	Cromwell leads discussions over settlement of the nation (monarchy?) in a conference at the Speaker's house.
26 December	Hales committee for law reform commissioned.

1652

April	The outbreak of the first Anglo-Dutch war.
July	Cromwell's tacit support for peace petition.
13 August	Fourteen-point reform petition of officers.
November	Second discusion with Whitelocke over settlement.

1653

1 April	Rump's non-renewal of the Commission for the Propagation of the Gospel in Wales.
20 April	Expulsion of the Rump.
10 May	Henry Cromwell marries Frances Russell.

4 July	Opening of the Nominated Assembly.
13 November	Lambert presents The Instrument of Government to the Council of Officers.
12 December	Conclusion of the Nominated Assembly.
16 December	Cromwell installed as Protector.
22 December	Powell and Feake imprisoned; Harrison loses his commission.

1654

18 March	The commission of Triers established by Protectoral ordinance.
20 March	Declaration of a Fast day to be observed on 24 March.
12 April	Ordinance for Anglo-Scots Union.
April	Peace with the Dutch.
Spring	Campaign for religious reconciliation and the gospel in Scotland.
9 May	Declaration of a day of Thanksgiving.
21 May	First arrests in Gerrard's plot.
August	The commissions of Ejectors established by Protectoral ordinance.
4 September	Cromwell's opening speech to first Protectorate Parliament.
12 September	Speech to Parliament on the constitution.
September	Cromwell hurt in a coaching accident in Hyde Park.
November	Funeral of Cromwell's mother.
December	Start of expedition to the West Indies.
December	Biddle condemned.
December	Attempted conciliation with Feake, Simpson etc.
23 December	Motion (dropped) that Cromwell be offered the crown.

1655

22 January	Parliament dissolved.
March/April	Penruddock rising in the west of England suppressed.
April	An expedition to establish an English Caribbean base defeated at Hispaniola.
May ~	Support for Piedmontese Protestants.
June	Venner plot.

July	News of Hispaniola débâcle reaches London.
9 August	Commissioning of Major-Generals.
September	Trial of John Biddle for blasphemy.
6 December	Day of Fasting and Humiliation.
Mid-December	Cromwell's interview with Ludlow.
Winter 1655–6	Attempts to prevent conjunction of Royalists and Fifth Monarchists.

1656

11–18 March	Meetings of Fifth Monarchists to consider legitimacy of violence.
17 April	Archbishop Ussher's funeral.
12 May	Henry Vane's *A Healing Question* questioning the legitimacy of the Protectorate was published.
1 August	Cromwell/Ludlow interview: 'consent'.
12 August	Vane before the Council over *A Healing Question*.
20 August	Writs issued for second Protectorate Parliament.
12 September	Opening of the second Protectorate Parliament.
17 September	Cromwell's opening speech.
September	Sindercombe's plot.
October	Hyde Park interview with George Fox.
31 October	Nayler case before committee of 55.
11 December	Council orders release of Vane, Feake and Rogers.

1657

13 January	Thurloe reports the Sindercombe plot to the House.
19 January	Ashe's amendment in favour of an 'ancient constitution'.
23 February	Vote for kingship and a second chamber – 150:52 (Packe's Bill).
27 February	Cromwell's angry speech to 100 officers.
5 March	Conciliatory army deputation to Cromwell.
23 March	Anti-Spanish treaty signed with France.
23 March –	Cromwell sees Fox twice this week.
March–May	Kingship negotiations.
25 March	Vote for kingship – 123:62.

31 March	Humble Petition and Advice presented to Cromwell.
3 April	Cromwell's first refusal of the crown.
9 April	Arrest of Venner conspirators.
6 May	Cromwell looks ready to accept kingship.
8 May	Cromwell's final refusal of the Crown.
25 May	Humble Petition and Advice presented with Lord Protector rather than King.
May	*Killing No Murder.*
26 June	Cromwell's second installation as Lord Protector.
11 November	Marriage of Frances to Robert Rich.
18 November	Marriage of Mary to Lord Fauconbridge.

1658

20/25 January	Cromwell's speeches to both Houses.
4 February	Dissolution of second Parliament.
4 June	Battle of the Dunes ~ acquisition of Dunkirk.
6 August	Death of Elizabeth Claypole.
19 August	Cromwell seriously ill.
3 September	Death of Cromwell.
4 September	Embalming of his body.
20 September	Lying in state at Somerset House.
10 November	Private burial.
23 November	State funeral.

1661

26 January	Cromwell's body exhumed.
30 January	Corpse displayed and mutilated at Tyburn.

Index